Truth and Lies in Literature

Truth and Lies
in Literature

ESSAYS AND REVIEWS

by

STEPHEN VIZINCZEY

Selected and introduced by
CHRISTOPHER SINCLAIR-STEVENSON

The Atlantic Monthly Press
BOSTON / NEW YORK

FIRST AMERICAN EDITION

LIBRARY OF CONGRESS CATALOG CARD NO. 86-70253

PRINTED IN GREAT BRITAIN

Contents

[v]

Acknowledgments

No writer can survive without the support of at least a few people who believe in him, and so I owe a debt of gratitude to those editors who commissioned most of these reviews: Michael Ratcliffe, who was then literary editor of *The Times*; and Rivers Scott and his successor Nicholas Bagnall, literary editors of *The Sunday Telegraph*.

I am grateful also to J. W. M. Thompson, editor of the *Sunday Telegraph*, who sent me to Sicily; John Higgins of *The Times*, who commissioned the longer essay on Kleist; and Walter Karp, who asked me to write about the execution of Imre Nagy for *Horizon*. I wrote about Lucien Leuwen for Mary-Kay Wilmers of the *London Review of Books*, about George Lukács for William Webb of *The Guardian*, and reviewed *The Death of My Brother Abel* for Robert Wilson of *USA Today*.

Lewis Lapham, editor of *Harper's* commissioned the title essay. I wrote two versions for him: one is here; the other, focussing more specifically on the politics of literature, is in *Harper's*.

I owe special thanks to Christopher Sinclair-Stevenson, my editor and publisher, who selected these pieces as worth reprinting and ordered them in a way that makes sense. His creative editorial work prompted me to improve the material, and I cut, expanded and rewrote accordingly.

The bulk of the text is still as it first appeared. Acknowledgment for permission to reprint is made to *The Times*, *The Sunday Telegraph*, *The Guardian*, *Writers' Monthly*, *Horizon*, *USA Today* and *Harper's*.

Introduction

Stephen Vizinczey is a man of strong, indeed passionate, views. He is not a graduate of the milk-and-water school of criticism, content to write elegant, urbane disquisitions on this or that, a mandarin of the British literary tradition. His pen is sharp, and often dipped in acid. He is not, therefore, a popular writer. Writers who strip away the emperor's new clothes seldom are.

He was born in Hungary in 1933, was educated at the University of Budapest and the Hungarian Academy of Theatre and Film Arts. Three of his plays were banned by the communist regime. He fought in the 1956 revolution and escaped to the West. His knowledge of English was almost non-existent. But, like Conrad and Nabokov before him, his ear for the nuances and resonances of English was remarkable. He has never lost his Hungarian accent, but he writes like a magician. Oddly, though perhaps not oddly, he learned his craft while working for the National Film Board of Canada, writing documentaries, and later editing a literary/political magazine, *Exchange*.

When his first novel, *In Praise of Older Women*, was published in 1965 (he took the risk – he had to take the risk – of publishing it himself) Stephen Vizinczey became immediately famous. It has been called a modern erotic classic, an erotic novel in which sexual experience is not a torment, a post-pornographic book. It seemed, in an uncanny way, to catch the mood of, to encapsulate, a generation. Sex was no longer a furtive occupation to be conducted in secret and more often than not in sorrow or guilt. It was suddenly acknowledged to be glorious, liberating, actually enjoyable. Again, it was not an entirely popular view, and many critics greeted it with hostility or silence. Even so, *In Praise of Older Women* has gone through thirty-six printings in English; it is still in print.

Vizinczey moved to England in 1966, and published a collection of philosophical and political essays, *The Rules of Chaos*, three years later. His second novel, *An Innocent Millionaire*, did not appear until 1983. Like its predecessor, it divided critical opinion. Some dismissed Vizinczey as a thinking man's Harold Robbins; others saw past the thin veneer of the adventure novel into the layers of subtlety beneath. Brigid Brophy spoke of the book's ironies, of the energy of invention, of the perfect pitch of the narrative tone. Anthony Burgess, who shares Vizinczey's sheer love of words, was both entertained and moved. 'Here is a novel,' he said, 'set bang in the middle of our decadent, polluted, corrupt world that in some curious way breathes a kind of desperate hope.'

Stephen Vizinczey's new book, like *The Rules of Chaos*, is a collection, containing both despair and hope, praise and prejudice. He has three great literary heroes, Stendhal, Balzac and Kleist, and all three are represented. Other writers are here: Tolstoy and Gogol, Nerval and Rousseau, Thomas Mann and Norman Mailer. There are essays on the nature of cruelty and of death; on feminists and male chauvinists; on anthropologists and sociobiologists; on religion and politics; on critics, charlatans, heroes and murderers.

The book also contains two autobiographical essays, one a remarkable meditation on George Faludy's poem 'The Execution of Imre Nagy' and Hungary's long history of fighting, losing and enduring ('Hungarians love a loser'), the other a writer's ten commandments. The latter produces a curious, vivid identikit picture of this most individualistic of writers. 'Thou Shalt Not Drink, Smoke or Take Drugs'; 'Thou Shalt Not Have Expensive Habits'; 'Thou Shalt Dream and Write and Dream and Rewrite'; 'Thou Shalt Not Be Vain'; 'Thou Shalt Not Be Modest'; 'Thou Shalt Not Let a Day Pass Without Re-reading Something Great' (the list includes Kleist, Swift, Sterne, Shakespeare, Mark Twain, 'almost everything by

Pushkin, Gogol, Tolstóy, Dostoevsky, Stendhal and Balzac'); 'Thou Shalt Not Worship London/New York/Paris'; 'Thou Shalt Write to Please Thyself'; 'Thou Shalt Be Hard to Please'.

A voluptuary with ascetic habits? An immodest man without vanity? An internationalist who despises great cities? The apparent contradictions are intriguing. But what emerges most forcibly is Vizinczey's blazing conviction that a writer must write for himself above all and must at all times keep his critical faculties finely honed. James Thurber once wrote a book called *Lanterns and Lances*, and the title could as easily apply to this book. Vizinczey's lanterns shed light, often dazzling, on dark corners, often murky ones. His lances are sharp and pointed, with a devastating cutting edge. Both are wielded with brilliance.

CHRISTOPHER SINCLAIR-STEVENSON

A Writer's Ten Commandments

This was written in response to a request from Raymond Lamont-Brown, editor of Writers' Monthly, *who asked me for something 'full of sound, practical advice for people who in many cases are quite new to the business of writing'.*

1. THOU SHALT NOT DRINK, SMOKE OR TAKE DRUGS
To be a writer you need all the brains you've got.

2. THOU SHALT NOT HAVE EXPENSIVE HABITS
A writer is born from talent and time – time to observe, to study, to think. So you can't afford to waste a single hour earning money for non-essentials. Unless you were lucky enough to be born rich, you had better be prepared to live without too many worldly goods. True, Balzac got special inspiration from running up huge debts and buying things, but most people who have expensive habits tend to fail as writers.

At the age of 24 after the defeat of the Hungarian Revolution I found myself in Canada with about fifty words of English. When it got through to me that I was now a writer without a language, I took an elevator to the top of a high building on Dorchester Street in Montreal, intending to jump. Looking down from the roof, terrified of dying but even more afraid of breaking my spine and spending the rest of my life in a wheelchair, I decided to try to become an English writer instead. In the end, learning to write in another language was less difficult than writing something good, and I lived on the edge of destitution for six years before I was ready to write *In Praise of Older Women*.

I couldn't have done it if I had cared about clothes or cars – indeed, if the only alternative I saw had not been the top of that skyscraper. Some immigrant writers I knew took jobs as waiters or salesmen to save money and create a 'financial base' for themselves before trying to make a living by writing; one of them now owns a whole chain of restaurants and is richer than I could ever be, but neither he nor the others returned to writing. You've got to decide what is more important to you: to live well or to write well. Don't torment yourself with contrary ambitions.

3. THOU SHALT DREAM AND WRITE AND DREAM AND REWRITE

Don't let anybody tell you you're wasting your time when you're gazing into space. There is no other way to conceive an imaginary world.

I never sit down in front of a bare page to invent something. I daydream about my characters, their lives and their struggles, and when a scene has been played out in my imagination and I think I know what my characters felt, said and did, I take pen and paper and try to *report* what I've witnessed.

When I've written and typed my report I read it over and find that most of what I've written is (a) unclear or (b) inexact or (c) ponderous or (d) simply could not be true. Thus the typed draft serves as a kind of critical report on what I imagined, and I go back to dream the whole thing better.

It was this way of working that made me realise, when I was learning English, that my chief problem wasn't the language but, as always, getting things right in my head.

4. THOU SHALT NOT BE VAIN

Most bad books get that way because their authors are engaged in trying to justify themselves. If a vain author is an alcoholic, then the most sympathetically portrayed character in his book will be an alcoholic. This sort of thing is very boring for outsiders. If you think you're wise, rational, good, a boon to the opposite sex, a victim of circumstances, then you don't know yourself well enough to write.

I stopped taking myself seriously at the age of 27 and since then I've regarded myself simply as *raw material*. I use myself the same way as an actor uses himself: all my characters – men and women, good and bad – are made up from myself plus observation.

5. THOU SHALT NOT BE MODEST
Modesty is an excuse for sloppiness, laziness, self-indulgence; small ambitions evoke small efforts. I never knew a good writer who wasn't trying to be a great one.

6. THOU SHALT THINK CONTINUALLY OF THOSE WHO ARE TRULY GREAT
'The works of genius are watered with its tears,' wrote Balzac in *Lost Illusions*. Rejection, derision, poverty, failure, the constant struggle against one's own limitations – these are the chief events in the lives of most great artists, and if you aspire to share their fate you should fortify yourself by learning about them.

I've often taken heart from re-reading the first volume of Graham Greene's autobiography, *A Sort of Life*, which is about his early struggles. I've also had the chance to visit him in Antibes, where he lives in a small two-room flat (a tiny place for such a tall man) with the luxuries of benign air and a view of the sea but few possessions apart from books. He seems to have few material needs, and I'm sure this has something to do with the inner freedom which radiates from his works. Though he claims to have written his 'entertainments' for money, he is a writer who is directed by his obsessions without regard to changing fashions and popular ideologies, and this freedom is communicated to his readers. He liberates you from the weight of your own compromises, at least while you read him. This kind of achievement is possible only for a writer of Spartan habits.

None of us has a chance to meet many great men in person, but we can be in their company if we read their memoirs, journals and letters. Avoid biographies, though – especially dramatised biographies in the form of films or television series. Almost everything that comes to you about artists through the media is sheer bunk, written by lazy hacks who don't have the faintest notion of either art or hard work. The most recent example is *Amadeus*, which tries to convince you that it is easy to be a genius like Mozart and very hard to be a mediocrity like Salieri.

Read Mozart's letters instead. As for specific literature on the writing life I'd recommend Virginia Woolf's *A Room of My Own*, Shaw's preface to *The Dark Lady of the Sonnets*, Jack London's *Martin Eden* and, above all, Balzac's *Lost Illusions*.

7. THOU SHALT NOT LET A DAY PASS WITHOUT RE-READING SOMETHING GREAT

In my teens I studied to be a conductor, and from my musical training I picked up a habit which I think is essential also for writers: *the constant, daily study of masterworks*. Most professional musicians of any standing know hundreds of scores by heart; most writers, on the other hand, have only the vaguest recollections of the classics – which is one reason why there are more skilled musicians than skilled writers. A violinist who had the technical proficiency of most published novelists would never find an orchestra to play in. The truth is that only by absorbing perfect works, the specific ways great masters have invented to develop a theme, to construct a sentence, a paragraph, a chapter, can you possibly learn all there is to be learned about technique.

Nothing that has already been done can tell you how to do something new, but if you understand the masters' techniques, you have a better chance to develop your own. To put it in terms of chess: there hasn't yet been a grandmaster who didn't know his predecessors' championship games by heart.

Don't commit the common mistake of trying to read everything in order to be well-informed. Being well-informed will allow you to shine at parties but is absolutely no use to you as a writer. Reading a book so you can chat about it is not the same thing as understanding it. It is far more useful to read a few great novels over and over again until you see what makes them work and how the writers constructed them. You have to read a novel about five times before you can perceive its structure, what makes it dramatic, what gives it pace and momentum. Its variations in tempo and time-scale, for instance: the author describes a minute in two pages then covers two years in one sentence – why? When you've figured this out you really know something.

Every writer will pick his own favourites from whom he thinks he can learn the most, but I strongly advise against reading Victorian novels, which are riddled with hypocrisy and bloated with redundant words. Even George Eliot wrote too much about too little.

When you are tempted to overwrite, read the short stories of Heinrich von Kleist, who said more with fewer words than any other writer in the history of Western literature. I read him constantly, along with Swift and Sterne, Shakespeare and Mark Twain. At least once a year I reread almost everything by Pushkin, Gogol, Tolstoy, Dostoevsky, Stendhal and Balzac. To my mind Kleist and these 19th-century French and Russian novelists were the greatest masters of prose, a constellation of unsurpassed geniuses such as we find in music from Bach to Beethoven, and I try to learn something from them every day. This is my 'technique'.

8. THOU SHALT NOT WORSHIP LONDON/NEW YORK/PARIS

I often meet aspiring writers from out of the way places who believe that people who live in the media capitals have some special inside information about art which they do not possess. They read the review pages, watch arts programmes on television, to find out what is important, what art really is, what intellectuals should be concerned about. The provincial is often an intelligent, gifted person who ends up following some glib journalist's or academic's notion of what constitutes literary excellence and betrays his talent by aping morons whose only talent is for getting on.

Even if you live at Land's End, there is no reason for you to feel out of touch. If you have a good paperback library of great writers, and if you keep re-reading them, you will have access to more secrets of literature than all the culture phonies who set the tone in the big cities. I know a leading New York critic who has never read Tolstoy and is proud of it too. So don't waste time worrying about what is the declared fashion, the right subject or the right style or what sort of things win prizes. Anybody who ever succeeded in literature did so on his own terms.

9. THOU SHALT WRITE TO PLEASE THYSELF

No writer has ever managed to please readers who were not on approximately his own level of general intelligence, who did not share his basic attitude to life, death, sex, politics, money. Playwrights are lucky: with the help of actors, they can broaden their appeal beyond the circle of kindred spirits. Yet only a couple of years ago I read the most condescending reviews in the American papers for *Measure for Measure* – the play itself, not the production! If Shakespeare can't please everyone, why should you even try?

This means there is no point in forcing yourself to be interested in something that bores you. When I was young I wasted a lot of time trying to describe clothes and furniture. I didn't have the slightest interest in clothes or furniture but Balzac had a passionate interest in them which he managed to communicate even to me while I was reading him, so I thought I had to master the art of writing exciting paragraphs about cupboards if I was ever to become a good novelist. My efforts were doomed and used up all my enthusiasm for what I had been trying to write about in the first place.

Now I only write about what interests me. I don't look for subjects: whatever it is that I can't stop thinking about – that is my subject. Stendhal said that literature is *the art of leaving out*, and I leave out everything that doesn't strike me as important. I describe people only in terms of their actions, statements, thoughts, feelings, which have shocked/mystified/amused/ delighted me in myself or others.

It isn't easy, of course, to stick to what you really care about; we would all like to be thought of as people who are curious about everything. Who ever attended a party without faking interest in something? But when you write you have to resist the temptation, and when you read over what you have written, you must always ask yourself, 'Does this really interest me?'

If you please yourself – your *real* self, not some fanciful notion of yourself as the noblest of persons who cares only about the starving children of Africa – then you have a chance to write a book that will please millions. This is so because no matter who you are, there are millions of people in the world who are more or less like you. But no one wants to read a novelist who doesn't really mean what he writes. The trashiest bestseller has one thing in common with a great novel: they are both *authentic*.

10. THOU SHALT BE HARD TO PLEASE

Most new books that I read seem to me half-finished. The writer was satisfied to get things more or less right, and then moved on to something new. For me writing becomes really exciting when I go back to a chapter a couple of months after I've done with it. At that stage I look at it not so much as the author but as a reader – and no matter how often I rewrote the chapter originally, I can still find sentences which are vague, adjectives which are inexact or redundant. Indeed I find whole scenes which though true add nothing to my understanding of the characters or the story, and so can be deleted.

It is at that stage that I ponder the chapter long enough to learn it by heart – I recite it word-for-word to anyone who is willing to listen – and if I cannot remember something, I usually find that it wasn't right. Memory is a good critic.

Writers' Monthly, July 1985

France

Why Eng. Lit. Is Not Enough

The recent publication of *The Wild Ass's Skin* (a philosophising tale in which everybody talks too much) and a *Selected Short Stories* of Balzac (which leaves out the two best ones, *The Abbé Birotteau* and *Colonel Chabert*) may suggest to the uninformed that Penguin are scraping the bottom of the barrel as far as the European classics are concerned. The sad truth is that dozens of masterpieces – among them Stendhal's *Lucien Leuwen* and *Italian Chronicles* and Balzac's own magnificent *Droll Stories* – still have not found their way into paperback.

All the more reason, then, to treasure the riches already available in Penguin Classics, from Balzac as well as other giants of 19th-century fiction. Indeed, I could do no more useful service to readers than to urge them to look on the Penguin racks for Balzac's *Old Goriot*, *The Black Sheep*, *Lost Illusions*, *Cousin Pons* and *Cousin Bette*, and for any and all books by Stendhal, Gogol, Dostoevsky or Tolstoy.

What a pity that these great novelists' masterpieces are not everybody's old friends!

The teaching of English literature instead of literature is to my mind the most harmful of all wrong-headed educational practices, robbing our intellectual and artistic life of a great deal of wisdom and inspiration. It is as though we had a system of musical education teaching not music but only English music, and there were hardly any musicians or music lovers in England who had ever heard a single piece by Mozart.

Luckily it is agreed by all concerned that music has to do with music, not xenophobia, that Beethoven's symphonies can stir Englishmen more deeply than Elgar's – that, in short, the best is the nearest to us.

Most educators haven't yet reached such elementary under-standing of the universality of great literature, or rather, they don't seem to be aware of how little of it there is. The exclusive preoccupation with native authors stems at least partly from the belief that there are multitudes of important writers in every corner of the world – a fallacy deriving from the inability to distinguish between the gifted and the uniquely profound.

This is a universal failing. Thus, when French students study drama they are given Racine rather than Shakespeare, as if the two were interchangeable in regard to their usefulness to developing minds, as if the French playwright's Greeks were closer to the French than the English playwright's Greeks, Moors, and Danes. Only those who perceive equally little in lesser and greater writers could fail to see the reason to venture abroad for more.

There is, of course, the argument that a writer's virtues are inseparable from his language, which is indeed often true of poetry. However, it does not hold true of prose or even of drama written in verse. To begin with, the most moving, most enlight-ening part of any fiction is the story; it is not through words but through structure that a writer depicts how things fit together in the world, and characters reveal their innermost being not through their speeches but through their actions.

As to language itself, I would argue that literature is not about language but about life; it is not about the sounds of words but about their meaning, and the writers who are most important to all nations are those who depict humanity in the most meaningful way – which is why the greatest French playwright is Shakespeare in French.

Students here are, of course, lucky to study Shakespeare rather than Racine, Swift rather than Voltaire, but they are real losers when it comes to the 19th-century novel. The fact is that none of the great 19th-century novels was written in English.

People who first discovered the joys of reading through Dickens, Thackeray or George Eliot and who have endowed these authors with the vitality of their own youth are bound to disagree, but, considering the odds, the wonder is not that no one wrote a great novel in 19th-century England, but that anyone managed to do it anywhere at all.

The governing ideas, the accepted ways of seeing things have always been false everywhere: classes and nations seek reassurance and self-justification rather than knowledge, and the pressures on writers to document the falsehoods of their age have been irresistible in most periods of history.

One of these pressures was mentioned on this page a couple of weeks ago by Dame Rebecca West, when she noted that writers have to conform to popular political attitudes if they are to enjoy ample success. This has always been so and in regard not only to political but also to religious, philosophical, psychological and above all sexual attitudes, all of which invariably involve hypocrisies and evasions.

Thus, to depict people as God would see them, to portray conflict-torn society without succumbing to party spirit, to render the powerful without flattery and the downtrodden without consoling white lies, to write without either servility or the indulgence of compassion, requires not only genius but the rarest combination of historical circumstances.

In the past 2,000 years there has been only one Shakespeare for the world's stage, and it is positively miraculous that novelists of Shakespearean stature could emerge in both France and Russia in the same century.

There must be more reasons for this than we could fathom, but I suspect that the development of Gogol, Dostoevsky and Tolstoy had a great deal to do with the all-pervading sense of the impermanence of the Russian way of life, shared even by the Tsars, and with the large number of educated, leisured but impoverished noblemen and doubting monks who were ready to listen to new answers to every question. There was a hunger in Russia for all sorts of panaceas – most of them deadly – but also for the truth.

In France the upheavals of the Revolution, the Napoleonic conquests, defeats and final débâcle and the Bourbon restoration raised people high and cast them low with the drastic swiftness of great drama; dukes became coachmen, coachmen became dukes, the official truth changed by the day, and the best minds were curious to know how it all came to pass.

By comparison, the situation for great fiction in England was uniquely unfavourable. The success of the Industrial Revolution, the power and glory of the British Empire assured the educated classes that they knew what they were doing; they had the wisdom and contentment of success; they were filled with certainties.

There was an approved way of living, and those who broke the code were heinous criminals, if caught. Life was seen, if not lived, according to the rules, and there was a stupefying degree of hypocrisy about lust, greed and ambition. It could be said of English fiction of the time what Balzac's d'Arthez said of Walter Scott in *Lost Illusions*:

> Walter Scott is without passion; he knows nothing about it; or perhaps it was prohibited by the hypocritical morals of his country. For him woman is duty incarnate. With rare exceptions his heroines are absolutely the same.... Woman brings disorder into society through passion. Passion is infinite in its manifestations. Therefore, depict the passions and you will have at your command the immense resources which this great genius denied himself in order to be read by every family in prudish England.

If passions were shown they discredited their characters like the plague. Neither Dickens nor Thackeray (nor Flaubert, when the French bourgeoisie, too, was caught up in the complacency of the great boom) could have created brilliant, lovable, enviable adulteresses like Stendhal's Mme de Rênal or Gina Sanseverina. The point is not which writer was free to approve *vice*, but that Stendhal, who had lived through the retreat from Moscow, could portray people in the light of their own lives rather than in the light of the dominant but ephemeral mores of the historic moment.

All this is by way of suggesting that the greatest 19th-century English novelists are Gogol, Dostoevsky, Tolstoy, Stendhal and

Balzac in English. There are nuances which were bound to be lost, and there are some wilfully stupid mistranslations (such as *A Harlot High and Low* for Balzac's *Splendours and Miseries of the Courtesans*), but just the same there is no greater intellectual thrill than reading these Penguin authors.

The only greater thrill is to read them again and again. Reading *The Charterhouse of Parma* once is about as absurd as listening to *Così Fan Tutte* once; it is only after the first half-a-dozen times that one is sufficiently well informed to share the vision of genius.

If this sounds somewhat daunting, I should perhaps mention that reading Stendhal makes being in love sweeter, and Balzac's *Cousin Bette* is the best present a loving wife could give to a restless husband.

The Sunday Telegraph, August 14, 1977

Putting Rousseau Down

The Making of a Saint: the Tragi-Comedy of Jean-Jacques Rousseau, by J. H. Huizinga (Hamish Hamilton)

There are books which are a labour of love; this one strikes me as a labour of spite. J. H. Huizinga writes about Rousseau with such mindless animosity that one would think the man had done him some personal injury instead of being dead for nearly 200 years.

Rousseau, of course, was far from being a saint (he gave away his five children to an orphanage), but *The Making of a Saint* gives us no idea that he had anything but faults.

There is hardly anything on record that Rousseau did, wrote or said that is not twisted in some way to discredit him. Whenever the author of the *Confessions* approves of himself, it is proof of his 'insane conceit'; when he regrets, criticises or condemns his own conduct, it is proof of his masochism. He is censured for being 'feeble' and 'timid', and also for having 'formidable nerve'.

Speaking of Rousseau's admirers, Mr Huizinga says: 'If they thought him a Christian saint, they were buying not a pig in a poke but a frog in a dog-collar, self-inflated to the point where he seemed more than once to identify himself with Christ.' Let's overlook the pig, the frog and the dog; it is the 'seemed to' that is crucial. Rousseau never identified himself with Christ, and expressed horror of an admirer who did, but the 'seemed to' lets out the sneer while also dispensing with the need for accuracy. Indeed, within half a page Mr Huizinga backs down to allow that Rousseau's 'assimilations with Christ are but implicit . . .'

Mr Huizinga does not hesitate to attribute to Rousseau the most unlikely attitudes and thoughts. He derides him for his morbid sensitivity ('his feeble soul, so sensitive and thin-skinned as to make him suffer every pin-prick as if it were a thrust to his heart') but also accuses him of a thick hide: Rousseau, he claims, 'would doubtless agree that bad publicity is better than no publicity.'

Having planted this Hollywood notion on an 18th-century French philosopher, Mr Huizinga tries to justify the calumny by actually quoting Rousseau, who said: 'I would rather be forgotten than be thought an ordinary man.' This surely shows a preference for no publicity rather than bad publicity; but then Mr Huizinga gets quite a lot of things wrong. He even mis-counts the years of his subject's life, speaking of 'his death at the age of 68'.

But to give the flavour of the book, perhaps I need only mention that the chapter devoted to Rousseau's mistress Thérèse Levasseur (a sensible girl, but unable to read) is entitled *The Maestro and the Moron*.

As for the feeble maestro, the uninformed reader would have no way of learning that Jean-Jacques Rousseau (1712–78) was one of the most forceful and gifted men of the 18th century.

The son of a Geneva watch-maker, apprenticed to an en-graver at the age of 12, he made himself, without benefit of further formal education, first a music teacher and composer of light operas, and then the leading philosopher and novelist of continental Europe. Under the *ancien régime* the bare facts of such a career were heroic – all the more so because some of his works were banned or burned and he was driven into exile – and he inspired millions of gifted but poor young men to defy the world and to better themselves against all odds. Perhaps this is why so many of them thought of him as a 'saint', revering him for their own aspirations.

But Rousseau's social disadvantages and his troubles with the authorities pale beside the curse of a physical ailment. According to Dr Elosu's *La maladie de Jean-Jacques Rousseau* (cited in Jean Guéhenno's biography, translated by Doreen and John Weightman), 'from his birth to his death Rousseau never completely emptied his bladder, and all his life oscillated between the discomfort of partial retention and the agony of total retention'.

Since there was no treatment for the infection of his urinary organs, he suffered from all kinds of unexplained fevers and ailments; worse, he had to wear a catheter.

Perhaps the meanest thing in this very mean book is that its author relegates Rousseau's illness to a few vague references by way of explaining particular incidents, which leaves the reader with the impression that it was a temporary or at worst recurrent condition rather than a constant torment – as if it had nothing to do with his 'fluctuations of mood', his irritability or how difficult he was to get along with.

Although Rousseau's condition made lovemaking either impossible or painful, Mr Huizinga, apparently maddened by the fact that his subject's work attracted so many female admirers, has the temerity to sneer at him as 'Don Juan Jacques' and to insist that he 'was allocated more than his fair share of the joys of life, [as] no one has attested more fully than the "unhappiest of mortals" himself'.

Thus Rousseau's gift for enjoying life in spite of his affliction, as demonstrated on so many pages of the *Confessions*, goes unacknowledged and is used simply to rob him of sympathy, while Mr Huizinga continues to berate him for his unnatural self-pity.

The relegation of Rousseau's illness to a small detail is all the more deplorable because it is the key to much of his writing. It seems to me, for instance, that his exaltation of feeling over reason and action has a great deal to do with the fact that, more often than not, he had to sublimate his sexual longings.

As a novelist, Rousseau's significance is historical rather than literary. *La Nouvelle Héloïse*, laden with high-mindedness to compensate for sexual deprivation, is about a girl and her tutor whose passionate epistolary romance is allowed to culminate in one night of lovemaking before she is married to an elderly

[18]

gentleman and devotes the rest of her life to estate-management and maternity.

It gives one some idea of the position of women, even of high-born ladies, in 18th-century France, that this fictional statement that whatever romance existed in life was before marriage, and what could not be helped was actually 'right', made women worship Rousseau as the wisest and noblest of men.

As a philosopher, Rousseau is wrongly considered the father of totalitarian ideologies on account of his (highly metaphysical) concept of a 'general will' and the consequent supremacy of the state over the individual. In the heat of the Second World War, Bertrand Russell wrote that 'Hitler is the outcome of Rousseau', and this has become a kind of received opinion.

Even as a philosopher, Rousseau was an artist rather than a theorist, who expressed not so much new ideas as a new attitude, a new way of living, and did it in the most eloquent language, the most striking paradoxes. To borrow a phrase from Peter Brook, Rousseau brought about a 'change of perception' – the perceiving of the possibility that one could rethink everything for oneself. As Mme de Staël said, 'he has invented nothing but he has infused everything with fire'.

Rousseau's 'Man was born free, and everywhere he is in chains' will no doubt go on echoing through the ages. However, he is important to us chiefly as the author of the *Confessions*, a masterpiece of psychological realism and psychoanalysis. 'I have displayed myself as I was,' he wrote, 'as vile and despicable when my behaviour was such, as good, generous and noble, when I was so.' Whatever his misjudgments or self-delusions, they become transparent as in a good novel: Rousseau is so truthful about the details that the reader can understand him better than he does himself.

The Sunday Telegraph, January 18, 1976

One of the Very Few

True greatness is like infinity, we cannot measure it. As a rule, attempts to assess works of art impair even our ability to experience them. Treating creative achievements as if they were sociological or historical surveys or exercises in pious intentions, much of literary scholarship is employed in destroying the vital distinction between the ordinary and the extraordinary – in the kind of barbaric incomprehension that would describe a woman's glance by saying that she had twenty-twenty vision. This pedestrian *seriousness*, which Stendhal was the first to recognize as the malignancy of modern culture, dominates teaching to this day, with the result that only readers with indestructible sensibilities can possibly survive becoming educated about literature.

Literary education is the chief instrument for alienating the young from good writing, and particularly from the classics. The pedantic lectures about this or that novelist's brilliant portrayal of a bygone age in which hardly anyone is interested propagate the fallacy that the great writers of the past wrote about things dead and gone. But calumny is truth misapplied. What gives deadly credibility to the socio-historic-moralistic misinterpretation of literary works of art is the abundance of dated novelists who were indeed little more than chroniclers of their society and righteous spokesmen of its delusions. Such writers suffered, if not from lack of talent, then from an overdose of their solidified culture and its conventions. Orwell said of Dickens's characters that they were prototypes of their trade or class rather than individuals, representing social functions rather than particular human beings. The same could be said of most fiction written in England or elsewhere in periods of real or apparent social stability when people's roles and relationships were preordained and permanent, and even their feelings, thoughts and motives were expected to conform to defined patterns. In a world where everyone knows his place, few have a chance to know themselves, let alone others; when people are typecast for life, the performance becomes indistinguishable from the actors. Again, it is Orwell who points out that Dickens, though a deeply compassionate man and a radical by the standards of his age, presented his 'good' lower-class characters as cheerfully content with their station: the poor may bewail starvation but not poverty, the servant may resent his mistreatment but not his servitude. Many Victorian novelists' ill-famed portrayal of sex is matched by their equally false and spiteful denigration of social ambition: the antithesis of the contented servants and saintly wives is that heinously maligned character, Becky Sharp.

At such times human desires which transcend the status quo – the most lively, best inspirations of our nature – are considered evil, because they reach beyond the realm of conceivable possibility. Just as Thackeray, for all his unwilling admiration of Becky's charm and spunk, sees her determination to rise in the world as proof of her essential wickedness, so Flaubert conceives Madame Bovary, who longs to escape from a loveless and dreary marriage, as a vulgar woman whose emotional ambition can only be stupid and destructive. The point is not that these writers were reactionaries: a romantic revolutionary like Victor Hugo or a radical social critic like Ibsen suffers from the same superficiality when he defines his characters in opposition to their social roles. When people tend to appear only in a certain standard way (within not only a rigid social system but also within a rigid ideology like late-nineteenth-century determinism in western Europe), it is difficult to get to know them. Social stagnation poisons perception down to the minutest false details, for it makes people appear only as their moral, ideological or social functions. And this is so because we observe only what we expect to see; the unexpected is unnoticed, denied, or condemned. When too many things are taken for granted, it is next to impossible to perceive the truth.

Thus even many of the 'classics' lose their appeal as soon as the world is transformed, as soon as we alter our expectations of how people should feel and behave. We are always disinclined to differentiate between the way things are and the way we think they should be, but we prefer our falsehoods to be contemporary.

This is said not to offend the dead but to separate them from the living – and to suggest the advantage enjoyed by those independent spirits who have sought to understand reality at times of political upheaval and drastic social change, when they could not only perceive but experience the relativity of appearances and governing ideologies. It is when no one's position is safe and no idea can be taken for granted that truths about our existence are allowed to surface. Danger is the muse of fiction. It is under her spell that we find those writers who (with luck to their genius) penetrated behind the social facade, beyond the slanted vision of their age and re-created our destinies as if seen through the eyes of God. Stendhal was one of these very few: he wrote in the eternal present tense.

*

No other great prose writer, in fact, had quite his opportunities to catch people between their acts, to perceive the actors behind their text and performance. Marie-Henri Beyle, whom we know as Stendhal, was born in 1783, in Grenoble. His father was a pious, prosperous and fanatically royalist lawyer; the family home, dominated by the spirit of feudal France, was appropriately situated in the rue des Vieux-Jésuites. Young Beyle was five years old when Louis XVI's France declared itself bankrupt, six when the Revolution erupted; his tenth birthday fell not on 23 January 1793 but (retroactively) on 3 pluviôse I, the year when the King was executed and Christianity officially abolished. Of all these events the changing calendar may seem the least cataclysmic, yet what is so matter of course, so natural, as our way of marking dates? Consider suddenly being told that this was Frostymonth of year II, and not the end of the month but the beginning – from then on you would be wary of taking anything for granted. It was thus that young Beyle became used to momentous surprises, which abound in his great novels. At sixteen he left Grenoble to study in Paris, and entered the capital for the first time on 19 brumaire – the day after General Bonaparte, the defender of the Revolution, overthrew the Directory of the Revolution.

Thanks to the patronage of Pierre Daru, his distant cousin and one of Napoleon's chief aides, Beyle spent the greater part of the next fourteen years in Napoleon's orbit, first as a junior officer and later as an administrator, through twelve campaigns, from the triumphal entries into Milan, Berlin, and Vienna to the burning of Moscow and the retreat of 1812. He witnessed the rise and fall of the great Bonapartist heroes and potentates and saw many of them rise again as craven courtiers to the vengefully renascent Bourbons ('*ces Bourbons imbéciles à faire vomir*') and survive unscathed when Charles X himself was overthrown in 1830. Beyle watched the July Revolution from the arcades of the Théâtre Français, having seen his contemporaries play all the parts available in the human comedy.

Under the new constitutional monarch, Citizen King Louis-Philippe (no less despised as '*le plus fripon des* Kings') he was appointed to the consulate of Civitavecchia: Beyle, who had no illusions left about the world, ended his life, fittingly, as a diplomat. On 22 March 1842 he collapsed on the street in Paris, never to recover consciousness. During his fifty-nine years he had lived under ten regimes in France and six different constitutions, and had been known as a 'cynic'; he took nothing on trust and passed on no lies.

The classic example of his lightning exposé of social reality is his portrayal of the battle of Waterloo at the beginning of *The Charterhouse of Parma*. 'He has created only a few episodes of this rout,' wrote Balzac in his review, 'but so suggestive are his brushstrokes that the mind sees beyond the given details, taking in the whole battlefield.' Later Tolstoy said that he learned from Stendhal how to describe battles, how to disregard the grandeur of armies for the experience of individuals. But not even *War and Peace* has a scene as poignant as the Waterloo in *Charterhouse*. Stendhal conveys it through a description of sixteen-year-old Fabrizio del Dongo's enthusiastically fumbling attempts to join Napoleon's last stand. At the end, Fabrizio isn't even certain whether he has been in that glorious battle, as he has seen only smoke, confusion, a friendly *vivandière* with her little cart, stragglers bargaining for horses and food, shooting, stealing, maiming – and the mysterious spectacle of people who have suddenly ceased to live.

Through the buildup and letdown of Fabrizio's expectations, Stendhal can make us see not only beyond the details of the battle but beyond the confines of the period, beyond the glittering slogans and delusions that unite men in self-destruction. The solitary corpses on the field of Waterloo are the foundation of the principality of Parma, a totalitarian state that belongs to all ages. But it is, to borrow Valéry's phrase, one of the 'characteristic magnitudes' of Stendhal's whole œuvre to show the world in the light of this truth: each man is alone in history.

*

It was in Civitavecchia that he wrote an account of his childhood and youth as *The Life of Henry Brulard*. Quite apart from its merit as a report on the making of a master, it is a most amusing masterpiece in itself. In English, only Bertrand Russell's joyous irony can give any idea of its lighthearted spirit, the offhand sincerity and easy clarity that the stupid mistake for shallowness. Readers of *Henry Brulard* could pursue further the parallels between these two enemies of humbug; here it is perhaps enough to mention that both grew up without friends of their own age, in the company of 'strangers'. Stendhal was seven when he lost his mother, whom he loved so passionately that her death seems to have destroyed every trace of filial sympathy for his father. As he recalls in the book, he overheard the priest saying that Mme Beyle's death was the Will of God, an opinion with which the bereaved husband piously concurred; and that took care of both God and Beyle *père*, as far as young Henri was concerned. From then on, his lifelong aversion to 'little white lies' was hardened by constant exposure to the pretensions and hypocrisies of his father and Aunt Séraphie, who came to take his mother's place – relatives he could not identify with and had no wish to excuse.

When a family servant died, the aunt was worried about little Henri mourning him too excessively:

> Séraphie, seeing me crying for poor Lambert, had a row with me. I marched out to the kitchen, muttering as if to revenge myself on her: 'Infamous, infamous!'

In a household of *ultras*, he was a staunch republican. Here is his account of a family scene that took place after Chérubin Beyle was arrested and released by the kindly representatives of the 'Reign of Terror' in Grenoble:

> Two or three months after this incident, which my family never stopped complaining about, I let slip an innocent remark which confirmed my wicked character. They were expressing, in their genteel way, the horror they felt at the mere mention of Amar's name.
>
> 'But,' I said to my father, 'Amar put you down on the list as notoriously *suspect* of not loving the Republic. It seems to me certain that you do not love it.'
>
> At this, the whole family turned crimson with indignation. They nearly locked me up in my bedroom; and during supper, which was announced shortly afterwards, no one addressed a single word to me. I pondered deeply over this. Nothing could be truer than what I had said, my father gloried in execrating *the new order of things* (a fashionable expression among the aristocrats at the time) – so what right did they have to be indignant?

Children's pitiless common sense is proverbial, but most of them grow weary of using it in the face of adult protest. They fear rejection, retribution, or simply being wrong; so they cease to observe and learn to believe. Even when they think 'differently' they tend to do so in groups, preferring to put their faith in shared opinion rather than in what they perceive to be true. Henri Beyle, however, remained stubbornly loyal to his own senses.

He was eleven when he forged a letter in the name of the commander of the revolutionary youth army, ordering Citizen Beyle to send his son to join *les bataillons de l'Espérance*, and deposited the paper at the door to the landing of a staircase *inside* the house. When he was found out, he was sent to his grandfather's study to wait for the verdict: in this royalist family, he was 'in the moral position of a young deserter about to be shot':

> There I amused myself by tossing into the air a ball of red clay I had just molded. . . . The fact that I had committed forgery worried me a little.

When he was called to face his judges and sentenced to three days' exile from the family table, he recovered his spirits:

> 'I'd rather dine alone,' I told them, 'than with tyrants who never stop scolding me.'

Apart from his secret qualms about the forgery, the account of Stendhal's boyhood does not record a single occasion on which he showed any sign of doubting himself just because everybody in sight disagreed with him, while he is often shown simmering with rage because of his family's inability to grasp that 'two and two make four' (one of his favourite and characteristic remarks). For two years, Henri also waged a relentless war against his detested tutor, the Jesuit abbé Raillane, who insisted on teaching him Ptolemaic astronomy because, he said, 'it explains everything and is also approved by the Church'.

> When we went for walks along the Isère . . . he used to take me aside and explain to me how imprudent I was in my speech. 'But, sir,' I used to say to him, in effect, 'it is true, it's the way I feel.'

[26]

'Never mind about that, my little friend, you must not say it, it will not do.'

But it was the Jesuit's advice that would not do for Henri, and he remained imprudent all his life. Scholars to this day reproach him for his arrogance. True, it is the stuff insufferable know-alls are made of, but it is also a vital attribute for people who know how to count. Without that wicked self-conceit, no artist could maintain the courage of his insights, the daring to create, to play God.

At the age of seven he had already decided he would grow up 'to write comedies like Molière and live with an actress'. Fortified by his future glory, by the Revolution, by his reading (*Don Quichotte, Les Liaisons dangereuses*), he 'breathed revolt' and resolved to excel in his beloved mathematics because 'it would get him out of Grenoble'. Finally, at the turn of the century and the Lausanne Gate, he mounted a horse to start on his decisive journey to Italy with the First Consul's triumphant army. He had never had a riding lesson, but didn't think that he couldn't ride just because he hadn't learned how, or at any rate it didn't occur to him that he should confess his ignorance and ask for advice; so he leaped on a mean-tempered beast which went berserk under him and galloped across a field of willows, heading for Lake Geneva. An officer's orderly pursued them around the field for a quarter of an hour and, after a perilous struggle in which he risked breaking his own neck, brought the horse to a halt. By way of thanks, the pale young man questioned his rescuer with regal disdain: 'What do you want?'

Yet what is pride but a keen sense of solitude? Henri could not admit that he needed help, because he could not conceive of anyone wishing to give him a helping hand. He even suspected the orderly of saving his life only to arrest him, and thought of drawing his pistols. Clearly, life was going to be a fight between H.B. and the world. He was to be his own hero.

*

Still, how unlike Stendhal, the dreariness of most independent spirits! He fought with the world like an ardent lover with his mistress – none of her real or imagined slights could prevent him from loving her with all his heart. His joyful sensations were always keener than his bitterest thoughts.

> I wanted to cover my mother with kisses, wishing away all clothes. She loved me to distraction and used to hug me all the time, and I returned her kisses with such fire that she was often obliged to draw away from me. I loathed my father when he came in and interrupted our kissing. I always wanted to kiss her on the breast. Kindly remember that I lost her in childbirth when I was scarcely seven years old.

This recollection in *Henry Brulard* is noted by many commentators as evidence of his 'Oedipus complex' – an example of how Freudian asides miss the point. A 'complex' is a manifestation of thwarted feelings, of conflict between impulse and some imperative norm of behaviour, implying inhibition and guilt; nothing could be further from Stendhal. The love and charm of the woman closest to him prompted him to respond with his whole being; his senses, his emotions were too powerful to be managed by concepts, moral or otherwise; so he could not react 'selectively'. The idea of 'mother' could never be as real to him as the actuality of her physical being. His senses absorbed the world so vividly that they etiolated all mental considerations. It was this that allowed him to perceive and convey life in its *immediacy* (that is, in its reality) which for most of us is buried under concepts or clouded by emotions storming in the void of abstractions. But perhaps the easiest way to describe the unique is by its common opposite. People who can be overwhelmed by the mental image of dominoes while looking at maimed and dead Vietnamese manifest an incapacity to 'receive' the world which is the exact antithesis of Stendhal's extraordinary ability to absorb the reality of each moment. After his mother's death he became bitter and moody, but he was quickly brought to life by all impressions – a vibrant breast, a beautiful landscape, or a song.

In the end, it was music, the language of the emotions, that acquainted him with his true nature. 'I was truly born in La Scala,' he records of his arrival in Milan. The opera, the then beautiful and spirited city, Renaissance art, women – all that Italy had to offer to a young aide-de-camp of a liberating army – awakened sensibilities unequalled in the history of the novel.

There was no clue about a gesture, a glance, an intonation, the mood of a scene that he missed, and he extended the limits of prose to realms that only music or the visual arts could reach. He wrote volumes on both music and Italian art, and (although the best of these was his carelessly brilliant *Life of Rossini* and he compared his intentions to Correggio's) he could well be introduced to strangers as the Mozart and Botticelli of literature. Like Mozart, he re-created life's passions in their full force yet without exaggeration and with the elegance of absolute precision (for great passions assert themselves with clarity and cannot mix with sentimentality). And his characters, like Botticelli's figures, are both real and *singular*. Stendhal, like Botticelli, could paint grace – which accounts for the fascination of his women. He didn't hesitate to repeat himself in describing the heroine of each of his three great novels (Mme de Rênal in *The Red and the Black*, Mme de Chasteller in *Lucien Leuwen*, the Duchessa Sanseverina in *The Charterhouse of Parma*) as 'a woman whose beauty is the least of her charms'. This description will make sense to anyone who has seen *The Birth of Venus*, even if he hasn't read the novels, and the memory of the painting can suggest to him the extra dimensions of Stendhal's art.

It was the fruit of a lifetime of passionate adventure. In Milan, the eighteen-year-old aide-de-camp fell in love promptly and hopelessly (the hopelessness is assumed, as he was too overwhelmed to make advances), but the sensation of proximity to Gina Pietragrua was exquisite bliss, as were the little affairs, the music of Cimarosa, plays and paintings, and animated conversation in the salons. Having experienced the rare sensation of 'five or six months of divine, total happiness', he decided that it was the best thing in the world and dedicated the rest of his life to *la chasse au bonheur*.

It was an uphill struggle. The few exalted months ended by his contracting venereal disease, a shock that would dampen any young man's spirits. Not Beyle's. 'I'm horribly sick today,' he writes in his *Journal*. 'I shall go out tomorrow.'

At the beginning of 1802, he returned to Grenoble on convalescent leave and promptly fell in love with Victorine Mounier, whom he followed to Paris in April, without leave from the army. As he recalled in one of the obituaries he wrote about himself, 'The minister [Daru] was angry and B. resigned his commission.' But Victorine moved to Rennes with her family, and Beyle began to court his fourteen-year-old Parisian cousin Adèle, until he succeeded with her mother instead. For three years he lived on a small allowance from his father and devoted his full time to reading, going to the theatre and trying to write comedies. To get him to do some honest work, as he notes in the same obituary, 'his father tried to starve him into submission. B., more determined than ever, set about studying how to become a great man.' The plays didn't come off but he achieved his second childhood ambition: the actress Mélanie Guilbert, who had rejected him in Paris, became his mistress when he followed her to Marseilles and even took a job with an exporter of foodstuffs to prove his devotion. In less than a year he was back in Paris, making his peace with Daru, and was dispatched on the emperor's service to Brunswick, where he paid court to Wilhelmina (a virtuous girl engaged to someone else) and heard for the first time *Così fan Tutte* and *Figaro*.

On an extended 'assignment' in Paris, he gorged himself on the theatre, books, conversation in the salons, dancing lessons, Spanish lessons, but after four months was ordered back to the war commissary in Strasbourg and followed the army to Vienna in the spring of 1809. Eventually he persuaded Daru to attach him to Napoleon's court in the capital, as inspector of the royal households and furnishings, and enjoyed a 'brilliant year' in Paris in 1811, keeping an actress, Angeline Bereyter, and making a declaration of love to Daru's wife. Receiving a firm but friendly refusal, he travelled to Milan to see his first hopeless love, Gina Pietragrua. This time he was lucky, left the next morning for Bologna, Florence, Rome, and Naples, and was inspired to write a history of Italian painting. This happy interlude was followed by the Russian campaign, in which Beyle, always a bored but competent administrator, distinguished himself as organizer of food supplies on the retreat from Moscow. 'The farther he ran away from danger, the more it terrified him,' he wrote in another of his premature obituaries. 'He reached Paris in a state of anguish, as much physical as mental. A month of good food, or rather of sufficient food, restored him.' On Daru's insistence, he took part in the campaign of 1813 in Poland, as intendant to 'a most hidebound general', but fell ill with some pernicious fever and in a week was reduced to such a feeble state that he had to be sent home to France – only to steal his way back to Italy, to recover his health at Lake Como. He returned to the service, but when his career collapsed with the Empire in 1814, he sold his apartment and furniture, carriage and horses, and caught the first stagecoach to Milan, to spend the next seven years in Italy, 'the land of sensibilities'.

When the tempestuous affair with Pietragrua came to an end, he met in Milan's radical *carbonari* circles his most hopeless love of all, the haughty Mathilde Viscontini-Dembowski, who held him at arm's length for three years. However, the Austrian police didn't know what to make of this Frenchman who was so fond of the company of passionate and subversive Italians, and in 1821 they delivered him from Mathilde's tormenting presence by hounding him out of Milan. On his way back to Paris, he was wavering between the desire to kill himself and the fear that his friends would laugh at him:

'What if the worst happens?' I cried out, 'what if those dried-up friends of mine guess at my passion – and for a woman I haven't slept with!' . . . I entered Paris, which I found worse than ugly, an insult to my grief, with one single idea: *not to be found out*.

Memoirs of an Egotist

He was thirty-eight years old at the time. Some of his critics describe him as 'a perpetual adolescent', 'a child who never grew up'; like a child, he was the fool of all his impulses, too rash, too excitable, too much in the grip of his impressions to cope successfully with the world. Whatever he got out of life, he had to go a long way and pay dearly for it. He was a poor, sick, unlucky devil who made a meagre living from his books on music, painting, and travel and by writing reviews for English journals. What could be a more painful sign of an all-around failure than the fact that, pushing forty, he couldn't wear a new coat without his friends suspecting that it was bought for him by a woman?

The bare facts of his life would indicate rather the making of a French Dostoevsky, a man who had become an expert on suffering, on the crazy, stupefying whirlwind of emotions. To some it may seem pathetic that this man considered himself – both in his life and work – a success at *la chasse au bonheur*. Yet nothing sums him up with greater exactitude than his own credo:

'Genius is the torch that lights the way to the art of happiness.'

This great art, in fact, must rest on a keen awareness of life's miseries. For what relevance, what truth could there be in a happy-go-lucky ignorance of the sufferings which are our common destiny? Stendhal's genius is rooted in his refusal to paint mirages, in his rejection of the pretty daydreams that only increase our disappointments. As a seventeen-year-old soldier, on his way to Milan and the dedication to *bonheur*, he went through his first battle, in which he discovered that the true source of happiness was simply *being alive*; so he could embrace and in a way wring satisfaction out of everything that happened to him: the joy of surviving was his keenest pleasure. 'To live is to feel, to have *powerful emotions*,' he writes, which is not at all the self-evident insight it may seem. He submits to all sensations if they are intense enough: even deeply felt defeat is victory. What matters is to experience to the full the miracle of existing. (In

[32]

this, too, he is akin to Mozart: his divine lightheartedness suggests all of man's sufferings.) It is a clue both to his character and his work that he correctly advises readers not to bother with him if they have never spent at least six months in the agonies of love.

The demonstration that our happiness depends on our actual feelings and not, as it is commonly supposed, on our situation, is another of Stendhal's characteristic magnitudes. In *The Charterhouse of Parma*, Fabrizio, the young veteran of Waterloo, who is trying to make his fortune in Parma under orders from his adoring Aunt Gina and her lover the Prime Minister, and who eventually becomes an archbishop, is happiest where everyone expects him to be the most miserable – in prison. He falls in love with Clélia Conti, the prison governor's daughter, and, to his great surprise, the mere glimpse of her through a hole in the wall turns out to be more thrilling than anything he has experienced in the world outside. For weeks Fabrizio foils all attempts at rescue, and even after his reluctant escape he longs to return to his cell in the Farnese Tower.

'Stock response', which is usually discussed in terms of aesthetics, is in truth one of the great problems of our lives: we continually *expect* ourselves to react in a certain way. We not only presume that we can foresee future events, we even presume that we know our future feelings about them, and this is the source of much of our unhappiness. No writer can help to cure us of this self-inflicted misery so much as Stendhal; the novelist whom Freud called 'a genius of psychology' shows the continuous tension in our consciousness between our expected and real reactions. One way to describe his first great novel, *The Red and the Black*, is to say that it is an ironic tale about a young man who is so determined to put himself in 'happy situations', so certain he knows what will give him happiness, that he fails to notice when he actually *is* happy.

That we count on our stock responses is most evident in our attitude to money. As for Stendhal, he was not only poor but 'childishly' capricious and irresolute in his material ambitions. Despite his high standing in the Napoleonic era, his many contacts among the Old Guard and his willingness to use them, he could never persist in his attempts to get rich. Invited to *ask* for the post of director of provisioning in Paris under the Bourbons, he declared that he was in an admirable position to accept it. The man who did ask for the post retired after four years, 'tired of making money'. Stendhal spent this time in the country where 'sunshine costs nothing', enriching his senses with music, art, the maddening Gina and the unattainable Mathilde.

The violent changes in the social order in France carried wave after wave of newcomers to power and riches, bringing 'everything' to people who had thought that all they were missing in life was position and possessions. Their disappointment produced the first epidemic of the malaise that afflicts the suddenly affluent classes of today, the source of which is simply that we cannot make love with unresponsive objects, no matter how hopefully we labour to obtain them, no matter how we overlay them with sexual symbolism. We have a *static* relationship with whatever we possess; it is a spell of death. Stendhal had a profound understanding of this existential flaw in the prizes of the rat race. In the minor character of M. de Rênal, *The Red and the Black* portrays the frustrations of success in the minutest detail. Mayor of Verrières, rich manufacturer, rewarded and decorated as a loyal *ultra*, owner of the town's handsomest new house and most spacious gardens, an heiress wife and three sons, M. de Rênal strives and continually fails to wring satisfaction out of his deals, honours, and acquisitions – like an unhappy fish in a silver bowl trying to find out why swimming in the stagnant water of confined space is not made more pleasurable by the preciousness of the container.

Stendhal preferred to travel. During his jobless years in Paris, he contrived two more trips to England, three to Italy and a leisurely tour as far south as Barcelona, mystifying his rich friends. Here is his description of one of them, the Baron Adolphe de Mareste:

Lussinge, then aged thirty-six or thirty-seven, had the head of a man of fifty-five. He was moved profoundly only by events which touched him personally; then he went mad, as at the moment of his marriage. . . . He had a mother who was a miser but also quite demented and capable of giving everything she owned to the priests. He decided to get married; this would be an occasion for his mother to make pledges which would prevent her from giving her property to her confessor. . . . Finally he married a perfect dolt, big and quite handsome, if she had only had a nose. . . . With her dowry, his salary as an official of the Ministry of Police, his mother's endowments, Lussinge had an income of 22- or 23,000 pounds a year around 1828. From that moment, he was dominated by one single emotion: the *fear of losing*. Despising the Bourbons (not as I did, from political virtue, but despising them for their clumsiness), he got to the point where he couldn't hear about their blunders without flying into a rage. He had a sudden, blinding vision of danger to his property. . . . In our political discussions he used to say to me: 'It's easy for you to talk! You – *you* have no fortune.'

Stendhal immersed himself in company instead – how wholeheartedly can be gathered from the wit and verve he brings to these portraits of his contemporaries in *Memoirs of an Egotist*. This is how he describes General Lafayette:

A great height, and on top of this tall body, an imperturbable visage, cold, impassive like an old family portrait, the head covered with a disheveled curly wig; this man, dressed in an ill-fitting grey coat, limping a little and leaning on a stick, entering the salon of Mme de Tracy (who called him, with an enchanting ring in her voice, *mon cher Monsieur*) – this was General de La Fayette in 1821.

That *cher Monsieur* of Mme de Tracy's (and said in that particular tone) caused, I think, some distress to M. de Tracy. It wasn't that M. de La Fayette had been intimate with the lady, nor was M. de Tracy, at his age, at all worried about that sort of thing; it was simply that the sincere, unforced and unassumed admiration of Mme de Tracy for M. de La Fayette made him too evidently the most important person in the salon.

Novice though I was in 1821 (I had always lived in the illusions of enthusiasm and passion), I worked that out *all by myself*.

I sensed also, without being told, that M. de La Fayette was, quite simply, a Plutarch hero. He lived from day to day, without too much *esprit*, and like Epaminondas, performed whatever great action presented itself to him. And in the meantime, in spite of his age (he was born in 1757, like Charles X, with whom he took the Tennis Court Oath in 1789), he was singlemindedly devoted to putting his hand up the skirt of every pretty girl, without the slightest embarrassment and as often as possible.

While waiting around for great actions, which don't present themselves every day, and for the opportunity to fondle bottoms, which hardly occurs till after midnight, M. de La Fayette expounded, without too much elegance, the commonplaces of the National Guard. A good government – and the only good government – is one which guarantees the citizen safety on the highway, equality before the judge (and a fairly enlightened judge), the money he's entitled to, passable roads, fair protection abroad. So arranged, the matter isn't too complicated. . . .

As for me, accustomed to Napoleon and Lord Byron (and, I might add, Lord Brougham, Monti, Canova, Rossini), I immediately recognized greatness in M. de La Fayette and never changed my opinion. I saw him during the July Revolution with his shirt in tatters; he welcomed all the intriguers, all the fools, everyone who made a bombastic approach to him. He was not so cordial to me – he plucked me and gave my post to a vulgar secretary, M. Levasseur. It never entered my head to be angry with him or to venerate him less, any more than it would have occurred to me to blaspheme against the sun when it was covered by a cloud.

M. de La Fayette, at the tender age of seventy-five, has the same failing I have. He is now infatuated with a young Portuguese, eighteen years old, a member of M. de Tracy's salon and a friend of his daughters . . . He thinks of no one but her, he imagines that this young Portuguese (and every other young woman) will favour him, and the amusing thing is, he is often quite right.

Stendhal could afford to be generous to Lafayette. For six years, by his own account, his hopeless love for Mathilde Dembowski plunged him into despairing celibacy, but when he recovered in 1824, he took as his mistress one of the most desirable women in France, the Comtesse Clémentine Curial. ('It was Clémentine who caused me the greatest misery when she left me . . . she was the wittiest of them all.') Several affairs later, while he was writing *The Red and the Black*, a young Sienese lady living in Paris, Giulia Rinieri, fell in love with him (he was forty-seven, poor, fat, gouty, and intermittently syphilitic) and he requested her hand in marriage. Her guardian-uncle, the Tuscan ambassador, suggested a brief postponement.

Though he was regarded as a dangerous liberal – Metternich personally vetoed his appointment to Trieste in 1830, and he was lucky to obtain even the consulate of Civitavecchia – he continually risked his job by abandoning it for months at a time, visiting Naples, Florence, Siena, the Abruzzi, Bologna, Ravenna, going on archaeological digs in the Roman country-side. Granted sick leave for three months, he stayed away for three years, touring France, Switzerland, the Rhineland, Holland and Belgium, and frequenting the theatres, cafés and salons of Paris. Here he was also reunited with Giulia Rinieri, who had married her cousin only to join her middle-aged lover wherever and whenever she could. ('Giulia, who at first seemed the weakest, surpassed them all in strength of character.') In ten years he wrote *Memoirs of an Egotist*, *Italian Chronicles*, *Lucien Leuwen*, *The Life of Henry Brulard*, *Memoirs of a Tourist*, *The Charterhouse of Parma* and *Lamiel*, not to mention his voluminous correspondence, but his itinerary was still that of a student sowing wild oats. At fifty-seven he had his 'Last Romance' in

Rome with the Contessa Cini. A year later he suffered his first attack of apoplexy ('there is nothing wrong with dying in the street,' he wrote to his friend Di Fiore, 'as long as one doesn't do it on purpose') but recovered for one more brief affair.

Looking out over Lake Albano toward the end of his life, he thought that his whole history could be summed up by the initials of eleven women and 'the inanities and follies they inspired me to commit'. Yet those who run wild must have the strength to run: it takes an extraordinary man to have the emotional energy, the spontaneity to be childish at fifty. As he put it, 'to possess a strong character one must have had an extensive experience of the disappointments and miseries of life: then one either desires constantly or not at all'.

The critics who complained of Stendhal's 'childishness' and 'immorality' missed the source of his genius, the strength which allowed him to keep his youthful responsiveness even as he grew old and wise. When he manifested a heedless capacity for both joy and sorrow to the end of his life, he was giving us a clue to the abilities which enabled him to write the most intensely alive novels in literature. He himself understood very well the springs of his inspiration:

> After the adventures of early youth, one's heart chills to sympathy. Losing childhood's companions through death or absence, one is reduced to spending life with indifferent acquaintances, forever measuring, ruler in hand, the considerations of interest and vanity. Gradually, tenderness and generosity dry up, and before a man is thirty he finds that his gentle and loving emotions have become petrified. In the midst of this arid desert, love strikes a spring that gushes forth with fresher and more abundant feelings than those of childhood.
>
> *On Love*

Stendhal was one of those rare souls who never stopped desiring *to be alive, to be in love, to be free*. These three desires dominate his works.

*

However, as Balzac said, we owe Stendhal to the contrast between the North and the Mediterranean: the man who wished to be described on his tomb as 'Arrigo Beyle Milanese' was still obsessed by French logic. In a sense the 'perpetual adolescent' Beyle was but an experimental subject for the 'cynic' Stendhal, who thus became master of both passion and irony. His childhood friend and maternal grandfather, Dr Gagnon, never ceased to impress upon him the importance of *knowing the human heart*, and Stendhal, his magnificent pride notwithstanding, dissected his own as if it were a guinea pig. Which accounts for the difference between his personal memoirs and *Journal* and most other writers' fiction: he talks about us even when he is concerned only with himself, while they write about themselves even when portraying others. And what he learned in the laboratory of his *Journal* he applied to the world of his novels. If his main pursuit was happiness, he also knew that it was the essential pursuit of all human beings, and his characters stand out so sharply because he asked the most vital and revealing questions: what gives them joy? what is it they truly love and hate?

His first masterpiece, *On Love*, grew out of his struggle to understand his insensate passion for Mathilde Dembowski. Since it was this work which provoked most critics to call him 'cold' and 'a cynic', it may be instructive to record how he finished it at the age of thirty-nine:

> I went up to my charming room on the third floor and cried as I corrected the proofs of *On Love*. It's a book that I wrote with a pencil in Milan, during my lucid intervals. Working on it in Paris hurt me. I never wanted to finish it.
>
> *Memoirs of an Egotist*

On Love is the distillation of *Beylisme*, the art of keeping one's head while losing one's heart. In *Being and Nothingness*, Sartre (who owes a great deal to Stendhal and little to the German philosophers he quotes at such length) cites this duality as an example of 'bad faith'. In fact, it is the schizoid aspect of literary genius: absolute involvement and absolute detachment.

[39]

It is also the secret of great acting. The fact that 'Stendhal' (derived from the name of a Prussian town) was only one of the hundred and twenty-nine pseudonyms that Beyle invented for himself ought to discourage anyone from presuming to understand him too well. Still, his fondness for assuming different identities betrays at least one other striking ability. All writers must have something of the actor in them – to create a character is to impersonate him – but there is no doubt that Stendhal was the greatest actor even among the master novelists. In *The Life of Henry Brulard* he recalls that in his youth at Napoleon's court, he acquired many powerful enemies by unconsciously mimicking their expressions, and growing old in Civitavecchia, he often stood in front of the mirror, imitating postures and gestures which he found particularly striking. Balzac and Tolstoy portray a wider range of characters but it is Stendhal who plays his heroes and heroines to the hilt.

> Everybody in France knows the story of Mademoiselle de Sommery, who was caught in the very act by her lover and denied it brazenly. When he protested, she cried out: 'Oh, well, I can see that you no longer love me – you would rather believe your eyes than what I tell you!'

On Love argues that she was nearly right. Her outburst, quoted in the book, carries *ad absurdum* one of its main themes: we become aware only of what we wanted to know in the first place. Strictly speaking, Stendhal examines only the relationship between love and consciousness, but with such lucidity that he reveals the connection between all thoughts and emotions. *On Love* is thus the most useful commentary on the novels to come.

The wisdom of the English language designates 'state of mind' as an emotional condition rather than a state of knowing – and this notion is also Stendhal's point of departure. He analyzes how our beliefs and opinions are formed by our psychological needs, how we reason to distort reality by accepting, rejecting, or twisting the facts of life to fit our inclinations. This process he calls *cristallisation*: the evidence crystallizes on the thread of feeling in a new and unrecognizable shape – like the 'diamond'-encrusted bough he once saw in the salt mines of Hallein. We may think we know everything about wishful thinking and emotional judgment (particularly in our opponents' views) but it is *On Love* that blows these phenomena up to their true proportions, by describing the process in its painful details and showing that each human being is subject to it: we all remake the world in the image of our feelings.

Illuminating the ways in which we wilfully fool ourselves, *On Love* sold seventeen copies in the year of its publication, and Stendhal's analysis of self-deception has still to be fully appreciated. By one of the characteristic modes of 'crystallization', we reject its significance by slighting it as a truism. Yet a truth seems obvious only when we understand it in the most superficial way. Facts are rarely obscure; our problem is to detect their relevance, their *meaning*. Thus, while we claim to know all about the ego's interest in our thinking, we continue to waste an inordinate amount of energy on the pretence that our beliefs, principles, opinions, our reasoning powers themselves are not in the pay of our emotions. This pretence (which is responsible for so many evils, from sexual prudery to ideological wars) is what Stendhal understood by *affectation*, a prime target of his irony and a current in the tension he creates in his novels.

*

Writing to Sainte-Beuve in 1834, Stendhal said: 'If I meet God after my death, I'll be very surprised, but if he allows me to speak, I'll have plenty to say to him.' He tells it all to his readers, and a lot of it concerns the affectations of envious malice.

Even today, when literature presents a crowded gallery of outsized monsters, madmen and sadists to demonstrate man's inhumanity to man, writers are curiously reticent about sheer everyday malice. It appears to be so basic to our nature that it has to be denied. The received notion is that there is very little malice in the world and a lot of paranoia. But Stendhal isn't shy about spite – he shows up the claim that 'all the world loves a lover' for the brazen lie it is.

[41]

On Love advises the reader who is lucky enough to be passionately in love not to confide in his best friend, because 'he is certain that if what you say is true, your pleasures are a thousand times better than *his* and make you despise him'. Which is how malice is born. We hate ourselves for our miseries and suspect everyone else of hating us too, or else we simply envy the more fortunate and imagine that they look down on us because we look up to them; and so we hasten to forestall their disdain by despising them first – like the generals who advocate the 'first-strike' nuclear strategy, urging their nation to be the first to fire its missiles, as a prudent preventive measure. *Malice is preemptive contempt.*

In *Lucien Leuwen* Stendhal describes the mood of a group of army officers in a provincial garrison as they learn that a new lieutenant is arriving from Paris. All they know about the newcomer, Lucien, is that he is a rich banker's son and has lived in the capital; but as they are bored with their own cramped, penurious lives, they imagine Lucien will despise them, and so they have no trouble in 'seeing through him'. They decide that he is overbearing, stupid, weak and worthless before they can possibly have any notion of what sort of person he is, and they employ all the mean little tricks of army life to make him pay for his 'conceit'. What might have been an easy satire on provincials becomes in Stendhal's hands the analysis of a common human trait: any sign of happiness in others strikes most of us as an offence, which we feel compelled to revenge. Lucien's father has just as many enemies in the political and financial world of Paris as his son has in the provinces, because he is cheerful and witty by nature and is suspected of having unlimited wealth and influence. *Lucien Leuwen*, by the way, is still the most up-to-date novel on modern politics and, along with *The Charterhouse of Parma*, allows the reader to discover the inspirational role that spite plays in political theories, stratagems and intrigues.

The master of irony doesn't miss out on the one-sided nature of malice. The people we envy rarely feel enviable. The rich lieutenant Lucien, whom the other officers despise for his 'arrogance', is miserable, lacks self-confidence and envies in his turn the officers who have made it in the army without their fathers' help. At the court of Parma, a careless sign of favour from the ruling monarch is enough to make the lucky courtier, Fabrizio, an object of hatred although he is so depressed that he is thinking of suicide. People don't really have to be better, better off, more intelligent or (worst crime) happier than we are – the mere suspicion that they might be is enough to convince us of their contempt for us and inspire us to retaliate.

'The passionate pride of the mediocre.' The phrase is Sartre's but the revelation is in Stendhal's novels. In *The Red and the Black*, Julien Sorel, a miller's son, is beaten by his father for reading books – a sign of the boy's wish to be superior. The rationalization is that he is 'lazy'. When Julien becomes tutor to the mayor's children and exchanges his peasant jacket for a smart black suit, his own brothers ambush him in the woods and leave him lying in his blood for the tailor's art. In Stendhal's world, as in ours, most people have a greater interest in beating down others than in bettering themselves.

The spitefulness of the Stendhalian characters depends not on their fixed 'character' but on their emotional state. Julien Sorel (who suffers as much from imagined slights as from the real spite he's subjected to) is finally condemned to death because he refuses to humble himself before the jury, and yet he is capable of despising his devoted mistress, Mme de Rênal, as an empty and selfish woman whenever he suspects her of pride.

On every page of Stendhal's novels, the characters are ready to change their attitudes toward people, to persuade themselves of new and 'impartial' judgments and act upon them, at the moment their ego is wounded.

It must be emphasized that none of this is on a complaining note: the gasping self-pity which turns most books on the human condition into nauseating revelations of the authors' deep sorrow for themselves is alien to Stendhal's realism. Far from sentimentalizing his characters' misery, he shows it as the chief inspiration for evil. He is teaching the reader to be beware of himself, *beware of the unhappy*.

We may become virtuous (or at any rate harmless to ourselves and others) if we are truly happy, for contentment is a generous and even humble state of mind. This is the importance of love – yet love, too, has its rationalizations.

Mme de Rênal grew up in a convent and has no thoughts or desires other than the ones her education allows her to have. Submissive and timid, sincerely devout, she is a faithful wife and a loving mother; she is also a snob, a provincial *bourgeoise* who dutifully detests Napoleon (Julien's secret hero) and is held up by all the petty tyrants of the small town as an example to their wives. Until the arrival of Julien in her household, the word *amour* means nothing to her but vile, revolting debauchery. When she falls in love with him, she can explain her sentiments: she is overjoyed that her children have a kind tutor who doesn't beat them, she feels sorry for this poor miller's son, she is concerned with his well-being out of Christian charity. And so she is 'perfectly happy, thinking of nothing but Julien, without the slightest notion of reproaching herself'. When she can no longer remain unaware of her love, she admits it to herself by disclaiming it: 'This fit of madness will pass.'

She is relieved that she has nothing to fear. It is by such twists of consciousness that she finally becomes his mistress.

Julien, for his part, inflamed by ambition, has firm and considered opinions about the worthlessness of all other emotions. He prides himself so much on his rationality that while he is head over heels in love with Mme de Rênal, he still pretends to himself that he is playing with her.

Affectations like these produce the charming ironies in our lives, but the irony is in a contradiction that can grow to ruin us. When Julien leaves her, Mme de Rênal convinces herself that the void left by his absence is *remorse*, guilt, proof of her sin; and when she is asked for a character reference to pave the way for his marriage to the daughter of a marquis, she is persuaded that she owes it 'to the sacred cause of religion and morality' to write a letter that will cut off both his marriage and his career. Julien, resolved to act and speak only to get ahead, doesn't realize his passion for Mme de Rênal until (a fanatical believer in calculating every move) he rushes back to Verrières and tries to kill her.

In short, no naïve rationalist could be pleased with Stendhal. If you appreciate yourself for your opinions and principles, if you think they place you above less high-minded people, he isn't your author. None of his books can be read without acquiring the uneasy feeling that we know nothing of a person if we only know his views. He is the novelist who puts ideas and ideologies in their place: if they are relevant to the character, they are expressions of an inner condition; if not, they are meaningless – or worse, they are poison.

But what of the feelings that lead us to false ideas? Stendhal isn't party to the kind of cynicism with which we protect ourselves from involvement. People are ever ready, he notes in *On Love*, to ridicule the madness of all absorbing interests, in order to encourage themselves to have none. The affectation that wisdom lies in the absence of emotion is inspired by the most contemptible emotion of all, the dread of feeling, which leads us to what he calls (in English) the *dead blank*.

We cannot escape from the domination of our psychological state, the only question is which emotions will master our being. This is from *On Love*:

> While the zealous nobody is consumed by boredom, avarice, hate and all the icy and bitter passions, I spend a cheerful night dreaming of her.

*

As both capitalist and communist states – not to mention the technological world – have evolved under the illusion that men purposefully built them, ideological optimism seeps into every niche of our lives. It is made worse by mass culture which feeds our most destructive illusions, fostering the belief that if we're only justified (and who isn't?) – if we only calculate things correctly, if we only *do the right thing* (and who doesn't?) – then the future must yield the desired results. There must always be a way. And so hubris turns hope to false certainties, everyone expects to be a winner, and each morning is a mind-blowing surprise.

Which is why we need Stendhal more than perhaps any other generation: his novels show us how the future works. Tolstoy wrote the best study on the tenuous connection between men's aims and life's results, but it is Stendhal who exposes at every turn the fundamental condition of our lives. Chaos is his specialty.

There is, to begin with, his understanding of the chaotic contradictions within each character. We cannot count on people to act in the way they have led us to believe they always would. The provincial prefect in *Lucien Leuwen* risks losing his job and his chances of advancement, the fruits of long years of shameless servility, by throwing the by-election to the opposition candidate in a sudden fit of wounded vanity. Lucien's father, the rich Parisian banker who acts and talks like the prototype of the successful capitalist and believes in nothing but money and power, in fact has so little interest in either that, to everyone's surprise, he dies a poor man.

Irving Howe pays Stendhal a misleading compliment when he praises the extreme political sophistication of *The Charterhouse of Parma* because the head of the liberal opposition party in the principality, Fabio Conti, is also the despot's craven prison governor, ever ready to connive in the murder of Ernesto IV's victims. Stendhal is much more sophisticated than that. Seeing through the transparent dissimulations of power politics is child's play compared with his accomplishment in describing the true relationship in the consciousness of each of his characters between their ideas, principles or intentions and their real nature.

The result shows society in a light that makes the image of a neat and tidy world of oppression (where even treacherous liberals pursue basely but simply their self-interest) look like just another daydream, an altogether too orderly and rational nightmare. *The Charterhouse of Parma* reveals modern totalitarianism operating under the same old anarchic non-rules as the Wars of the Roses. If the liberal prison governor is ready to sacrifice Fabrizio's life to the Prince's spite (and his own), it is Conte Mosca, the Prince's avowedly opportunistic and efficiently ruthless prime minister, who organizes the prisoner's escape. (*'Here I am, committing high treason,' the Conte said to himself, wild with joy*.) One cannot even rely on politicians to be consistently vile, any more than one can count on them to keep faith with their noble speeches.

Beyond the darkness that descended on Europe with the victory of the Holy Alliance, there is the darker world of unpredictability.

Stendhal doesn't only suggest this, he proves it. His heroes and heroines are armed with all the best weapons against the world and exploit to the full every conceivable opportunity to achieve their aims. They do not fail, they are defeated.

Julien Sorel, the commoner determined to get to the top, is a near-genius. At the age of fourteen he has the wit to recognize from a single trivial incident the fact that in post-Napoleonic France a peasant boy cannot hope to rise in the red coat of the army, that the only way up is in the black cassock of the church.

All at once, Julien stopped talking about Napoleon; he announced his intention of becoming a priest and was constantly to be seen in his father's sawmill, memorizing a Latin Bible that the curé had lent him. This good old man, marveling at his progress, spent whole evenings teaching him theology. In his company, Julien expressed nothing but pious sentiments. Who could have guessed that this pale, gentle, girlish face concealed the unshakable determination to risk a thousand deaths rather than fail to make his fortune?

Determination, self-denial, intelligence, imagination, dreams of glory – and a series of lucky and unlucky accidents – carry him from the sawmill to the Rênal household to the seminary at Besançon to the Hôtel de La Mole in Paris, as private secretary to a powerful aristocrat. For all his calculations, he is trustworthy and loyal, as well as efficient, and is soon entrusted with all the Marquis de La Mole's business affairs and dangerous political intrigues, handling them better than the Marquis himself, who wishes that his son could be more like Julien. When the 'monstrously proud' Mathilde de La Mole falls in love with him and invites him to her room at midnight, he

[47]

suspects a trap: he is convinced that the young noblemen, her brother's friends, want to kill him and are planning an ambush; yet he keeps the date, pistols in hand. He wouldn't excuse himself if he were careless; he never wants to say 'I didn't think of that'. He always thinks of *everything*. Even the things he doesn't calculate work to his advantage: when Mathilde becomes pregnant she insists on marrying him, and the enraged Marquis is eventually forced to set about turning his secretary into an aristocrat. Julien becomes the Chevalier de La Vernaye, lieutenant of hussars, stationed at Strasbourg with his horses, his uniforms, his liveried servants. He is intoxicated with ambition.

> . . . he was already calculating that he would have to be more than a mere lieutenant at twenty-three in order to be commander-in-chief by thirty at the latest, like all the great generals. He thought of nothing but glory and his son.

At this moment, the Marquis has already received the letter of denunciation from Mme de Rênal.

The significance of her letter is that it brings Julien to realize what has mattered most to him in life. The realization comes to him too late; this is his tragedy. But as far as his social ambitions are concerned, he has done everything humanly possible. He was found wanting in nothing, no one could have done things better. Yet in truth even his temporary successes are due rather to accident than to his calculations and efforts, and in the end he is beaten.

Had Julien been any less willing or capable, his story would have been inconclusive. Indeed, literature is crowded with the misfortunes of weak or obsessed characters who are overwhelmed by life, leaving both themselves and the reader *at a loss*. Such characters – even as conceived by Dostoevsky or Kafka – may be moving and convincing but their very helplessness limits their relevance: one can never be certain that a saner or stronger man would not have done better in their place. The limits of the human condition haven't been tested. We're left with a bewildering sense of the 'mystery' of life, which can exercise our compassion and feed our self-pity but which adds little to our understanding of the rules of existence.

Stendhal has no use for the art of the inconclusive. After his first novel, *Armance*, he discarded half-hearted characters who could not probe the ultimate limits of passion, will and capability. Although he condemned Napoleon for 'robbing France of her liberties', he never ceased to be a fascinated admirer of the intelligence, energy, ingenuity, courage and determination that allowed a Corsican nobody to become an emperor. Like Tolstoy after him, he saw Napoleon as the definitive *doer*, the explorer of the possibilities of human mastery over events. And so he creates Napoleonic characters. Julien often compares himself to the young Bonaparte, and the comparison is justified by his talents and actions. There is no 'mystery of life' in the Stendhal novel: whatever his central characters are trying to do, the reader can take it at the end that the thing *has been tried*.

Even such a spirited woman as Anna Karenina compares unfavourably with one of Stendhal's least strong-willed heroines, Mme de Rênal. She is timid and can be bullied by her confessor into ruining Julien and herself, but her failure is in misunderstanding what happens to her, not in weakness of character. After Julien's attempt on her life, she doesn't hesitate to expose herself to ridicule and condemnation in a public effort to save him. She *thinks* of suicide but she carries on until her heart stops beating.

However, no character, male or female, can compare with Gina Sanseverina of *The Charterhouse of Parma*. There is nothing in the world she doesn't know: she understands men, she understands politics, she knows how to charm, she knows how to fight. This woman is never deceived by false notions: she even knows herself. She is also highborn, rich and powerful. Conte Mosca, the prime minister of Parma and a profound master of diplomacy and intrigue, is her slave. Without even trying, she can inspire passions that lead men to risk their lives and commit murder to please her. It has been noted that she makes even literary critics lose their heads; to quote only Balzac, she is 'frank, naïve, sublime, submissive, witty, passionate . . . she embodies the genius of Italy'. There has never been a real or imaginary human being so well equipped to get what she wanted from life – or who wanted it so badly. 'The universe is a footpath to her passion.' She wants her nephew. Everything she does, she does for Fabrizio. He has the most sincere affection and admiration for her, but he has fallen in love with Clélia Conti, and there isn't a thing that she can do about it.

Her love rejected, her life in danger, she hears loud voices in the house at midnight:

> 'Good!' she thought, 'they're coming to arrest me. So much the better. That will give me something to do, fighting them for my head.'

The Duchessa Sanseverina not only illuminates the impossibility of controlling our destiny, she even reconciles us to it.

*

Readers who have yawned through one too many 'serious' novels need not keep their distance from Stendhal. His works are not displays of ponderous fatuity, devised to prove how deep the author's mind is and how difficult his craft. They are not the sort of books that are trumpeted by the culture phonies like Sainte-Beuve who dictate literary opinion in every age and every country and who are unfailingly opposed to art – perhaps for the simple reason that they are chiefly interested in art, while art is chiefly interested in life. Such people can easily live with falsehood because they are horrified of nothing but vulgarity – that is, reality without the cushioning of affectation. They considered Stendhal cheap, vulgar and 'inartistic' in his time and even today they cannot write of his works without condescension. Stendhal is too lively for them, even in the grave.

This needs saying because Stendhal's dedication 'to the happy few' has been picked up by these precious few as a slogan of their caste. He detested these bookish 'halfwits whose vanity compels them to talk about literature and make a pretense of thinking', and it was primarily their mob that he meant to exclude from the happy circle of his readers (which he hoped would contain 'beings such as Mme Roland and M. Gros, the geometrician' – his old mathematics teacher in Grenoble). In his day they praised and admired writers who are now completely forgotten or still remembered for their monumental achievements in melodramatic absurdity, tortured psychology and unnatural style – Chateaubriand, Alfred de Vigny, Eugène Sue, Fenimore Cooper, Walter Scott. Sainte-Beuve considered Stendhal's novels literally beneath notice and even denied himself the satisfaction of attacking them in print for fear that negative reviews might encourage some perverse reader to buy them. *The Charterhouse of Parma* received one single review (a favour from the *Revue de Paris* to Stendhal as one of its contributors) in the year of its publication – an outrage which finally prompted Balzac to set down his sixty-nine-page *Etudes sur M. Beyle*, 'in admiration, compelled by conscience'.

However, Balzac, of all people, couldn't help noting that M. Beyle was 'very fat' and (while spelling his subject's pen name 'Stendahl') castigated him for 'negligent errors' of grammar and style – concluding with the suggestion that he should polish his manuscript to achieve the poetic perfection of Chateaubriand. No wonder Stendhal took two weeks to compose his thank-you note, grateful though he was for Balzac's many true insights. The three drafts of his answer give us some idea why he is above all *a good read*. 'I've been told,' he wrote to Balzac, 'that I should give the reader a rest from time to time by describing landscape, clothes, etc. But those things have bored me so much in other books!' He wouldn't inflict on his readers the sort of 'obligatory' passages he himself found tiresome – which is why he is one of the few authors we can read without skipping. Excusing his negligent errors on the grounds that the book was dictated in just over nine weeks (I don't believe it!), he confided innocently that he had never thought of the *art* of writing a novel and had no idea that there were rules about it. As for what Balzac had called 'that character of perfection, the seal of irreproachable beauty which Chateaubriand and de Maistre gave to their beloved books' –

While I was writing *The Charterhouse*, I sometimes read a few pages of the Civil Code in order to catch the right tone. . . . I could never read twenty pages of M. de Chateaubriand; I almost had to fight a duel because I made fun of 'the indeterminate crest of the forests' . . . I find M. de Maistre insupportable. No doubt that's why I write badly – from an exaggerated love of logic.

He confessed that he knew of only one rule in writing: *to be clear*. ('I often reflect for a quarter of an hour whether to put an adjective before or after a noun. I try to recount (1) truthfully, (2) clearly, what goes on in a human heart.') Out of gratitude for Balzac's enthusiastic review, he made the (unkept) promise to 'improve' his language; but there was no doubt in his mind about who was right. As he had already written elsewhere: 'Only a profound mind would dare a straight style. That's why Rousseau put so much rhetoric into *La Nouvelle Héloïse*.'

Unappreciated by his contemporaries, he wrote for future generations, and this has a direct bearing on the fact that his masterpieces have the pace, economy and tension of good thrillers. Assuming that his future readers would neither know nor care about the period he lived in, he found it easy to ignore the great ephemeral issues of his time, the sort of front-page problems that find their way into most novels and date them in a few decades, if not a couple of months. His novels include nothing which is not of the utmost significance to the characters or their story. Balzac, who spoiled some of his own works by excessive documentation of the purely temporary, identified Conte Mosca of *The Charterhouse of Parma* with Count Metternich; Stendhal's response to the suggestion was cool:

I had no intention of portraying M. de Metternich . . . I dream of having some little success around 1860 or 1880. By then there will be very little talk of M. de Metternich . . . Death makes us exchange places with such people.

Stendhal isn't for scholars or the luckily limited number of literary intellectuals: his theme is the human emotions we all share. He doesn't count on pleasing pretentious women or 'practical' men who are too busy making a hundred thousand francs a year and meeting a weekly payroll of two thousand workers to *waste their time* on anything but useful facts, nor the student who is 'so delighted with having learned modern Greek that he's already thinking of taking up Arabic'; but he doesn't exclude from his happy few the sort of people who strike it rich on the Bourse or in a lottery. Such emotion-stirring gambles, he thinks, are quite compatible with the feelings inspired by a great painting, a phrase of Mozart's or a look in a woman's eyes.

As Balzac said, Stendhal can be read 'with bated breath, craning neck, goggling eyes, by anyone who has an imagination, or even just a heart'.

*

Writers who stuff their readers with the most preposterous lies, appearing more ignorant of real life than one would have thought possible, are usually called romantics. It's a nice and reputable word, as if believing in a lot of nonsense were a harmless and even perhaps admirable pastime. The adjective 'romantic' has also been applied to Stendhal, with absolutely no justification, by dried-up critics who are shocked by the very idea that men and women can be possessed by feelings. Those who call him a cynic and complain that he robs us of our illusions are at least stating a fact.

We live in a haze of illusions, never quite certain who we are or where we are, each suffering our own 'anxiety neurosis' and 'identity crisis'. When Stendhal robs us of our false notions about love, reason, action and history, he clears away the haze and allows us to touch ground. 'This is life,' the reader can say, 'this is what it means to be a human being, this is what I must cope with.'

Freeing life from its lies, he also communicates its *force*, which fills our senses, our emotions, our impulses, but which we learn to betray.

Most of our adult life is spent in little compromises which

[53]

enable us to get along with other human beings but also reduce our feeling of individuality, our sense of our own uniqueness and importance. We're keenly aware – more so perhaps in this age of overpopulation and mass communication than ever before – that each one of us is a superfluous nonentity in the scheme of things. This makes it easier for others to handle us and more difficult for us to have faith in ourselves – which is why all tyrannies make humility the greatest virtue. This virtue, this servility, this denial of self which is euphemistically called 'conformism', even swamps our will to live.

The mainspring of all Stendhal's work is the emotional tension between our immediate impulses, our true feelings, and the pressure to check them for the sake of our social role. In this tension we often warp and even exchange our living self for a kind of functioning machine. This is Julien Sorel's keenest torment: his own powerful impulses conflicting with what he conceives as the necessity to make all his words and gestures conform to an expected and supposedly successful pattern. But this problem isn't confined to the underdog and outsider: Lucien Leuwen, the rich boy, feels it just as keenly, as does Fabrizio del Dongo, the Italian aristocrat.

For the impulsive, passionate, 'childish' Stendhal, it was the problem of his life – spending as he did many years in the army, at court, in the diplomatic service (not to mention the all-important literary salons), where every look, every gesture, every word had its consequences – and facing even worse hazards in the constant company of the women he worshipped and so desperately wanted to please. To adjust or to be oneself – this is the drama that is always there, in every moment that we spend with others. Stendhal had to face it also as a writer: should he or shouldn't he play literary politics? should he or shouldn't he apply the 'poetic' style? As Valéry wrote, 'he was divided between his great desire to please and to achieve glory and the *mania*, the *sensual pleasure*, of being himself. . . .'

Julien Sorel, condemned to the guillotine for the attempted murder of Mme de Rênal, is offered the chance of a pardon if he will only publicly repent his sin and undergo a religious

[54]

conversion. However, this young man, this most cynical opportunist who prided himself on never uttering a word in earnest, has come to realize that we can depend on absolutely nothing in this world, neither on hopes realized nor hopes thwarted – that we're rich or poor, defeated or victorious only in the way we feel about ourselves, and therefore nothing is worth so much as this feeling, the only thing we truly possess. And so he refuses to *pretend* any more, even to save his life. *'And what would I have left,' Julien answered coldly, 'if I despised myself?'*

The sensual joy that inspires Julien's decision is the Stendhalian beat, striking in the reader's own soul 'that which is fierce, jealous, and incommunicable'. No one can read Stendhal and feel redundant or altogether beaten. He rekindles our pride.

The Times, May 11, 1968

Stendhal's Torch of Genius

Stendhal: The Education of a Novelist, by Geoffrey Strickland (Cambridge)

Readers who get nothing out of fiction simply haven't yet found
the novelists who see and feel the world as they do. And they
should keep searching, for there is nothing so exhilarating, so
mind-blowing, as to experience other lives through the same
sensibilities, the same curiosities, the same inclinations, preoccupations, moods and responses as one's own – to say
nothing of finding one's half-formed thoughts expressed and
confirmed. Reading a novelist who is the same sort of person as
oneself (plus genius) is like going on a world tour without
leaving home.

These propositions are inspired by Stendhal, who was the
first to understand fully that literature is possible only between
like-minded and like-hearted authors and readers. It should be
said right away that Stendhal's own books cannot fail to annoy
those who take themselves very seriously.

He defined genius as 'the torch that lights the way to
happiness' and employed his sublime intelligence to ridicule
those *bad habits* which make people unhappy. Clearly, those
who are not prepared to blame themselves for their miseries
and are not about to laugh at their own bad habits tend to find
him an offensive bore. (They should try Balzac, who is more
fascinated by the harm people do to others than by the harm
they do to themselves.)

Also, those who are too sensible ever to have been carried to
unreasonable lengths by love and have never had the luck to

inspire passionate love in others, might as well skip Stendhal: he makes a great deal of the happiness they will never know, and they can only despise him for it. It was Stendhal, incidentally, who noted in his treatise *On Love* that a man cannot forgive even his best friend for being happy.

All this is by way of a recapitulation for those who have just come in and by way of comment on an unending literary dispute. Dead since 1842, Stendhal still attracts the kind of personal animosity and personal affection and enthusiasm which are usually generated only by living figures.

Professor John Bayley of Oxford, for instance, has just dismissed the author of *The Red and the Black* and *The Charterhouse of Parma* (which won the admiration of Balzac, Baudelaire, Proust, Valéry, Gide and Mr Bayley's very own Tolstoy, among others) as a clumsy writer and not really a novelist at all, while Geoffrey Strickland, in *Stendhal: The Education of a Novelist*, upholds him as one of the best.

I see from the acknowledgments that Mr Strickland was advised at one stage by Professor Vittorio del Litto of Grenoble, and though he isn't blessed with the magnificent Del Litto's irresistibly joyful passion for his subject, he scores quite a few points in his circumspect English way.

His study is particularly valuable in tracing Stendhal's philosophical development under the influence of Locke and Bentham and their French disciples, and in showing how he formed his theories about literature through his studies of Italian painting, music, Molière and Shakespeare.

I miss only any mention of Laclos, the first great psychological novelist and the first to create a hero whose feelings are the exact opposite of what he thinks they are and whose pride in his cold heart gives way to love only too late. Readers of *Les Liaisons dangereuses* and *The Red and the Black* will see that Laclos' work was a decisive inspiration for Stendhal and that the relation between them is not unlike the relationship between Haydn and Mozart.

But while it is difficult to conceive a full account of any genius's development, Mr Strickland goes a long way towards proving Jean Prévost's proposition that 'few men have pre-pared themselves for writing with so much effort and conscientiousness' as the young Stendhal.

It is important to stress this, for people who have not the slightest idea of creative work – and this includes many critics – tend to assume that masterpieces are tossed off more or less accidentally, and even among Stendhal's admirers there are many who underrate his critical writing.

In truth, of course, no one could create such a complex work of art as a great novel without knowing exactly what he is doing, and Mr Strickland demonstrates through his analysis of the *History of Painting in Italy*, *Comedy is Impossible* and *Racine and Shakespeare* that Stendhal was a profound thinker and critic before he became a profound novelist.

He believed that his first task was 'to know man perfectly' and that the most moving and therefore most illuminating way to convey what he learned was not through some long drawn-out account of an experience, but through just a *little true fact*, through a *particular impression*. This is what makes him, as Mr Strickland eloquently puts it, so 'tantalisingly brief and yet straight to the point'.

He didn't care much for descriptions of dresses and furniture, and he explains why in his article *Sir Walter Scott et La Princesse de Clèves*:

> . . . it is infinitely less difficult to describe in a picturesque fashion the costume of a character than to say what he feels and to make him speak. Don't let's forget another advantage of the school of Sir Walter Scott; the description of a costume and of the posture of a character, however minor he may be, take up at least two pages. The movements of the soul, which first of all are so hard to detect and then so difficult to express, with precision and without exaggeration or timidity, will provide the material for barely a few lines.

This is the place perhaps to note with disapproval that Mr Strickland's *Stendhal's Selected Journalism* is out of print and

English readers are deprived not only of Stendhal's reviews and articles in French but even of those that appeared originally in the *Edinburgh Review* and the *London Magazine*. It is a scandal how many classics of European literature are unavailable in English.

Mr Strickland notes that Stendhal was 'incapable of the servility of mind any political allegiance is likely to require' and his analysis of Stendhal's novels is particularly forceful and helpful because he never loses sight of the fact that Stendhal had no use for ideologies and systems but rather revealed the world by *examples*.

This makes the novels a series of dramatic discoveries by way of the 'little true facts', many of which Mr Strickland catches and holds up for us to reflect upon.

He notes, for instance, that Julien Sorel begins to feel remorse for shooting Mme de Rênal only *after* learning that he didn't kill her and she will recover; these are the sort of truths about the human soul that not a dozen writers in history have been capable of giving us.

Stendhal: The Education of a Novelist also supplies a much-needed critical appraisal of *Lucien Leuwen* (now about to be issued by The Boydell Press after being out of print for God knows how long). Stendhal noted in his *Journal* that the draft of *Lucien Leuwen* (which is all we have) was about 200 pages too long and he intended to cut 'pages and phrases'. I doubt that he could have cut 200 but he might have managed to get rid of 40 to 50 pages, improving the tempo of the work. But then all too many critics have pondered the imperfections of what is still a great novel, and in fact its immense virtues render its flaws more or less irrelevant. If *Lucien Leuwen* eventually becomes more widely appreciated in the English-speaking world, Mr Strickland and his book ought to be given some of the credit for it.

In the meantime I would advise readers who have ever been in love to grab any Stendhal they can lay their hands on. I'm only sorry that no one is thinking of bringing out his *Italian*

Chronicles, which are as breathtaking as Heinrich von Kleist's stories (also out of print in England).

The Sunday Telegraph, August 18, 1974

The Unfinished Masterpiece

Lucien Leuwen, by Stendhal, translated by H. L. R. Edwards, introduction by Geoffrey Strickland (The Boydell Press)

In his preface to *The White Devil* Webster speaks of 'those ignorant asses who visiting stationers' shops, their use is not to inquire for good books but new books'. I'm reminded of Webster by the fact that *Lucien Leuwen* was not translated into English until 1951, thirty-three years had to pass before it was reprinted, and, as far as I know, no publication has taken any notice of this reissue of *Lucien Leuwen*, one of the essential books of Western literature. True, it does not have the dramatic sweep of *The Red and the Black* or *The Charterhouse of Parma*, but in an important sense it is closer to us: it is the best novel ever written on parliamentary democracy, on that 'seductive blend of hypocrisy and lies which is called representative government'.

It is set in the reign of 'Citizen King' Louis-Philippe, brought to power by the revolution of July 1830. France has a constitutional monarchy, a legal republican party, a free press and a parliament elected by limited suffrage. Hence the need for hypocrisy and lies. The Prince if Parma could rely on his secret police; an elected government needs to impose its will by deception.

Once again, the hero is a young man who wants to succeed in the world and remain decent at the same time; the twin discoveries of self and society are to the novel what counterpoint is to music, and Stendhal is their unequalled master.

Lucien Leuwen is Stendhal's luckiest hero. Unlike Julien

Sorel or Fabrizio del Dongo, he has a jovial and affectionate father who believes that 'a son is a creditor given by nature' – a father, moreover, who is an extremely rich Parisian banker. When Lucien is expelled from the Ecole Polytechnique for taking part in a political demonstration, he wastes two years 'waging ceaseless war on cigars and new boots' but then decides to amount to something in the world and with his father's help becomes a subaltern in the 27th Lancers, mainly because he likes their uniform best.

The first thing he does as a soldier is to fall off his horse. When Stendhal was writing his great novels in the 1830s, more than three decades after the horse ran away with him at the Lausanne Gate, it was still one of his favourite motifs: evidently it was his way of tapping his subconscious and calling back the intense feelings of his youth, the enthusiasm and dreaminess of adolescence, which somehow suffused everything he wrote.

Lucien spurs his mount at the wrong moment because he is gazing at 'a young blonde with magnificent hair and a disdainful look' who is watching the parade from an upstairs window and who smiles (laughs at him, as he thinks) when he is thrown into the mud. Furious and infatuated, he devotes himself singlemindedly to winning her love.

To contrive an introduction to Mme de Chasteller he has to wangle his way into the salons of the local aristocracy – legitimist landowners resentful of their shrinking share of the budget. Only Stendhal could bring off a love story that meanders through a maze of political discussions, but then only Stendhal could make political discussions so enthralling. As Geoffrey Strickland writes in his brilliant study, *Stendhal: the education of a novelist* (Cambridge, 1974), he 'lacked the servility of mind which any political allegiance is likely to require' and with the impartiality of his critical intelligence saw the folly in every point of view. Lucien fears he is doomed to spend his life among 'legitimists who are mad, selfish and polite, adoring the past, and republicans who are mad, generous and dull, adoring the future'. This still seems to me a perfect description of the left and the right.

Mme de Chasteller's obdurate chastity is the only element in the novel that may seem dated, though its effect (Lucien's desperate conclusion that she cannot possibly love him – has even had a child by another man, unlikely though it seems – and his headlong flight back to Paris) still rings true of impatient young men today. Nor is there anything outdated about the power games in Paris.

When it came to that sort of thing, Stendhal had the unfair advantage of having seen a great deal more than most novelists. He had been an army officer, an administrator, a government official, a diplomat, and even a tax collector for Napoleon, 'nearly beaten senseless' by an angry mob – an episode which crops up in *Lucien Leuwen*. Having found that 'men nearly always lie when they talk about the motives of their actions', he does not accept the most boring and widely shared pretence about public affairs: namely, that political acts are committed for political reasons – in the public interest, or at least in the interest of some group or other. Even Marxists picture politicians as more-or-less disinterested representatives of an evil system, motivated by the desire to maintain the power of the exploiting class, rather than as what they are, hungry individuals out for themselves. Stendhal knew better. In *Lucien Leuwen* there are as many parties as there are characters.

'Always treat a minister as an imbecile, he has no time to think,' says Leuwen *père* to his son, whom he has just placed as administrative assistant to the Comte de Vaize, Minister of the Interior. Lucien gets the job because de Vaize is Leuwen's silent partner: the minister forewarns the banker about government decisions, and the banker buys and sells for both of them on the Bourse. Which is how many politicians who devote their lives to the public good end up as millionaires.

Of course, not all corruption has to do with money. Inspired by the admirable ambition to prove that he isn't just his father's son, Lucien works hard for the Minister he despises, trying to bribe the voters of Caen in order to prevent the election of a good man, the republican candidate. He fails in spite of his clever manoeuvres because the vain little Prefect of Caen would rather risk losing his job by ensuring the defeat of the government's candidate than co-operate with Lucien, who has offended his *amour-propre*. The Caen election is lost but Lucien's father, in 'a fit of ambition', gets himself elected deputy for the Aveyron department, acquires a group of followers in the Chamber who vote at his bidding and creates a parliamentary crisis to punish the Minister for failing to reward Lucien's efforts in a sufficiently impressive manner.

As you read this novel it dawns on you that the affairs of state will *always* be mismanaged, because people cannot help making public decisions for private and often idiosyncratic reasons. *Lucien Leuwen* is full of the kind of scandalous stories that financial editors and Westminster and Capitol Hill reporters love to tell their friends but never print for fear of libel. Only in fiction can the truth be told about the powerful.

Not that the truth is ever welcome in any shape or form. 'If the police render publication inadvisable there will be a delay of ten years,' wrote Stendhal in one of his prefaces to *Lucien Leuwen*. In the end he put it aside; he depended for his livelihood on 'the Budget', as he scornfully called the government, and could not afford to risk his post as consul in Civitavecchia. But he left an outline of the ending and 2,200 manuscript pages which are written with such force that the reader *sees beyond the given details* (to borrow Balzac's phrase) and completes the novel in his head.

The London Review of Books, February 20, 1986

Loving Bids for Freedom

Droll Stories, by Honoré de Balzac, translated by George R. Sims (William Reeves)

One of the glories of Western civilisation, Balzac's *Droll Stories* was first published in England in 1874, and I cannot think of a more fitting literary centenary to celebrate this year.

For one thing, *Contes drolatiques* is the most lively and profound fiction on sex. For another, this distinction hasn't won the book any wide circulation in its first hundred years in England, and there are multitudes of readers who haven't had the luck to experience this radiant work. It is as if hardly anyone in this country had heard *The Marriage of Figaro* or *Don Giovanni*.

Luckily, it is never too late to catch up with the immortals.

A London bookseller, William Reeves, has reproduced the 1874 edition, with all the famous illustrations by Gustave Doré, and, more importantly, in the original translation by George R. Sims – a work of art in itself, which has stood the test of time and still does justice to Balzac's merry text.

Perhaps the best way to describe the unique is by its common opposite. Most books with an erotic theme unsettle us because of the exaggerated claims made for the characters' emotions. For instance, lovers fall into each other's arms in the convenient solitude of an empty cottage or a deserted beach, and are so 'swept away' by passion that they 'forget the world'.

There is nothing to indicate whether or not they actually did forget about the world, but even if we accept that they did, we cannot take this as a sign of great passion, for the world was miles away to begin with. So the assertion of an overpowering passion makes us feel uneasy; it may strike us as obscene – that is, fraudulent.

For his part, Balzac fills his readers with the serenity of understanding.

We can see into his lovers' hearts, because he measures their amorous whims and passions on the scale of their conduct. Furthermore, to make their conduct as self-revealing as possible, he lends extreme consequences to their actions by placing them in the 15th and 16th centuries – violent periods of history when people risked a great deal by whatever they did. His characters are shown not only in the light of their actions but in the light of dangerous actions. Here suspense is depth.

There is no doubt, in *The High Constable's Wife*, whether or not the lady of the title and her new lover forget the world in each other's arms: they make love while her former lover is being noisily hacked to pieces under her window.

A few minutes later, the High Constable rushes into his wife's room with the head of the forgotten man:

> 'Behold, Madame,' he said, 'a picture which will enlighten you concerning the duties of a wife towards her husband.'
>
> 'You have killed an innocent man,' replied the Countess, without changing colour. 'Savoisy was not my lover.'
>
> You can imagine that the Constable was greatly embarrassed with the head of poor Savoisy, and . . . was growling to himself all sorts of words. At length he struck two heavy blows on the table and said, 'I'll go and attack the inhabitants of Poissy.'

One of the ways in which genius manifests itself is by the amount of information the writer conveys while apparently talking only of one thing.

In this brief dramatic scene Balzac demonstrates the lady's heroic presence of mind (her new lover is hiding in the cupboard, 'having no desire to cough'), while also conveying the gullibility of her murderous husband and the reason why the unlucky town of Poissy was razed to the ground.

This telling detail in turn shocks us into realising how little the ordinary citizens, as well as great ladies, mattered in the feudal world, depending for their very lives on the whims of their lords and masters.

In this social context, a woman's amorous longing to bathe 'in the waters of love' is identical with her refusal to remain her father's or husband's property, with her desire to assert herself as an individual.

Feminist critics have been arguing recently that most fiction on sex consists of malevolent fantasies of male domination, in which women are not people but mere figments dreamed up to boost the male ego. All too true. But Balzac's heroes are his heroines. He portrays not the dream of male power but its brutal feudal reality, which nonetheless fails to force spirited women to submit.

In seeking pleasure, the adulterous wife becomes the mistress of her own soul: in Balzac's hands, feudal relationships convey both the political and spiritual dimensions of sexual drives.

These often lead to long suffering or quick death, but also to triumphant comic scenes:

It was at this moment that the husband entered, his sword unsheathed and flourished above him. The comely Tas-cherette, who knew her lord's face well, saw what would be the fate of her well-beloved, the priest. She sprang quickly towards her husband, half-naked, her hair streaming over her, beautiful with shame but still more beautiful with love, and cried to him, 'Stay, unhappy man! Would'st thou kill the father of thy children?'

Balzac lacks the hypocrisy which rots many books as well as many minds. Rather than face the responsibility for their decisions, most people prefer to see themselves as falling leaves tossed about by the wind: they have 'no choice', life just sort of happens to them.

Sex-fantasy books cater to this self-deception: lovers are not only oblivious, they are practically unconscious, carried away by drink, excitement, force of circumstances; they themselves don't really have anything to do with it.

Such works merit the complaint that the characters are reduced to the level of animals, for they are denied their human attributes – self-knowledge, will, awareness of their freedom to choose. Balzac never fails to show that his lovers make their own bed, even if they wish to pretend otherwise.

This pretence itself is the theme of one of the most moving stories, *The Venial Sin*, concerning a virgin bride and her burnt-out husband, an old ape who 'saw clearly that God had amused himself by giving him nuts when his teeth were gone'.

After years of deprivation, she resolves to make love with a young page and goes to a great deal of trouble to be ravished unawares, so that she should commit a mere venial sin rather than a mortal one.

She pretends to doze off in a most tempting fashion in the presence of the inexperienced page, who is 'armed against his desire by his fear'. As he keeps hovering about her, she finally cries out: 'Ah, René, I am asleep!'

Comparisons are the shorthand of criticism, suggesting all that there is no time to say. So perhaps I ought to mention that Balzac has often and rightly been called the Shakespeare of prose. His poetic wit captures a surge of passion, a character, a relationship, with the magic power of exactitude, holding fast the fleeting moment for as long as the sun will shine.

The Sunday Telegraph, August 4, 1974

The Last Word on the Media

Lost Illusions, by Honoré de Balzac, translated by Herbert J. Hunt (Penguin)

Balzac is the Shakespeare of the novel and never more so than with *Lost Illusions*.

The central character, Lucien Chardon, a young provincial poet, goes to the capital to make it to the top in literature, and he does – he becomes one of the top fictional heroes, for he has the classic ambiguity of brilliant gifts and fatal flaws. He falls short of genius only in his lack of patience and his love of the easy life. He's handsome, charming, witty, clever, capable of keen sensations, deep emotions and profound reflections upon his predicaments; his initial responses and moral judgments are admirable. However, he manages to suppress them when there seems no other way to succeed. Giving up the austere life of a poet to become a powerful journalist, he makes his reputation by writing a vitriolic attack on a book he admires, praising it to the skies in another review (after the publisher buys his poems), and settling the 'controversy' under his own name in a third paper. Betraying his principles, friends, family, he understands and abhors his villainies but goes through with them just the same – the stakes are too high.

Coralie, the beautiful and spirited actress who throws out her rich protector for Lucien's sake, encourages him in his ambitious double dealings and even his gambling – so that he will have no time left to be seduced by other women. How the desire to keep a man can destroy him is one of those by-the-way insights that can be found on every page.

[69]

It is significant that the character of the lovable and noble-minded opportunist unfolds in the world of journalism:

> like all trades it has neither faith nor principles . . . Consequently, in due course, all journals will be treacherous, hypocritical, infamous, mendacious, murderous; they will kill ideas, systems and men, and thrive on it. They will be in the happy position of all abstract creations; wrong will be done without anybody being guilty. . . .

Through the debasement of Lucien, Balzac portrays all the human passions and interests which go into the marketing of information, everything that makes for the inescapable corruption of the business of communication. As the mass media had just got started in Balzac's time, the novel in this respect is more relevant today than when it was written. It is customary to cut the edge of the discoveries of great writers by sending them back to where they came from: if you hear that Balzac wrote about a bunch of dead foreigners, don't you believe it!

On one level, this novel is about manipulation, the victimization of the public as well as individuals. The last illusion Lucien loses is one that Balzac never had: that noble sentiments and the best and most compelling motives make a person any less *dangerous*, if there is something he really wants and you are in the way. The novel is full of good men who wouldn't hurt a fly, who deceive, betray, exploit, swindle, rob and ruin their fellow-men with reluctance, and only because there is no other way to get where they want to go.

The failure to appreciate this dark aspect of the nicest people brings about the ruin of both Lucien and his brother-in-law David Séchard, who doesn't flinch from hard work and deprivation and takes the honest man's road to success. He endures years of self-denial to invent a cheaper way of producing paper and then loses the fortune from it by relying on his lawyer, an old school friend, who can get the appointment he covets by helping to defraud him. Before consulting your solicitor, consult your Balzac.

[70]

As V. S. Pritchett said, Balzac's moral passion is one of his most striking qualities, but he is never depressed by villainy: the novel contains some of the most magnificent comic and tragi-comic scenes ever written, which convey the sheer fun, the excitement, the *art* of conning people. In this masterwork whatever is worth doing is worth doing well.

Balzac works with even more parallel predicaments than Shakespeare in *King Lear*, and they are interwoven to maximum effect. The supreme dramatist of fiction allows none of his characters to take up more space than their roles in the story can justify. If there is more to some episode characters than can be revealed in one book, they can become the central figures in another, but in the meantime Balzac keeps them in their place, to give his novel the speed and tension of a great play. And he has the rarest of all gifts: an absolute sense of timing.

To read *Lost Illusions* is to be pulled up, cast down, doused with hot and cold water: whatever emotions the reader is capable of, Balzac brings them out. It is the book you won't be able to put down even when you read it for the tenth time.

Jefferson said that the purpose of education is to teach people to recognize ambition in all its shapes and forms, so they can learn how to protect their freedoms. No writer (and certainly no school) offers a better education of this kind than Balzac.

The Times, June 24, 1971

The Man Who Told Us About Going Mad

Journey to the Orient, by Gérard de Nerval, selected and
translated by Norman Glass (Peter Owen)

Gérard de Nerval used to walk in the gardens of the Palais-
Royal leading a lobster on a leash of blue ribbon, because
lobsters didn't bark and knew the secrets of the deep. Once in
the Paris zoo he threw his hat to the hippopotamus so that the
poor beast could cover his head like a man; at another time he
threw off all his clothes in the street and, imagining himself
all-powerful, was worried that he might hurt the policeman
who came to restrain him. He was a sweet, appealing and
fascinating man, and though he could imagine himself to be
Napoleon's son or a prince of Aquitaine, he had a humble look
that would make strangers cry.

Nerval was one of those who gave a romantic aura to
madness and some credence to the notion that artists ought to
be unbalanced. But the drawbacks of a disordered mind can be
seen in *Journey to the Orient* (actually to the Middle East – a
voyage both of exploration and convalescence after his first
breakdown in 1841). The greater part of this abridged version
consists of his retelling of Oriental tales in which he succumbs
to his preoccupation with magic, miracles, the Cabala, the
Zohar, the Orphic mysteries and the cult of Isis, and his
multi-religious mysticism runs to extremes of obscurity and
inanity.

Born in 1808, the son of a surgeon in Napoleon's armies, he
never knew his mother, who sent him out to a wet-nurse and
followed her husband to Silesia, where she died of fever.

(Norman Glass writes aptly that Nerval was 'haunted by an absence' all his life.) He proved his extraordinary talent as a poet while still in his teens and had money for a few years, thanks to an inheritance, some of which he spent on the promotion of an indifferent actress. (He adored her for years but they never made love. This was one of the ominous signs: it was enough for him to love a woman to cease desiring her – though he kept buying huge beds.) Hounded by debts and helped by his friends, he became a moderately successful all-round man of letters, publishing translations, criticism, stories, and collaborating on plays with the elder Dumas. These 'normal' years were his apprenticeship, when he practised his talent to the point of acquiring absolute skill of observation and delivery. Without this perfected craftsmanship it is unlikely that he could have written with such classic clarity and simplicity even inside a mental home.

His marvellous stories about famous 'eccentrics', collected in *Les Illuminés*, would have made more sense to translate than the present volume. But while *Journey to the Orient* cannot stand on its own, it too has brilliant flashes. Best of all is the portrait of an unforgettably bossy slave girl who should delight any reader, but especially henpecked husbands and militant feminists – a character so idiosyncratic and yet so true to type that she can be read either for laughs or for inspiration. Even in a messy book there are signs of Nerval's luminous objectivity which never abandoned him altogether.

His great works in both poetry and prose, *Chimères*, *Sylvie* and *Aurélia*, were written in the appalling last two years of his life. (They were published earlier by Peter Owen under the title *Selected Writings*, now available also in Panther paperback.)

His attitude to his illness is best summed up in a letter he sent to Mme Dumas upon his first release from hospital after nine months of confinement, some of it in a straitjacket. 'Dear lady', he wrote, 'Dumas will tell you that I have recovered what is commonly called my reason, but don't you believe it. . . . In fact I was having an amusing dream, and I miss it.'

Aurélia is the story of his own insanity, told without a trace of self-pity or self-indulgence – a writer's triumph over his raw material if ever there was one. It is perhaps the best account of madness in world literature, surpassing even *Diary of a Madman*. Gogol's work is a masterpiece of premonition; Nerval brought back *Aurélia* from mental after-life.

This is what it was like to go mad one night in Paris:

Suddenly it seemed to me that the stars had gone out all at once, like the candles I had seen in the church. I thought I saw a black sun in the deserted sky and a blood-red globe over the Tuileries. I said to myself: 'The eternal night is beginning, and it's going to be terrible. What is going to happen when people notice that there isn't any more sun?' . . . Coming to the Louvre, I walked toward the square, and there a strange sight awaited me. Through the clouds scudding before the wind, I saw several moons passing at great speed. I thought that the earth had left its orbit and was wandering in the sky like a ship without a mast, approaching or receding from the stars as they grew bigger and smaller by turns. For two or three hours I observed this confusion, and then I made my way toward Les Halles. The peasants were bringing in their produce, and I said to myself: 'How amazed they will be when they see that the night doesn't come to an end. . . .' However, dogs were barking here and there and roosters were crowing.

Before confinement, he becomes quarrelsome:

I picked a fight with a postman who was wearing a silver badge on his chest. I insisted that he was Duke John of Burgundy and tried to prevent him from going into a tavern. For some peculiar and inexplicable reason, when he saw me threatening to kill him, his face became covered with tears. I was moved, and let him pass.

If there are more heartrending scenes in prose, told with fewer words and greater cunning, I haven't read them. The last pages of *Aurélia* were found on his body.

Several writers inspire greater admiration but none more

sympathy than Nerval. He slipped in and out of madness, using his saner moments to tell us all about it, and then he hanged himself.

The Times, June 5, 1972

Voice from the Fringe of Madness

Les Chimères, edited by Norma Rinsler (Athlone Press)
Gérard de Nerval, by Norma Rinsler (Athlone Press)
The Disinherited, by Benn Sowerby (Peter Owen)

> One winter night he gave up the ghost,
> Asking as he went away: 'Why did I come?'
>
> Nerval: *Epitaph*

Forlorn bewilderment has no more compelling poet than Gérard de Nerval – which is perhaps why he is becoming popular again in these bewildering times.

He was born in 1808 and was found dead one winter morning in 1855, hanging from the back gate of a filthy courtyard. Here is his portrait drawn by Heine, the authenticity of which is vouched for by the most keenly observant generation of Parisian writers, including Dumas and Balzac:

> He had the delicacy of a sensitive plant, he was good, he liked everybody, he was jealous of no one; he never swatted a fly; when by chance a mongrel bit him, he shrugged his shoulders.

His sonnet sequence, *Les Chimères*, with Norma Rinsler's commentaries, provides an excellent introduction to his poetry. Her general critical study, *Gérard de Nerval*, gives an equally illuminating account of his more extensive and no less significant prose works, *Sylvie*, *Les Illuminés* and *Aurélia*.

Nerval is one of those immortals who seem to generate unending argument as to whether they are major or minor –

[76]

which is to say that he is one of the greatest authors, but only on a very few subjects. In both poetry and prose he is the undisputed master of mental breakdown and elated or despairing hallucinations; and no novelist, with the exception of Graham Greene, can equal him on the subjects of finding oneself without divine guidance and the anguish of longing.

Nerval never knew his mother, who left him to follow her husband, a surgeon with Napoleon's armies, and died of fever in Silesia. In early childhood he lived happily with his uncle's family in the country, and after 1814 stayed with his father in Paris, where he became a member of a brilliant literary circle while still a schoolboy. At 18 he published his first collection of poems, at 20 a translation of Part I of *Faust* which prompted Goethe to prophesy that he would become a great poet.

First, though, he came by an inheritance and set off for Italy, turning into a restless and inveterate traveller, though travelling, he said, 'is a sad experience – to lose town by town and country by country all that beautiful universe which one created for oneself when young through books and pictures and dreams'.

Contact with women led to similar let-downs, and though he fell in love frequently, he was a lover rather like Octavius in *Man and Superman*: he worshipped the ground his goddesses walked on, but he didn't press them too much.

Benn Sowerby's useful biography *The Disinherited* is particularly good on his ethereal affair with the actress Jenny Colon, which culminated in his first breakdown in 1841. It is arguable, however, that the theatre, not the actress, was his undoing.

He founded a lavish theatrical magazine which folded in less than a year, consuming his inheritance and saddling him with debts for the rest of his life. He wrote 14 plays in collaboration with Dumas and others; only one was a hit and that, too, had to close because of a cholera epidemic. His anxiety about money was his doctors' greatest problem.

Dr Etienne Blanche is properly described by Mr Sowerby as a remarkable psychiatrist. Not unlike R. D. Laing today, he viewed certain kinds of madness as a fragile state of wisdom, and it was he who suggested that Nerval should write about his illness. The result was *Aurélia*.

Moving in and out of Blanche's clinic, Nerval retained his technical skill, his precision of language and his indestructible charm and humour, and completed his greatest works during the last two years of his life. It was his genius that he remained lighthearted and witty even while going mad.

Mr Sowerby quotes Nerval's greeting to a friend who came to visit him at the clinic: 'It is kind of you to come and visit me; this poor Blanche is insane; he believes he is in charge of an asylum, and we pretend to be deranged to humour him.' And he had marvellous fancies: the treasure of the Medicis was buried under a tree in the Tuileries, and the goldfish in the fountains swam to the surface to bring him messages from the Queen of Sheba.

He chronicled his torments with the spirited conviction that 'one man's experience is the treasure of all'. It would be a fine thing if these books would prompt further translations of Nerval's own works; there is too little of him available in English.

The Sunday Telegraph, November 18, 1973

A Horse at the Opera

The Philosophy of Jean-Paul Sartre, edited and introduced by Robert Denoon Cumming (Methuen)

. . .since I have lost the chance of dying unknown, I
sometimes flatter myself that I live misunderstood.

Sartre: Words

Robert Denoon Cumming's anthology is directed to readers
who are unfamiliar with Sartre. The irony of such an 'authoritative introduction' is that, while it promises an easier access to
the writer than his complete works, it is in fact far more difficult
and confusing, leaving the reader with a headache but no
memory of pleasure. The professor's 43-page introduction is
heavier going than anything Sartre ever wrote: it reminds me of
the *Carmen* I saw the other day at the Paris Opéra, in which the
producer – presumably to bring the opera closer to the audience
– has a real horse trotting noisily across the stage in the middle
of the habañera. The French can be just as great ignoramuses
as any American academic but, even so, Sartre is a famous
writer because he has, among other things, a greater facility
with words than Mr Cumming and has proved himself
eminently capable of introducing his ideas to the public.

Such a *salade* of a book is a more depressing sight in English
than in any other language, because since the late forties Sartre
has never had a fighting chance to enrich Anglo-American
culture. A truly original thinker needs to be fashionable to be
able to influence readers – only fashion can give people the
extra incentive they need to persevere with the hard work of

comprehending unfamiliar ideas. Unhappily, at the time when Sartre's works had the warm glow of having just been discovered by the world, cultural functionaries in Britain and America were busy fighting the Cold War on the wrong terrain and were keen to discredit him as a philosopher, novelist, and playwright, to undermine the influence of his un-American politics.

When *Encounter* was not expostulating on the puerilities of Bertrand Russell, it was publishing learned exposés of all the holes in Sartre's thinking. With so many pedants showing themselves so much smarter than Sartre, it was no wonder that his books never quite caught on, and our intellectual life is the poorer and more provincial for it. What a blow to Communism!

True, there are many holes in Sartre's philosophy and the reasons for them are often suspect. His attempts to marry existentialism and marxism may not be unconnected with the fact that after World War II a French writer hungry for readers had to be either a Catholic or a communist, because only the Church or the Party could boost books in a big way. But whatever the reasons for Sartre's twists and turns, he is a vital thinker. Here is one of his definitions of the existentialist concept of freedom:

> We don't say that a prisoner is always free to leave his prison (this would be absurd), nor that he is always free to desire to get out (this would be a self-evident truth without significance). What we do say is that *he is always free to try to escape.*
> *Being and Nothingness*

This is not a notion that the builders of the Berlin Wall want to put about, which is why most of Sartre's works have never been published in communist countries. His existentialism helps people to conceive choices, that is, freedom. You can't read Sartre and believe in determinism, which is the foundation of communist ideology and all totalitarian regimes. Tyranny feeds on the notion that you have no choice and must act the way you have to. If you accept that you're boxed in, you're easy to control. Sartre argues that, far from being boxed in, we choose even our past, in the sense that we choose its meaning, what is important about it and what isn't. As for the future, Sartre insists, sternly but correctly, that you're always free to commit suicide or desert, and thus you can never truthfully say that you have no choice and are not responsible for what you do. Such thoughts confront you with your cowardice and challenge you to be brave.

But whoever is interested in Sartre ought to read Sartre's own books as he wrote them. Since the beginning of literature, there hasn't yet been devised a better or easier way of getting to know a writer. I would suggest that they start with *Portrait of the Anti-Semite* – as good a first taste as any of Sartre at his most original and significant and most readable.

The title is somewhat misleading, for it isn't simply about anti-Semitism but deals with the logic of delusion and pre-judice: a standard work, one would think, at the time of Powellism. In one of his roles, Sartre is a part-time Freud of the conscious mind, the most profound analyst of the ways in which we form our misconceptions. I have no doubt that any reader of the *Portrait* would want to come back for more, in which case *Sketch for a Theory of the Emotions* (Methuen) would be an excellent entrée to *Saint Genet* (W. H. Allen) and *Being and Nothingness* (Methuen).

The last two are difficult and at times tiresome works, but they will yield pleasures and illuminations which will make the reader a wiser human being. They are extra windows cut in the walls of our ignorance.

The Times, January 11, 1969

Good Faith and Bad

Sartre, by Hazel E. Barnes (Quartet; Midway)
Camus and Sartre, by Germaine Brée (Calder & Boyars)
Between Existentialism and Marxism, by Jean-Paul Sartre (New Left Books)

'Hell is other people' is one of Sartre's perfect statements, evoking a whole world of misery beyond words. To add to it is to reduce its meaning.

Hazel E. Barnes demonstrates this in her *Sartre*. 'Hell is others,' she tells us, means that 'human relations anywhere are Hell'.

This book is in the fine old tradition of academic studies, rendering the subject either boring or incomprehensible or both. Plots of plays and novels are recounted, philosophies are watered down or thickened, to persuade us of the need for professorial expertise.

Such volumes about great writers appear every week. It is as if humanity's best communicators were retarded children whose incoherent babblings must be deciphered by specialists before we can possibly understand them. These products bring to mind another of Sartre's telling phrases: 'The passionate pride of the mediocre.'

The reader has but one defence: ignore books about writers and read the writers themselves. They are always more lucid, more amusing or, at the very least, more interesting opponents to argue with in one's mind than lecturing intermedaries.

In so far as Miss Barnes's book has a theme of its own, it is the utterly irrelevant as well as untenable proposition that Sartre is a consistent thinker. He burst on the literary scene in 1938 with *Nausea*, a brilliant and deeply-felt novel expressing his revulsion from the human race. Subsequently he developed a profoundly individualistic philosophy in *Being and Nothingness*, which he has increasingly diluted with collectivist presumptions about the perfectibility of men if only they could be cured of capitalism.

This doesn't strike me as very consistent – though of course if it were it would not make the slightest difference. Consistency is a virtue for trains: what we want from a philosopher is insights, whether he comes by them consistently or not.

Germaine Brée has a flair for the English language and is blessed with a critical intelligence, but her *Camus and Sartre* shares with Miss Barnes's work an undue emphasis on Sartre's *folie de marxisme*.

She gives an excellent account of the Cold War dispute between the humanist Camus and the fellow-traveller Sartre: the latter seemed to think at the time that literature was about loving the Soviet Union and hating the bourgeoisie, and neither Camus nor Miss Brée have had any difficulty in proving him a fool on that score.

Yet, as Nigel Dennis has recently argued on this page about Swinburne's passion for birching, aberrations are a dime-a-dozen and tell us nothing about genius.

The best introduction to Sartre is his own *Words*, a moving and illuminating self-portrait of the artist as a bookish and lonely child, a 'little shrimp of no interest to anybody' whose ungainliness and wounded sensibilities doom him to live forever in his head.

This goes a long way to explain his longing for revolutions, as a drastic way of mixing with the world. It also helps to explain the mathematical clarity and depth of his arguments when he gets hold of a fruitful idea.

The existentialist notion that we are free to change ourselves even if we cannot change our circumstances led him to a profound exploration of the choices open to us even in desperate situations. *Being and Nothingness* and *Saint Genet* (along with

Camus's *The Myth of Sisyphus* and *The Rebel*, which owe a great deal to Sartre) are our century's most inspiring treatises on inner freedom.

Perhaps even more indispensable is Sartre's analysis of the ways and means of self-deception, which he calls Bad Faith, the attempt 'to flee what one cannot flee'. He examines it from many different points of view – this is from his *Portrait of the Anti-Semite*:

> How can one choose to reason falsely? . . . There are people who are attracted by the permanence of stone. They want to be massive and impenetrable, they don't want to change: where would change lead them? It's a question of a fear of one's original self and a fear of the truth. And what frightens them is not the content of the truth, which they do not even suspect, but the form of it, this object of indefinite approximation: it's as if their own existence was perpetually deferred. But they want to exist all at once and right away; they do not want to acquire opinions, they want to be born with them. Since they have a fear of reasoning, they want to adopt a mode of life in which reasoning and searching have only a subordinate role, in which one never searches except for what one has already found and one never becomes anything except what one already is . . . Only a strong sentimental prejudice can give a lightning-like certainty, can hold reasoning at bay, can remain impervious to experience and subsist through a whole life. The anti-Semite has chosen hate because hate is a faith.

Of course, Sartre hates the bourgeoisie as the anti-Semite hates the Jew, and he indulges in a great deal of self-deception to satisfy his own craving for 'lightning-like certainty'.

Unkind critics use this to discredit him, but to my mind it only proves the authenticity of his theory of Bad Faith. He couldn't conceivably be so profound on the subject if he had no personal experience of what he is talking about.

Examples of self-deception abound in *Between Existentialism and Marxism*, a selection from his writings since 1960, but even at his worst he is stimulating to read.

In the present instance this is partly due to John Matthews's uncommonly lucid translation, but mainly, as ever, to Sartre's irrepressible passion for making sense of everything. A surfeit of this passion makes French intellectual life pretty deadly at times, but we could do with a bit more of it here in England.

Most inconsistently but quite brilliantly he now turns on the Soviet Union, in an essay on Czechoslovakia. The system, he writes, operates on the principle that 'men should be doubted rather than institutions', and that the nations of Eastern Europe are 'simply Russian peasants of 1920'. He now calls for revolutions in both East and West.

There are some flawless pieces in this collection. To read Sartre on Tintoretto's *St George and the Dragon* is like reading Kierkegaard on acting: a nearly complete account of all the things one can take in at a glance, an exhilarating demonstration of how the human brain can work on several levels simultaneously.

As for the three interviews with Sartre which are included here, they tell us more about his virtues and failings than a whole library of books about him.

The Sunday Telegraph, April 21, 1974

A Passion for the Impersonal

André Malraux, by Jean Lacouture (Deutsch)

One of the things they order better in France is the honour and attention they accord to intellectual activities – which may explain why they have had so many profound thinkers and also, alas, so many would-be intellectuals who are attracted by the glamour of it all and who, owing to their superior numbers, dominate and direct official culture.

Thus, if it is typical that the most lucid books ever written should be by Frenchmen, it is equally typical that even such wonders of the world as *The Charterhouse of Parma* and *Lost Illusions* were ignored or abused in France for many years. The French have the best thinkers and the biggest crowd of pseuds, and at present the grand old man of the pseuds, the species I would call culture phonies, is André Malraux, now 75 and the subject of Jean Lacouture's richly detailed biography.

Malraux is considered a great writer by the kind of people who admire an artist's social standing as much as his talent, by those for whom prestige shines like genius. 'I expected his prestige and his genius to illuminate his face,' wrote Claude Mauriac of meeting the famous novelist and man of action who was about to become a minister in de Gaulle's first government after the war.

André Malraux began to be famous back in 1924 when he went to Indo-China on a supposed archaeological expedition and, caught stealing a ton of stone carvings from the jungle temple of Banteai-Sre, was tried and convicted by the French colonial administration. Since it is a dear old custom in France that when someone who has put pen to paper is caught doing something criminal, he immediately becomes the great hope of French letters, most of the well-known writers of the time signed a petition vouching

> for the intelligence and real literary worth of this writer . . . whose already published works give rise to the highest expectations. [The already published works consisted of a few articles and essays.] They would profoundly deplore the loss resulting from the application of a penalty that would prevent André Malraux from accomplishing what we can all rightfully expect of him.

In fact, of course, imprisonment has always proved a marvellous thing for writers (to mention only Cervantes, Dostoyevsky and Solzhenitsyn), and if Malraux had gone to prison for three years, he might have acquired some inkling of our common humanity, the stuff of literature; but unluckily for him the appeal court let him off with a suspended sentence, and he developed an interest only in common causes.

He became one of the *engagé* writers of the 1930s who thought that Stalin should be loved because of Hitler, and he turned into a platform figure and public speaker, writing novels woven from popular left-wing delusions of the time, about the profound philosophising of terrorists, the revolutionary struggle in China (*The Conquerers, Man's Fate*) and the Spanish Civil War (*Days of Hope*). Still, all his novels bear re-reading and may survive, in which case everything else I say here is irrelevant.

The success of these books was enhanced by the notion that Malraux had taken part in all the Historic Struggles he wrote about. He had not actually been in the Kuomintang revolution as he claimed, but he did fight against Franco in Spain, as the leader of an air squadron he himself organised, and he later played a courageous and important rôle in the Resistance.

In *André Malraux* (translated by Alan Sheridan) M. Lacouture quotes many witnesses to his subject's extraordinary physical courage, but as I read about Malraux's brave deeds, I began to feel a renewed respect for Orwell and Koestler, who, however deeply involved they were in single-minded combat, still managed in their books to widen our awareness of the variety and complexity of human predicaments, while Malraux gave us arid treatises about Commitment and the Absurd seasoned with shoot-outs.

French communists have called Malraux a turncoat for deserting the political beliefs he held in the 1930s and becoming a Gaullist. It is even suggested by M. Lacouture that the only reason why Malraux didn't get the Nobel Prize for literature was that he was a member of de Gaulle's government, which was 'regarded as semi-fascist by a few puritan professors of the Stockholm jury'. (It was, of course, not the *puritans* who called de Gaulle's government semi-fascist, but in France one does not take the communists' name in vain – certainly not M. Lacouture, who writes with a kind of television impartiality.)

For my part, I don't think there's anything particularly important about the leftness or rightness of Malraux's political views. What is wrong with them is that they are received notions. Malraux thinks along with millions, whether they are pre-war Left or post-war Right. He doesn't seem to have an inner centre, he must always feel part of a crowd.

The most salutary lesson of this biography of a very brave man who 'liked nothing better than standing on some high point during the worst of the shooting' is that physical courage can save neither the individual nor society, let alone an artist, and that true strength is what Stendhal called moral courage, the courage to think on your own.

M. Lacouture quotes a comment on Malraux from Gaëton Picon which I believe sums up both the emptiness of the man and the falseness of his books:

> It is always, for Malraux, a question of escaping from oneself, of exchanging a subjectivity for something exterior. . . . He has a passion for history, for the event, the act, ideas, problems, artistic styles, great cultures; all forms of a single passion for the impersonal.

'What do I care about what matters only to me?' asks Malraux in his *Antimemoirs*: what is the point of uncovering the 'miserable little pile of secrets' that is a man? Horrified by his own individuality as well as by everybody else's, he confesses that he had no curiosity even about his friends. Sartre called him 'Being-for-death', and indeed this persistent flight from the self destroys a man, leaving him nothing but the craving to be loved and the worship of power.

Antimemoirs is surely one of the most pathetic books ever written: a writer looks back on his long life and finds hardly anything worth recording except his part in historic events and his formal meetings with the big shots of the world.

He is sympathetic and solicitous towards such diverse characters as Mao-tse Tung, Nehru and de Gaulle; there is nothing he could conceivably admire in them all except that they were all Men of History and sat at the top of the tree.

It is precisely in this reverence for power regardless of its nature that Malraux is so representative of the ever more vacuous French intellectual scene. There isn't much written in France today that either Catholics or Marxists could find offensive; the co-existence of these powerful and touchy majorities has given rise to a sort of *consensus ideology* which, by pretending that there is no conflict between totally incompatible and irreconcilable beliefs, reduces thinking to an exercise in diplomacy.

Malraux, who has been a bit of everything and has learned to talk out of both sides of his mouth, is ideal for the period. He says he was a Marxist as Pascal was a Catholic; he calls himself an agnostic but assures a priest that he, too, knows 'no one can escape God'. Now, anybody who tells you he is an agnostic while also asserting the existence of God isn't in the business of thinking; he is simply saying what he thinks you want to hear.

The only thing constant about Malraux, from his days of trying to lift bas-reliefs from the jungle to his time as de Gaulle's Minister of Culture, seems to be his love for art. As a minister he was responsible for the cleaning of great buildings, a practice which has spread all over Europe.

But while claiming that art is his religion, he did not hesitate to take the Odeon Theatre away from Jean-Louis Barrault (that great actor and director whom the French have to console them for not having Laurence Olivier) because he made the wrong kind of political speech and said some 'extremely malicious things' about Malraux himself. It seems to me that anyone with the slightest regard for art, let alone a religious dedication to it, would understand that one does not pull the stage from under the feet of a genius of the theatre, no matter what he says.

M. Lacouture's biography provides all the damning facts about Malraux and wraps them in expressions of admiration; but it is a book I would recommend to all young intellectuals as a kind of warning example.

The Sunday Telegraph, November 16, 1975

Cruelty and Death

Europe's Inner Demons

An Inquiry Inspired by the Great Witch-Hunt, by Norman Cohn (Sussex with Chatto and Heinemann)

Dear reader, don't ever utter that terrible word *interpersonal*. Its use is never justified and can only signify that the offender doesn't quite have a firm grip on his meaning. Such is the case with Professor Norman Cohn when he writes about 'interpersonal fears and resentments among the peasantry' and 'interpersonal fears and hatreds at village level', as if personal fears, hatreds and resentments were not between persons.

I could fill this whole review with complaints against the unthinking academic style, and I'm tempted to, because it is a scandal that taxpayers are fleeced of millions to finance a process by which students unlearn English and lose their capacity to think clearly, so that they can spent the rest of their lives in a fantasy world where villages in valleys and villages on mountaintops are all at the same level.

Well, so much about the way the book is written, let's see about the demons.

The most illuminating book on the great witch-hunts is still Hugh Trevor-Roper's *The European Witch-Craze of the 16th and 17th Centuries*. With classic brevity and lucidity, Professor Trevor-Roper portrays the witch-craze as an outcome of the impassioned conflicts of the Reformation and Counter-Reformation, and his book has the solidity of a true story.

Although much of *Europe's Inner Demons* deals with the build-up to the great witch-hunts, Norman Cohn's chief interest is not in the history of events but in the history of ideas, and his purpose is to trace the connections between the various calumnious fantasies which, from antiquity to the present, have enabled Europeans to eliminate their chosen victims with a clear conscience. This is a book on the common ideology of purges.

It seems, for a start, that the victims always had to be guilty of eating babies. Christians under the Roman Empire, heretics in the Middle Ages, 'witches' in the 16th and 17th centuries, Jews right up to our own time – all were tortured and killed in their turn on this self-same pretext.

Tales of orgies, evoking sexual jealousy, were similarly recurring calumnies that sanctioned mass-murder. Wishing to seize the wealth of the Knights Templars, Philip the Fair had most of the 4000 members of the order rounded up and tortured until they admitted to all possible outrages, including the crime of copulating with each other and with 'demons in the form of beautiful girls'. Who would have wished to save the life and property of such men?

Witches at the stake were paying for all the fun they had at the Devil's sex parties. At their nocturnal 'sabbats' they would worship Satan in the form of a goat or a cat, make a meal of children and wind up with

> an orgiastic dance, to the sound of trumpets, drums and fifes. The witches would form a circle, facing outwards, and dance around a witch standing bent over, her head touching the ground, with a candle stuck in her anus to serve as an illumination. The dance would become a frantic and erotic orgy, in which all things, including sodomy and incest, were permitted. At the height of the orgy the Devil would copulate with every man, woman and child present.

How was it possible for people to believe in such manifest absurdities?

For one thing, it was unhealthy to doubt them. Professor Cohn cites the case of the unfortunate Guillaume Adeline, a noted doctor of theology and former professor in Paris, who disputed the existence of witches' sabbats. He was arrested in

[94]

Normandy in 1453 and tortured until he confessed that he flew to the sabbat himself, that he found there a demon called Monseigneur who sometimes changed into a goat, and that he did Monseigneur homage by kissing him under the tail.

Perhaps because of his eminence, perhaps because he enjoyed the support of the University of Caen, Adeline was sentenced not to death, but to perpetual imprisonment in a dungeon, on a diet of bread and water. After four years of this regime he was found dead in his cell, in an attitude of prayer.

More importantly, human beings are not easily swayed by the evidence of their senses once they have set their hearts on seeing a demon. In Balzac's *Succubus* a strikingly normal if beautiful girl is seen as merely appearing *like* a normal woman. She can explain convincingly that she has no dealings with the Devil – but this too proves that she *is* a succubus (a demon in female form) for it is well known that Lucifer helps his demons to confuse the minds of God-fearing folk. When their beliefs are involved, people are no more capable of sound reasoning than of flying on broomsticks.

At the height of the witch-craze women would condemn themselves to death by voluntarily coming forward to confess to consorting with the Devil. Mr Cohn cites the happy exception of a woman at Breisach on the Rhine

who, feeling death approaching, confessed that she had been making love with a demon. It had given her such pleasure that she had resisted confessing for seven years . . .

The human race, of course, hasn't grown any saner, only changed its idiocies. If we're to profit from the history of the witch-craze, we ought to take to heart the point emphasized by Professor Trevor-Roper as well as Professor Cohn: it was the learned authorities of Church and State who created both the nonsense and the horror. 'The mass witch-hunt,' writes Professor Cohn, 'reflected above all the demonological obsessions of the intelligentsia.'

It is well to remember this whenever we think of experts,

whether they are authorities on winged goats or supersonic flight, on the ingredients of the Devil's brew or nuclear energy. Strange as it may seem, no amount of learning can cure stupidity, and formal education positively fortifies it.

The witches' sabbat itself has its academic advocates to this very day. In a book published as recently as 1972 a professor at the University of California maintained that sects of witches did exist, and if they didn't actually fly, they did worship the Devil and even ate children.

In truth, no witch society of any kind is known to have existed until our own time, when the ravings of the old demonologists have inspired a sort of pop cult 'culminating', as Professor Cohn says, 'in the foundation of the Witches International Craft Association, with headquarters in New York'.

The Sunday Telegraph, March 2, 1975

Wolves Dressed in Papal Robes

Cesare Borgia, by Sarah Bradford (Weidenfeld)

When Cesare Borgia, Duke of Valentinois, was informed that a man had been uttering scurrilous remarks about him, he had the offender's right hand cut off, his tongue cut out, and ordered his gaolers to display the severed hand at the prison window, with the tongue hanging from the little finger. 'The Duke is a good-hearted man,' said his doting father, Pope Alexander VI, 'but he cannot tolerate insults.'

This is one of the incidents related with telling detail in Sarah Bradford's *Cesare Borgia*, which is as much about the father as about his touchy son; these two most famously wicked characters of Renaissance Italy were inseparable in their crimes.

Rodrigo Borgia (1430–1503), who reigned as Pope Alexander VI for the last 11 years of his life, and his second son Cesare (1475–1507) both possessed that split sensibility so characteristic of the morally insane: thin-skinned and callous, they could be wounded by a word, but robbed, betrayed, maimed and murdered their fellow men as a matter of routine. 'Fellow men', though, is hardly the phrase to use in connection with the Borgias, who related to other people as a cook relates to chicken.

Their conduct showed the most brazen contempt for the religion they were supposed to represent. Rodrigo Borgia, far from observing his priestly vow of celibacy, used the revenues of the Church to finance a life worthy of a Roman Emperor, enriching himself, his mistresses and his children.

While still only a cardinal he managed to bestow lucrative

benefices on most of his relations; Cesare was an apostolic protonotary at six, a rector and archdeacon at seven, and bishop of Pamplona at 15. At 17, within a week of his father's elevation to the papal throne, he became Archbishop of Valencia, and a year later was made a cardinal.

Most oddly for a Pope, Alexander VI had the ambition to found a dynasty, to take possession of the Papal States and turn them into a Borgia kingdom. As a modest beginning to this insane enterprise, he carved off a duchy and two cities from the Papal States and gave them to his younger son, Juan. This provoked the murder of Juan by the Orsinis (themselves a charming bunch of Roman brigands), and Cesare, as the son most likely to succeed, renounced his cardinalate to further the establishment of a Borgia state through marital alliance and force of arms.

The first murder reliably attributed to Cesare Borgia was that of a Carmelite monk who preached in Rome against simony (the sin of trafficking in ecclesiastical offices), and many more deaths followed. 'Every night,' reported the Venetian Ambassador in 1500, 'four or five murdered men are discovered – bishops, prelates and others – so that all Rome trembles for fear of being murdered by the Duke.' Cesare arranged the murders, his father (who, as Pope, was heir to the personal wealth of all clerics who died intestate) turned them to account.

The Borgias' insatiable greed and love of display turned the capital of Christendom into the most sparkling and corrupt city in the world, where prostitutes were called *oneste* if they were rich. Fair Imperia, who survives as the heroine of one of Balzac's *Droll Stories*, lived in apartments of such splendour that 'the Spanish ambassador who visited her there preferred to spit in the face of a servant rather than on the floor for fear of spoiling the magnificent carpets'.

Yet for all their crimes and ostentatious corruption, it is not at all self-evident why the Borgias should be the most notorious villains of their time. This was an age when *virtù* meant strength and guile, when most Italian states were ruled by despots who, in Burckhardt's words, 'permitted themselves everything', and the Borgias of the Papal States were far from being the worst among Italy's unbridled rulers.

Ferrante I of Naples, for instance, not only murdered his enemies but embalmed them and dressed them in the clothes they wore when they were killed, and showed off the bodies as trophies to his guests. The Borgias, slightly more normal, preferred to entertain their guests in the Vatican with live whores.

The history of 15th- and 16th-century Italy is filled with stories of sons murdering fathers, fathers murdering children, husbands poisoning wives, wives cutting up husbands, in a mad pursuit of power, riches and pleasure. By contrast, the Borgias were a close-knit family. Mrs Bradford effectively defends Cesare against the charge of killing his brother Juan: he was devoted to his own blood and though he disposed of one of his sister Lucrezia's lovers and one of her husbands, it seems fair to say that he would never have murdered a Borgia.

To my mind, what set the Borgias apart, securing them a special place among history's monsters, was their unmitigated gall.

When, for example, the time came to end Lucrezia Borgia's first marriage and arrange a more politically advantageous one, her father and brother compelled her unfortunate husband to sign a paper declaring himself impotent, so that the marriage could be dissolved on grounds of non-consummation.

Anyone but Alexander and Cesare would have been satisfied with that, considering that they themselves had been Lucrezia's lovers and she was flagrantly promiscuous, but Alexander also arranged for a papal commission to 'examine the matter' and solemnly declare that Lucrezia was still a virgin. 'A conclusion,' wrote the Perugian chronicler Matarazzo, 'that set all Italy laughing . . . it was common knowledge that she had been and was then the greatest whore there ever was in Rome.'

The history of Italy's Renaissance princes has a special significance for English readers, because (mainly through Guicciardini's *Storia d'Italia*, translated in 1579) it was a prime inspiration for the Elizabethan and Jacobean dramatists to whom we owe most of our understanding of wickedness and the misuses of power. Macaulay, too, recommends this most instructive period of Italian history to the thoughtful reader who wishes to reflect upon the nature of men and the problems of right and wrong.

I'm afraid that Mrs Bradford's book can be very little help in this. She appears to have read everything, but while her book is rich in details, they are not held together by any clear vision or moral sense. She repeats every justification ever uttered in defence of the Borgias' crimes: she seems to think, for instance, that Alexander's corrupt practices are made less reprehensible by the fact that there were other corrupt Popes before him.

She is not quite as callous as an earlier Borgia biographer who refers to the poisoning of cardinals as an 'equivocal activity', but she, too, talks of 'deliberate poisoning', as if poisoning pure and simple would be less of a crime, and writes of the 'ruthless gangsterism' of Alexander while also claiming that he was a great Pope. Similarly she observes that Cesare was incapable of realising the effect of his actions (which made him a non-starter as a political and military leader), but also speaks of his 'genius'.

In short, Mrs Bradford seems to be under the spell of Machiavelli, who portrayed Cesare Borgia in *The Prince* as a ruler to be emulated by all those who wish to succeed in putting themselves above other men, because he knew how to break his word, how not to be good: he understood that it was better to be feared than to be loved, and that it was right to destroy 'all who were the blood of those ruling families which he had despoiled'.

The maxims of ruthlessness and unscrupulousness which Machiavelli propounds are still considered sound principles of *realpolitik*. But in fact Cesare Borgia, who lived by those maxims, obtained only the most fleeting victories at the price of universal odium. His success in infamy only made everyone wish that he were dead, and indeed within months of his father's death he was shipped off to prison in Spain, and before the age of 32 he was killed.

It seems to me that the Borgias' exploits tell us very little about the art of government and a great deal about the inability of human beings to handle too much power in anything but the most destructive and self-destructive way.

The Sunday Telegraph, July 4, 1976

Mind of a Mass Murderer

Into That Darkness: From Mercy Killing to Mass Murder,
by Gitta Sereny (Deutsch)

The Spaniards wiped out most of the original inhabitants of
Central and South America; Stalin, building a sadist's Utopia,
murdered even more people than Hitler; hardly a day passes
without news of some massacre.

Still there is something specially appalling about the Nazis'
'final solution' – the rounding up of men, women and children
and the herding of them with whips and dogs to make them run
naked, at the double, up the hill into the gas chambers. The
horror of it freezes the heart.

Places like Auschwitz were not the worst. The too-young,
too-old and too-weak were killed there without delay, but the
rest could do forced labour and if they withstood starvation and
disease had some chance of survival.

Chelmno, Belsec, Sobibor and Treblinka, however, existed
for the sole purpose of killing people: those whose trains
happened to be routed to these camps were dead within hours
of their arrival, except for a small number of 'work-Jews'
needed to burn the corpses and pack the valuables for shipment
to Berlin, and to do the cooking and serve the food for the
killers.

At Treblinka alone 1,200,000 people were murdered between
the summers of 1942 and 1943, and when it was all over – when
the camp was demolished to leave no trace of what went on,
and the bricks from the gas chambers were used to build a
farmhouse to make it appear that nothing but farming had been

done there for years – when the 'work-Jews' too had been shipped over to Sobibor to be gassed, and only a few women prisoners were kept back to wait on the last SS men who were getting ready to leave – the Unterscharführer in charge said to the three women as they finished serving lunch: 'Well, girls, it's your turn now.'

And Tchechia laughed and said, 'Aha, I never did believe your fairy-tale promises, you pigs. Go ahead, kill us. Just do me a favour and don't ask us to undress.'

Of all the harrowing details in Gitta Sereny's *Into That Darkness*, this is what haunts me most. One million two hundred thousand weren't enough for these men: they had to kill the very last three. The only victims who left Treblinka alive were those who had escaped in the uprising of August 2, 1943. Altogether 82 people survived the four extermination camps in Poland.

Based on interviews with these survivors, SS men and their relatives, prosecutors, diplomats, historians, priests, Miss Sereny's book is the most gripping and illuminating account of Nazi genocide that I have read, shedding light, as she intended, on 'a whole dimension of reactions and behaviour we have never yet understood'.

Her central character is SS Hauptsturmführer Franz Stangl, Kommandant of Sobibor and Treblinka, whom she first interviewed for *The Daily Telegraph Magazine*. He was the only death camp commander ever brought to trial, and the only one who ever told his story.

A master-weaver in Austria, worried about his lungs, Stangl joined the Austrian police force to escape the dust and earned his first medal for seizing a cache of illegal Nazi arms. Terrified of retribution after the Anschluss, and of his new boss from the Gestapo, he was easily persuaded to look after the administrative side of gassing the crippled and mentally retarded.

Neither in his early life nor later did Stangl exhibit the slightest tendency towards sadism: he was a *nice* man by conventional personal standards, whose dominant emotion was nothing more evil than fear. This was what led him first to 'mercy' killing and later to mass-murder.

Miss Sereny doesn't quite have the intellectual courage of her own discoveries, and is reluctant to accept that anything as forgivable as fear could be the chief reason for Stangl's appalling crimes against humanity; and she stresses repeatedly that his fears were often unjustified and may have been invented after the fact to mask crass personal ambition.

Going by the evidence she presents, however, it seems that Stangl was always more frightened than ambitious; and this forces me to conclude that fear is not an innocent emotion. *Cowards are dangerous.*

The corollary of this is also true, and I would say that even in far less extreme situations than those created by Nazi terror, even in our relatively humdrum situation in Britain today, a man cannot be decent unless he is brave.

Stangl's career, moreover, disposes of the pernicious theory of good intentions which is constantly dragged into discussions about atrocities to befog our minds and benumb our moral sensibilities, and I especially recommend *Into that Darkness* to those who believe that it makes the slightest difference *why* somebody does something.

One of the reasons why Franz Stangl took on the job of building Sobibor and running Treblinka was that, as a loving husband and father, he was afraid that his superiors might kill not only him but also his wife and children if he refused. No one could have arranged the death of millions out of greater regard for his family.

Still, how could a more or less normal man bring himself to run an extermination camp, to organise and keep organising the smooth, efficient killing of over 5,000 people a day? How could he do it? How was he able to perpetrate so much suffering and death? Why, by *thinking nothing of it.*

'Of course, as I said, usually I'd be working in my office – there was a great deal of paper work – till about 11. Then I made my next round, starting up at the *Totenlager*. By that time they were well ahead with the work up there.' [He meant that by this time the 5,000 to 6,000 people who had arrived that morning were dead. . . .] 'A transport was normally dealt with in two or three hours. At 12 I had lunch – yes, we usually had meat, potatoes, some fresh vegetables. . . .'

A man's virtues, it seems to me, are his abilities, and his vices are his deficiencies. Stangl lacked the imaginative ability to place himself readily in other people's shoes. He was, alas, quite 'normal' in this respect – which is why today's news reads the way it does. Most people are incapable of realising something merely because they see it with their own eyes: nothing is real for them unless they think about it and brood about it for so long that their weak faculties are stirred and they are finally able to *imagine* it: then it becomes real.

Stangl managed not to comprehend what he was doing while he was at Treblinka ('. . . of course, thoughts came,' he told Miss Sereny, 'but I forced them away. I made myself concentrate on work. . . .'), but after the war, when he was living in Brazil and read all the accounts of the Eichmann trial – and later when he was tried and imprisoned himself and had his conversations with Miss Sereny, lasting altogether 70 hours – he finally realised that the 'cargo' back in Treblinka was people. The day after he seemed to understand that he was guilty, he died.

Perhaps in a book review it is not out of place to note that the safety of the state depends on cultivating the imagination.

The Sunday Telegraph, September 8, 1974

The Latest Pseudo-Science

The Survivor: An Anatomy of Life in the Death Camps, by
Terrence Des Pres (Oxford)

If you are about to be run over by a car, you jump aside; if it
rains, you seek shelter; but if you are an academic and want to
make a book out of it, you write that

> human behaviour may be understood as 'a repertoire of
> possible reactions' to a range of possible events. The particu-
> lar response will depend on the situation being faced.

Terrence Des Pres, who was born in 1940, is trying to explain
the survivors of Nazi and Soviet death camps in terms of
Sociobiology, which is replacing Structuralism and the New
Linguistics as the latest and most fashionable of the pseudo-
sciences – the sciences of vacuities uttered in very specialised
language at great public expense:

> The biologist's assumption is that like any other animal, man
> possesses 'instinctive' forms of basic behaviour.

This is Mr Des Pres's sociobiological way of saying that –
although it would be premature to draw definite conclusions –
we may *assume* that there is such a thing as human nature.

He is dogmatic only about patent absurdities. 'Survivors are
not individuals in the bourgeois sense,' he declares. As the title
of his book suggests, he claims that there were no particular
survivors of the holocaust: just *The Survivor*, a single type of
human being, the mass-man.

This mythical mass-man is supposed to have managed in the

camps because he was forced to shed 'his illusion of separateness' along with the last vestige of culture and civilisation, and so came to appreciate that 'Life, the earth in its silence, is all there is.'

The burden of the message is that to survive in a world of atrocities one only needs to draw on the 'biological wisdom' with which 'all living creatures are endowed', making them realise that they 'need each other', so that they return to the community. The only way to live, in short, is in communion with others. 'What remains to us now is simple care, a care biologically inspired and made active through mutual need.' If there is a mention of intelligence in the book, or of any individual abilities or qualities of character, it certainly isn't emphasised.

What has struck *me* about the survivors of death camps whom I happen to know is that they are all formidable individuals who, apart from listening to the silence of the earth, also speak several languages. They are brainy, gutsy people with a highly developed sense of humour, which indicates an indomitable spirit and the ability to think at the speed of light.

This is why, incidentally, the survivors' own accounts of hell are far from depressing (as those who haven't read them might suppose), and I would like to recommend to anyone who missed them at least Evgenia Ginzburg's *Into the Whirlwind* and *I Cannot Forgive* by Rudi Vrba, the man who escaped from Auschwitz at the age of 19 to warn the Allied leaders and the Jewish Councils of the planned extermination of the Hungarian Jews. Also one cannot mention often enough that savagely funny masterpiece, *The Gulag Archipelago*.

These books, I believe, will be the enduring works of our age, not only for what they teach about the ways in which evil is perpetrated but also because they show how a man must be both his own master and his brother's keeper if he is to survive or die with dignity in this world.

Another extensively documented and impressive book, *Fighting Auschwitz: the Resistance Movement in the Concentration Camp*, by Józef Garlinski, is relevant here in showing that the so-called élitist philosophy which emphasises individual endeavour is in fact the most truly communal one – for everyone is better off cultivating what abilities and skills he has instead of subsiding into inertia with the thought that what people know or can do makes no difference.

'The greatest achievement of the underground,' writes Józef Garlinski, 'was to restore men's faith in themselves and their abilities.'

Against all evidence to the contrary, Mr Des Pres advocates the life-saving powers of sameness, uniformity and mindless collectivism. And all this apropos the victims of the Nazis – the arch-purveyors of biosocialism. For the Nazis, it was all in the blood; for the biosociologists, it is all in the cells.

Indeed, it is amazing to behold how a well-meaning young American academic comes to echo some of the basic tenets of Nazism. Mr Des Pres manages to convince himself, for instance, by the most spurious reasoning, that Western culture is a denial of death and hence a denial of life and ought to be discarded; he seems quite unaware that this was the kind of argument the Nazis used when they burned books and put the death's head on the SS cap. Certainly nobody could accuse the SS of denying death.

As for that Western culture with its 'contempt for life', I've been wondering whether Mr Des Pres is talking about the one created by Aeschylus, Dante, Donatello, Bernini, Mozart, Beethoven, Stendhal, Balzac, Dostoyevsky, Tolstoy, to mention but a few – or some other Western culture? 'And as for an ethic based on selfless love,' Mr Des Pres goes on, 'that dream cost 2,000 years of misery.' Deriding both individualism and the religious ideal of selfless love has been a peculiar feature of both Nazism and Communism.

It seems to me that one of the greatest dangers to Western societies is the uncontrolled expansion of the universities, by which millions of people are taking up intellectual professions without possessing any intellectual ability. Unable to comprehend complexities, yet having a degree to convince them that they ought to know the answers to the world's ills, they are grateful to any simplifier who tells them that there is more to be learned about the human predicament from a tribe of baboons or a gaggle of goslings than from the Bible or Shakespeare, or that the bewildering history of man can all be made clear and simple by the application of a few economic theories or the study of insects, which carry on their tiny backs the whole edifice of Sociobiology.

Which of the simplifiers will become most popular among the university-trained hordes who only require a simple ideology to feel that they have expanded their minds? The answer to that question may decide what sort of totalitarian society is going to evolve.

Insofar as good men and true can do anything about this, I think that it is time to start demanding at least the abolition of public grants for so-called inter-disciplinary studies. I submit that anyone who is trying to explain one thing in terms of something else has nothing important to say.

Mr Des Pres's book is a case in point. It is undoubtedly true that 'there is a bank of knowledge embedded in the body's cells' which prompts people to turn to each other in times of trouble, but it does not necessarily follow that the operation of the herd instinct is an aid to survival in a complex social situation of which the body's cells know very little.

Millions of people boarded the trains to the death camps without a struggle simply because *the others were doing it*. Man's compulsion to be part of his group, which may lead him to survival, has led him as often to death and destruction – and the Nazi movement as well as the resistance organisations in the camps grew from a biological urge of solidarity.

It may be true that 'beyond our lust for disaster there is another, far deeper stratum of the human psyche, one that is life-affirming and life-sustaining'; but such cheering generalisations seem inappropriate to Auschwitz, where the guards' life-sustaining stratum urged them to keep murdering prisoners rather than risk being sent to the front to get killed themselves.

In the case of indistinguishable insects it may not matter one way or the other, but when it comes to human beings and their communities, it makes a vital difference *whose* will to live or community spirit we are talking about.

The Sunday Telegraph, April 11, 1976

Cannibals and Christians

Alive: the Story of the Andes Survivors, by Piers Paul Read (Alison Press and Secker & Warburg)

Much of reading is daydreaming, and one can have a thrilling nightmare reading *Alive* – living through an air crash and an avalanche, through 10 weeks of suffering in ice and snow and thin air, subsisting on a diet of human flesh.

This is the book-length version of the 1972 news-story about the group of Uruguayan rugby players, their relatives and friends, who took a charter flight to Santiago with pilots who didn't quite know what they were doing, and crashed in the Andes. Out of 45 people on board, 29 were killed in the crash or the subsequent avalanche, and they were the only food available to the survivors.

It is no small matter to write a book which works as a dream. Piers Paul Read is a gifted writer and his narrative skill, praised by Graham Greene, is perfect. He can describe places, objects and events so lucidly that the reader sees them as if he were there. The heroic journey of two men back to the land of living things and the final rescue by overstrained helicopters have the chilling suspense of superb timing.

I have no hesitation in predicting that the book will be a best-seller – though this will be due to its limitations as much as its virtues.

For, if a book must be well written to work as a dream, it must not be *too* well written. Characters and ideas must be sufficiently vague to remain inoffensive to everyone, to allow the reader to identify himself with them without being disturbed by troubling insights. Any sort of distinct vision of life would challenge his preconceptions, force him to think, and wake him up.

Mr Read's handling of cannibalism illustrates how he manages to be explicit and vague at the same time. He shrinks from none of the physical details:

> Having overcome their revulsion against eating the liver, it was easier to move on to the heart, kidneys and intestines . . . Only the lungs, the skin, the head and the genitals of the corpses were thrown aside.

Later they even ate rotten lungs 'from the need of a new taste'.

He couldn't be bettered at describing the labour of breaking open a skull to get at the nourishing brain, only to find it putrid. But the real story of enforced brutalisation, the hardening of the spirit which finally allowed these people to feed on the corpses of their friends and acquaintances, is totally missing.

We are told that the survivors, practising Catholics, agreed that 'God wanted them to live, and he had given them the means to do so in the dead bodies of their friends.' One of them is quoted as saying that what they were doing was

> . . . like Holy Communion. When Christ died he gave his body to us so that we could have spiritual life. My friend has given us his body so that we can have physical life.

A great deal is made of the dead friends' willing sacrifice, though of course they did not choose to die. It is as if cannibalism were an expression of brotherly love rather than a measure of man's indifference to man, an indication of the lengths to which human beings will go in order to survive.

At one point Mr Read portrays one of the boys as moved by 'conscience' to overcome the 'primitive, irrational taboo' against cannibalism. (Surely it is the most civilised of taboos?) They embarked on cannibalism, we are told, in a 'sober and religious spirit'.

All such excuses and rationalisations are asserted on behalf of the survivors under the pretext of objectivity. You may take them as lies, wishful thinking or the plain and simple truth, depending on your point of view. However, it seems to me that leaving it an open question whether cannibalism is a necessary evil or a religious activity is a way of slanting the story.

I am not blaming the Uruguayans for eating what they could, nor for making a virtue out of necessity, but I object to the author's way of filling the void of psychological understanding with the theology of rugby players; declarations of faith are no substitute for moments of truth.

This instance, by the way, is an excellent example of how literary sins can be commercial virtues. 'Alive' has its shock value (what could be more revolting than eating corpses?) but the impact of the shock is softened by a sort of holy mist.

Indeed, although Mr Read tells a story that actually happened, and the characters have their photographs in the book, the result is 'real' only in the most tenuous sense of the word, in the mass-media sense.

Once upon a time impartiality used to be a brave witness, speaking the truth as he saw it, without fear or favour; now he is a television producer who never shows his face in front of the camera and is not going to alienate anybody. He transmits truth and falsehood, folly and wisdom with equal respect, or perhaps with the same polite scepticism – nothing is certain.

Mr Read treats even superstition and charlatanism with this sort of objectivity, as he recounts the desperate parents' efforts to find the site of the crash by consulting various clairvoyants. And conceding that a Dutch clairvoyant was blamed by the parents of one of the dead boys for sending search parties on a wild-goose chase to another part of the Andes, he notes that 'there were many things in what he had said which turned out to be true'.

This sort of fine balancing between accurate reportage and occult rubbish is very fashionable just now. Authors and publishers are not slow to ride the new wave of irrationalism while also remembering the multitudes out there in mental limbo who cannot bear the agony of making up their minds about anything.

Yet, as violent changes render the world less and less comprehensible, we need our wits about us more than ever and must insist that a gifted novelist like Mr Read make sense of what he is writing about. There is no way a writer can escape from judging the world and being judged for it in turn.

The Sunday Telegraph, May 5, 1974

Level Look at Death

Stay of Execution, by Stewart Alsop (Bodley Head)

This is a book for people with strong nerves; Stewart Alsop's account of life with leukaemia, *Stay of Execution*, is a truly scary experience. I must confess there were several paragraphs which I did not have the courage to finish reading.

The horror is not death, but helplessness: the innumerable blood counts, the transfusions, the 'hospital gowns open at the back, which seem to be designed to make the patient feel as unhappy and humiliated as possible', the painful marrow tests with long needles stuck deep into the bone at the base of the spine.

Mr Alsop has the heroic spirit and the talent to observe and recount all this with detachment, and even to remember funny verses. He quotes Belloc:

> Physicians of the utmost fame
>> Were called at once; but when they came
> They answered, as they took their fees,
>> 'There is no cure for this disease.'

It is, he writes in his diary, a most interesting experience, though he wishes he were not so personally involved. One of America's leading journalists and political commentators, he reasserts himself as a reporter even at the hospital for terminal cancer, and notes that between 20 and 30 per cent of the cases there were *induced by medicine*.

He is a master of understatement, which is a *sine qua non*, considering the subject. Meeting with his sister and two brothers to divide the contents of the old family house, he comments that 'the occasion is a melancholy one, and I'm not feeling well'.

But then it turns out that leukaemia is just like life: it's fatal, but not right away. Mr Alsop was told that he had incurable blood cancer in July, 1971; he is still with us, writing his column in *Newsweek*. So if *you* hear bad news, remember to take your time about getting frightened.

Fright, however, does throw a most revealing light on one's character and past: what memories will be dearest to you, what is it that you will want to think about until the very end?

Mr Alsop relives falling in love with his wife (an English girl whom he met here while serving in the British Army at the beginning of the war) and ruminates movingly about his children.

He also takes a new interest in his ancestors, since, as he says, he is likely soon to become an ancestor himself. He draws a striking portrait of several generations of Connecticut Yankees, who originally 'made most of their money in the West Indies trade, shipping rum north and ice south', and who counted among their ranks two Presidents of the United States, as well as a thief and a famous murderer.

On both sides they were patricians of the sort who would describe themselves as 'not *really* rich'. Related to the Roosevelts, they may at times have felt quite poor.

Mr Alsop himself has some odd ideas about his ancestry. Noting that none of his forebears on either side 'had ever taken any part whatever in any war' or 'ever worked for any appreciable length of time in a position of salaried dependence', he concludes that 'they just hated the idea of being in a subordinate and dependent position'.

He thinks that this had something to do with their genes. I'd think that it had something to do with having money.

Mistaking the opportunities of wealth for a family trait may suggest something of Mr Alsop's limitations as a political commentator, but it is one of the idiosyncrasies which help him to come alive in the pages of his book. He succeeds in recreating himself as a living literary character, a representative of the 'Eastern WASP Establishment', whose survival is assured in the reader's imagination and does not depend on transfusions.

However, what makes this book not only engrossing reading but also a significant document of courage and endurance is Mr Alsop's account of his struggle to come to terms with the course of his disease – the uncertainty, the unaccountable ups and downs, the hopeful releases from hospital, the sudden returns.

At the beginning, he used to whistle in the dark Churchill's seven-word speech to the boys at Harrow: 'Never give up. Never. Never. Never. Never.' Yet, as he eventually came to realise, 'A dying man needs to die, as a sleepy man needs to sleep.'

It is as if he were on a voyage of discovery, finding out not just for himself, but for the rest of us as well, how much we can take – or would want to take – and how long we can or should hang on to life.

The Sunday Telegraph, March 31, 1974

Honour, Mafia Style

A Man of Honour: the Autobiography of a Godfather, by Joseph Bonanno with Sergio Lalli (Andre Deutsch)

Mafioso means 'spirited, brave, keen, beautiful, vibrant and alive'. So say many Hollywood movies, some of which are financed by the Mafia, and so says the possibly retired New York crime boss Joe Bonanno in his ghosted autobiography.

With the gratefully acknowledged help of the ghost, his editor and his lawyer, Bonanno lies his way through the book in a sentimental yet wily manner, the way criminals lie after they have discussed their problems with experts, mixing half-admissions with denials and sheer obfuscation – the way juries get conned.

He mentions, for instance, that his father Salvatore stole a gold candelabrum from his monsignor when he gave up studying for the priesthood, but adds that this was done to 'dissolve his obligations to the church and bring him home regardless of his mother's objections'. Unless you are very much on the alert, you are left with the impression that poor Salvatore could not have got out of the seminary to kill two men and take over leadership of the family gang, if he had not stolen the gold.

The father's murders are admitted in this fashion: 'Not long after Salvatore Bonanno returned home, two members of the Buccellato clan met their death.' Bonanno brags about his tough, manly father, but leaves room for reasonable doubt. You can't convict.

Joe Bonanno is a loving son. He recalls fondly his father's resourcefulness on another occasion when he stood trial for the murder of a neighbouring farmer. To discredit the chief witness against him, Salvatore told the judge that he had slept with the witness's wife and that the testimony was the revenge of a cuckolded husband. To prove this vile calumny he cited intimate details of the woman's anatomy, obtained from an unscrupulous midwife. Bonanno reports gleefully that his father was acquitted and ever after the little boys of Castellammare made the sign of the horns with their fingers when the husband passed them on the street; he doesn't say what happened to the young wife.

At any rate, it was from this thief, murderer and wrecker of other people's families that Joe Bonanno learned the meaning of manhood and the sanctity of family life and honour, and he faithfully upholds 'the Tradition' in America.

He admits to being a bootlegger, loan sharker and gunman for Maranzano in New York. (The way he actually puts it is: 'I was much like a squire in the service of a knight.') In 1931, after Maranzano's murder, he became the Father of the Castellammare Family, the youngest Mafia boss in New York, who also reigned the longest. We learn of his iron-fisted rule indirectly, through his account of how he showed mercy towards one of his goons who wanted to quit working for him and join Bonanno's cousin in Buffalo. Bonanno's top men told him that the man 'deserved a traitor's punishment', but he said no. 'My men, *not accustomed to such leniency* for those who betrayed our Family, looked at me with dismay . . . mercy was a luxury . . . I was too sensitive, too scrupulous.' (All italics are mine.)

In other words, his men had become accustomed to hearing him order the execution of anyone who wanted to quit his service. 'The archetypical Sicilian is stoic, self-possessed and given to violence only to restore order, not out of display.' He expects you to think well of him because he didn't kill anybody just to show off.

While he is away in Arizona there is an 'insurrection in progress' in the Bonanno Family and he rushes back to New York to restore order. 'The shootings of the period, however, cannot rightly be said to have constituted a war – the Bananas

War, as it was dubbed in the press.' (It isn't as though *hundreds* of people had been killed.) 'Some people were killed and some were wounded. For the most part, they were men of inconsequential position.' (It isn't as though they were *important* people.)

The book exudes moral insanity in the way most modern fiction does: victims tend to become worthless and insignificant as they are killed, while most of the space is given over to the inner life of the hero. And the inside of Joe Bonanno is just wonderful. There is nothing there but good feelings and high ideals, noble motives and a longing for philosophical discussions. Since he has never seen himself in the light of the consequences of his actions, it is perfectly natural for him to complain that people are not interested in 'my deepest thoughts, my meditations and my philosophy . . . in my insights about honour, family, trust'.

He is a philosopher, but agents of the FBI and the US Drug Enforcement Administration are 'a pack of jackals'. They 'broke the law' when they tapped his phone. Policemen perjured themselves to get him indicted. There is no such thing as organised crime. It is just a loose relationship between people committed to the Tradition. 'What Americans call the Mafia' is a fiction of 'police mentality', the work of a sensationalist press 'going on a verbal rampage'.

The book is evidently aimed at the sort of readers who are not bothered by contradictions, who need to be told who Garibaldi was and know so little about the subject that they are unaware that *everybody*, in Italy as well as America, calls the Mafia the Mafia. The Prefect of Palermo is also the High Commissioner for the Co-ordination of the Struggle Against the Mafia.

Bonanno categorically denies any involvement in prostitution and drug trafficking. However, as one of the five Family bosses of New York, he was a member of the 12-man policy-making Commission which presided over the national Syndicate of organised crime, and the Syndicate made most of its money from illegal gambling and narcotics. It is also a fact that Carmino Galante, one of Bonanno's group leaders, whose existence seems to have slipped Bonanno's memory, has been convicted of dealing in heroin. And according to the Italian journalist Antonio Padalino, the Sicilian allies of the Bonanno family were the Spatola-Inzerillo-Bontade gang who made their millions transporting the White Death to America.

Everything gets twisted in this book. For a short time under Mussolini Palermo had an honest Prefect, Cesare Mori, still revered in Italy today, who tried to root out the Mafia and imprisoned great numbers of them, until he got to their aristocratic patrons and Mussolini recalled him. From this Bonanno makes out that the Mafia were good anti-fascists and that he himself came to America as a political refugee from fascism. He is also the descendant of a great artist (Bonanno of Pisa, of course) and a prince, and exhibits a coat of arms on page 193 to prove it.

A Man of Honour is a mendacious work of disinformation designed to improve the public image of gangsters and to discredit the people who are trying to protect us from them. What I find most troubling about it is the way the originators of this criminal nonsense, the New York publishers Simon & Schuster, ignoring what Mafia family men do to other people's families, acclaim Joe Bonanno as one of 'the famous and powerful men in that shadowy, fascinating world (which) represented an expression of the deepest ethnic roots of the Sicilian people . . . in which loyalty, honour and family ties were paramount'.

How dare they? How dare they claim that 'organised crime' is *misunderstood* by the US government? And how dare they put organised crime in quotation marks, at a time when organised crime is selling drugs to Nato soldiers as well as school children, bombarding the cities of Western Europe and North America with tons of heroin which are as devastating as the German rockets of World War II? Well, they don't see any problem with it. Michael Korda of Simon & Schuster, whom Joe Bonanno humbly thanks 'for recognizing the true me', launched this book on America – on voters and potential jurors – with national publicity and a first printing of 75,000 copies.

The Guardia di Finanza has intelligence that the Mafia have been trying to buy newspapers in Italy to improve their image and support their friends. In New York they don't have to bother: Michael Korda is there running a big publishing conglomerate on the principle that '*I don't think it's up to us to make a moral judgment*' and selling *A Man of Honour* on the pretext that it is just 'Mr Bonanno's view of organized crime and his view of the Mafia tradition'.

But deception is not a point of view, and in this case it is enemy propaganda in time of war. Incidentally, have you read that fascinating autobiography published during the Blitz, Josef Goebbels' *A Man of Truth*?

The Sunday Telegraph, September 4, 1983

The Brave Men Who Fight the Mafia

What do you do if your son witnesses a murder and is so upset that he keeps shaking and crying and cannot be calmed down? You take him to the doctor.

This is a bit of history from Corleone, a small town south of Palermo. On the night of 10 March 1948 a boy who had been guarding his father's sheep among the rocks ran home sobbing that he had seen a man killed. He was so hysterical that his father eventually took him to the local hospital. There he was attended by Dr Navarra, who questioned him and gave him an injection to calm him down. The boy died before morning.

The head of the local carabinieri, Captain Carlo Alberto Dalla Chiesa, summoned another doctor, who examined the body and found that the cause of death was poisoning. Confronted with the death certificate and autopsy report, Dr Navarra was shocked: he must have taken the wrong ampoule from the medicine cabinet. 'You can see what a difficult calling this is, when such an unhappy accident can befall even a conscientious doctor like myself,' he said to the captain.

Don Michele Navarra was the district doctor, chief physician of the hospital, superintendant of the health insurance schemes for nine communities, the man who got out the vote for the government, a Cavaliere of the Republic (a title awarded to him on the recommendation of the then-Prefect of Palermo), and a big landowner. He was also the mafia lord of Corleone, who had ordered the murder that so upset the boy and had poisoned him to eliminate the only witness. But in the absence of decisive proof, there was no way Captain Dalla Chiesa could move against the town's most prominent citizen.

It was another physician, the young GP who had made out the certificate confirming death by poisoning, whose career was broken. He didn't feel safe in Corleone, or indeed anywhere in Italy or Europe, and took a boat to Australia.

A few months later Dr Navarra himself was murdered by his own hit man, Luciano Liggio, who in his turn became *il boss*. (Italians like to use the American words for organised crime, just as Americans like to use the Italian words, evidently wishing to distance themselves from their most appalling fellow-citizens.) According to prosecutors, Liggio still runs the mafia in Corleone, though he is in prison in Milan for killing Dr Navarra. The state finally managed to prove this one murder against him, thanks to Justice Cesare Terranova's handling of the first trial of the case. There is no capital punishment in Italy, and Liggio is serving a life sentence.

As for Justice Terranova, *i killer* gunned him down one morning on his way to work. Liggio was tried last winter for ordering the assassination, but he was acquitted, as in seven other trials for fourteen other murders, on the grounds of insufficient evidence. There were no witnesses willing to die for testifying against the defendant.

*

Monreale, the beautiful hill town above Palermo, celebrated for its 12th-century cathedral and cloisters with their still intact Byzantine mosaics, is also a place with secrets about heroin deals. Monsignor Notto, an aide to Cardinal Pappalardo who teaches part-time at a school in Monreale, has tried to discuss organized crime – a subject now taught in more than 200 schools in Sicily – but he is always met with sullen silence. The first thing children seem to learn in Monreale is that they don't want to know about the mafia.

Captain Emanuele Basile, head of the Monreale carabinieri, did want to know and must have learned something, for on the evening of 4 May 1980 he was shot dead on the street by three gunmen in a car, as he was returning home with his wife and their small daughter.

The carabinieri gave chase to the murder car, which was found abandoned at the end of a lane. Minutes later three young men from well-known mafia families were picked up on the outskirts of town, the first two racing towards Palermo in a car belonging to the third, who was found a couple of hundred yards away trying to climb a high wire-mesh fence. In search of lemons, he said. The three were already suspects in the murder of another police officer, and none of them could account for their flight from the scene of the crime. Or rather, questioned separately, they all gave identical answers: they were returning from assignations with young married women, whose names they could not reveal, because they were *men of honour*.

To kill a man in front of his wife and child and then claim gallantry as an alibi strikes me as a uniquely Sicilian combination of unpardonable crimes.

But juries are no braver than witnesses in mafia trials. Last March 31st the three young men charged with murdering Captain Basile were acquitted, like Liggio, on grounds of insufficient proof. Ordered to compulsory residence on Sardinia by the magistrate investigating the other murder case, they disappeared two weeks later, presumably taken off the island in a motorboat. One even left a goodbye note. There are new warrants out for their arrest but no one thinks they will be caught, unless the FBI finds them in the States.

The outrage that swept Italy about their acquittal and subsequent escape has created popular support for a proposed law, backed by all three police forces as well as the magistracy, which would have mafia murders tried only by judges; perhaps the new parliament will finally act. In the meantime, the only thing Monreale could do about Captain Basile's murder was put up a marble plaque at the spot where he was gunned down. It was unveiled at a little ceremony on the 4th of May this year, the third anniversary of his death.

Not quite six weeks later, on the 13th of June, Captain Mario D'Aleo, Captain Basile's successor, was also murdered. He had no children; he was only 29 years old and wasn't married yet. The killers shot him outside his fiancée's flat.

[125]

'We need special laws for Sicily!' said Dr Elda Pucci, the new mayor of Palermo, a reform Christian Democrat, a pediatrician and the first woman to become mayor of a major Italian city. What is needed, in fact, are new rules of evidence which would allow the manifestly guilty to be convicted even if they have killed or terrorized all the witnesses.

*

At this point a glossary might be helpful.

la morte bianca. Italians call heroin the White Death. The mafia exports about 3½ tons a year to North America, about a ton to the rest of Western Europe, but there is plenty of it left over and the new plague is raging throughout Italy. In the last couple of years drug addicts have become visible in every big Italian city. There are districts where up to twenty per cent of young people are on heroin. In the first six months of this year 139 Italians died of drug use, and those who are still at the stage of losing their teeth and their minds turn their private hell into a social calamity. A few weeks ago a drugged woman staying at a *pensione* in Rome threw her landlady's baby out of a window. Others go about smashing faces for the price of the next fix, making it inadvisable to stroll around looking at those magnificent monuments by moonlight. The rabble of muggers and thieves are too spaced-out to be used by organized crime, but they serve as a kind of diversionary force, helping to spread disorder, confusion and fear.

narcolire. The billions made from the drug traffic are worse than the drug, for they have turned families of Sicilian peasant bandits into international business oligarchies with all the capital they need to invest in criminal undertakings and, simultaneously, to acquire status, education, legitimate corporations, political connections and even political office. Lately all their profits have come to be called *narcolire*, though they also include, through inflated contracts for public works, billions of the regional development funds Rome has sent to Sicily. There is a Sicilian proverb, *la fonte della ricchezza è il pubblico denaro* – the fount of riches is public money – and proverbs are a fount of wisdom.

gli insospettabili. Remember those old movies in which gangsters disguised themselves as priests or nuns? Today Italy has gangsters who *are* priests and nuns. Just about a month ago police in Naples arrested Sister Aldina Murelli, who had been carrying messages, including assassination orders, from the imprisoned camorra boss Raffaele Cutolo to murderers and extortionists still at large. She almost bit off a policeman's finger when they came to arrest her in the nunnery.

Then there are the professional men. Dr Michele Navarra was an exception back in 1948; today there are hundreds of mafiosi who have gone to university and entered the professions without ever leaving the family business. The Calabrian gangster who cut off young Getty's ear was a practising surgeon. In addition, there is a large group of middle class professionals – doctors, lawyers, accountants, bank officials, entertainers, politicians, bureaucrats – who form a kind of fifth column of organized crime. Right now the popular television presenter Enzo Tortora is in Rome's Regina Coeli prison, charged with being a sworn member of Cutolo's gang, and three magistrates are being questioned by police about 'informing and protecting' other camorra bosses.

fenomeno mafioso. The mafia now involves so many people, from all classes and all regions of Italy, that Italians have begun to talk about it as a kind of impersonal force of nature. To mention only the three largest groups, there is the Sicilian mafia, now also established in northern Italy, the camorra of Naples and Salerno, and the Calabrian 'ndrangheta.

They all do everything, but the mafia's specialty is heroin, the 'ndrangheta's is kidnapping, while the camorra is into extortion and cocaine. Each group is a concentration of economic, social and political power supported by a guerrilla army of thugs. Italy has not so much a crime problem as a civil war in which only the enemy has licence to kill.

Anyone who stands up to them has to be good and brave.

*

Beware of public officials who have expensive pleasures; they can't afford them on their salaries. Ernesto Di Fresco, President of the Province of Palermo until his arrest last November on charges of corruption, may yet be found innocent of the charges, but he is very fond of girls, gambling and flashy sports cars. During the visit of John Paul II to Palermo Di Fresco drove behind the Pope's white Land Rover in his open Ferrari – a conspicuous display of wealth which may have been the cause of his downfall, setting people thinking not only about the super-expensive car but also the absurdity of such a childish show-off being a leading light of Sicilian politics.

Most public men in trouble seem to be like stupid children who must have new toys all the time or they will go crazy. They don't seem to be aware that there are pleasures in life which don't cost a lot of money.

By contrast, Gaetano Costa, the Chief Prosecutor of Palermo, was fond of good pasta and *dolci*, pleasures that even an honest prosecutor can afford. He was also fond of walking, good talk, books. He was an intelligent man, the proof of which is that he lived happily with an intelligent woman for decades. (Signora Costa is now a popular and effective member of the Sicilian assembly.)

In June 1980, Gaetano Costa was confronted by a typical problem facing prosecutors: what should he do about a crook who was high up in the world? From investigators on the trail of big heroin shipments from the Sicilian mafia families to their American relatives, Costa had received incriminating evidence about Rosario Spatola, who had never killed anybody and had probably never seen heroin, but who made all the crimes worthwhile by investing the *narcolire* in legitimate enterprises. An unlicensed milk vendor on the streets of Palermo only a few years previously, Spatola had thousands on his payroll, that is, he controlled thousands of votes and had money to contribute to Christian Democratic Party funds, which bought him powerful protectors in Rome. Overriding the opposition of other prosecutors who wanted to do nothing, Costa signed the papers authorizing the prosecution of Spatola and the rest of the

Bontade-Inzerillo-Badalmenti gang. A few days later he was gunned down in the street.

*

Criminals think that the past can be wiped out: that's why they believe in murder. They think that when they kill somebody, that's the end of him. But the dead cannot always be cowed; some of them even grow in the grave.

While he was alive, Pio La Torre argued in vain for a new law which would make involvement in any association *di tipo mafioso* a criminal offence, abolish bank secrecy and allow the confiscation of all funds and property originating from criminal activities. Such measures would have gone a long way to destroy the economic and political power of organized crime, but La Torre was a communist deputy, secretary of the PCI in Sicily, which meant that at least half the country wasn't interested in what he had to say about anything. However, when he was gunned down on the 30th of April last year, he became a man whose proposals had to be listened to.

They were endorsed by the former carabiniere captain of Corleone, now General Dalla Chiesa, the organizer and first commander of Italy's anti-terrorist forces, a sort of latin Sir Robert Mark who grew with the country's crisis to become a national hero. Arriving to attend La Torre's funeral as the newly appointed Prefect of Palermo, he asked for the same kind of co-ordinating powers against the mafia that he had used so effectively against the terrorists, and he demanded the enactment of La Torre's proposed law which would give him the authority to get at the mafia's money, to storm their financial strongholds.

The government was stalling. There was quiet but effective opposition from bankers, mafiosi politicians and other *insospettabili*, highly vocal opposition from civil libertarians, including mafia attorneys. But law number 646, which became known as the La Torre Law, was passed in a matter of days after General Dalla Chiesa himself was gunned down with his young wife Emanuela and their bodyguard in another ambush last

September. There was no way politicians who wanted to be reelected could deny Dalla Chiesa's last request.

The new Prefect of Palermo, Emanuele De Francesco, also appointed as the government's 'high commissioner for the fight against the mafia', was given all the special powers that Dalla Chiesa had begged for in vain.

As for Public Prosecutor Gaetano Costa's ghost, he kept national attention focussed on Rosario Spatola and his gang, who were handed over to instructing magistrate Giovanni Falcone.

The dead also fought in the election. Last month's poll was an unqualified success from the point of view of the fight against organized crime. In the list for Western Sicily three mafia lawyers, one of the jurors who acquitted the murderers of Captain Basile, and Ernesto Di Fresco were all defeated. The fall in the Christian Democrat vote has strengthened the hand of the reformers within the party, led by Professor Sergio Mattarella, whose brother Piersanti, Christian Democrat President of the Region, was murdered by the mafia for his attempts to cleanse his party and the administration of corruption. Among those elected, Sergio Mattarella came out far ahead of the once all-powerful Attilio Ruffini, nephew of the late Cardinal Ruffini and three times a minister, who was backed in the previous election by *il big* of 1979, Rosario Spatola.

*

With the authority of the La Torre Law and the help of the Guardia di Finanza, Falcone traced the flow of *narcolire* through the banks and apparently legitimate companies, collecting in the process enough cancelled cheques and other financial records to fill a safe and two cupboards. The significance of the La Torre law, the thoroughness of Falcone's work in preparing the case for trial, may be judged by the results. Spatola and his associates were convicted and sentenced to prison terms totalling 400 years. The Gambino brothers who handled the American end of the *same* heroin deals – and who were the first to be found out, by way of an unclaimed suitcase full of heroin which kept riding around the Alitalia baggage conveyor belt at Kennedy Airport – were acquitted in New York.

Born in Palermo, Giovanni Falcone first wanted to be a priest but then studied law and after graduation joined the Ministry of Mercy and Justice, which is what Italians call their Home Office. He enjoys swimming, fishing and reading – inexpensive pastimes. At the age of 44, he has already been instrumental in putting behind bars more than a hundred mafiosi who have had people shot to a pulp for a great deal less.

To avoid the fate of their colleagues – Terranova, Costa, Montalto, Caccia – many magistrates are refusing to handle mafia cases, or asking for transfers to safer jobs, or simply quitting to go into private law firms. Italy's administration of justice is improving with danger. The sort of people who shouldn't have been judges, investigators, prosecutors in the first place are taking to their heels.

Falcone is one of those who didn't run. Heading the investigation of the Dalla Chiesa murders, he has just issued nine arrest warrants for the men who organized the killing, the *mandanti*, of whom the best known are the Catania building contractor Benedetto Santapaola and the new drug bosses of Western Sicily, the Greco brothers, Filippo Marchese, Rosario Riccobono and Liggio's lieutenant Salvatore Riina from Corleone. (The six men charged with the actual killing were arrested last October.) A so-far unpublished report on events leading up to the assassination has identified several members of the *alta mafia* who opposed the granting of special powers to Dalla Chiesa and did so '*for a specific political project of the mafia*'.

Eventually there should be a political earthquake. But nobody can stop Falcone from exposing the guilty, no matter who they are. Under Italian law no one, not even the Minister of Mercy and Justice, can tell a magistrate how to conduct his investigations or remove him from a case, unless he is charged with some crime. The only way to remove an honest magistrate is to kill him; that is why so many of them get killed. Falcone could quit, of course, but he doesn't, accepting the pressure of living in danger and yet under guard.

He is guarded by 24 agents in three shifts around the clock: young men in jeans and tee-shirts, with guns in their shoulder bags, great actors and acrobats. I'm told they are ace marksmen, but having eight of them always around you, even outside your bedroom at night, must be a strain. Falcone wouldn't say that there was anything unusual about his work, or that he had any particular motivation; he didn't even admit to seeing much difference between himself and a mafioso – an attitude which must be helpful in interrogations. I asked him what he would want to say as a kind of last message in case he too gets murdered. '*Niente*,' he said. 'I did my work like everybody else.'

Falcone betrays something of the tension he lives under only by refusing to divulge his wife's first name and saying with some relief that they have no children. Children are hostages to fortune; they can be kidnapped.

*

Palermo may be the world capital of crime but it is full of the kind of brave, spirited people who must have made London a great place during the blitz. The journalists of *L'Ora* and the *Giornale di Sicilia* are certainly among them. *L'Ora* is a left-wing paper, the *Giornale* is conservative, but in their relentless exposure of crime and corruption there is no difference. An editor of *L'Ora*, Mauro di Mauro, disappeared without trace; the *Giornale*'s chief reporter on crime and the courts, Mario Francese, was gunned down on a busy street. The young man with the big moustache and the telephone is his brilliant successor, Franco Nicastro, going after the latest news on murderous crooks and drug-traffickers. His wife has already had a phone call from them – a voice saying in thick Sicilian dialect, 'we don't like the things your husband writes'. They have one small child and another on the way, but they take Cardinal Pappalardo's advice not to give in to fear.

Unlike his predecessor Cardinal Ruffini, who never denounced the mafia, the present Archbishop of Palermo is leading a church crusade against organized crime. The Sicilian Bishops' Conference, which he heads, excommunicated mafiosi and even those members of mafia families who know about crimes and keep silent. This year when the Cardinal went to say Easter Mass at Ucciardone prison, not one of the 1,090 inmates showed up. 'The mafia has excommunicated the Cardinal,' people joked in Palermo. Some think it means that the mafia has decided to kill him.

Cardinal Pappalardo still walks around without armed guards, however, even in districts infested by *i killer*, preaching courage not just with words but by example.

The Sunday Telegraph, July 24, 1983

POSTSCRIPT: In contrast to the men I wrote about in 1983, behold the spokesman for President Reagan's Commission on Organized Crime. Speaking of the successor to murdered crime boss Paul Castellano, he says it is mobster John Gotti 'who is likely to determine the future of organized crime in the United States for the rest of the century'. Most Americans would expect the future of organized crime to be determined by investigators, district attorneys and judges – not by a convicted assassin who, for reasons far from clear, had to serve only two years for a contract killing.

And I can't help thinking of Cardinal Pappalardo when I read in today's *New York Times* that Cardinal O'Connor decided 'after prayer and consultation' not to permit a public requiem mass for Castellano. The Cardinal's spokesman said they wouldn't want to be 'appearing to condone the *alleged* crime syndicate'. The Sicilian Bishops' Conference excommunicated not only mafiosi but also members of their families 'who know about crimes and keep silent'; Cardinal O'Connor provided these unrepentant enemies of men and religion with the comfort of a private memorial mass and a priest at the graveside.

(Roosevelt Island, December 20, 1985)

Germany

The Power of Pretentiousness

The Death of my Brother Abel, by Gregor von Rezzori, translated by Joachim Neugroschel (Elizabeth Sifton Books – Viking)

This book illustrates perfectly why most intelligent people have given up reading fiction. Presented as a great German novel, 'a landmark in twentieth-century literature', it is in fact a big mindless mess. The first-person narrator himself describes it as 'this book with no solid ground plan or outline, no foundation-laying idea, no shaping principle, this book which increases and proliferates like a cancer, nourished by my moods and whims . . .'

One of the narrator's whims is to refer to the Holocaust as 'immoderation' and to regret the passing of anti-Semitism. 'What a lovely tension . . . has been lost to us because of German immoderation! Europe without hatred of Jews – why, that's like faith in God without the devil. The loss of a meta-physical dimension. A loss of eroticism. Never does my heart fail to quicken at the thought of the passionate caresses I provoked in Nuremberg when I held the black-haired girl from the death camp in my arms and whispered into her ear, "Kike bitch!" and she drummed her fists on my chest and gasped, "You filthy goy!" '

Only someone of stunted sensibilities, with the small brain and thick skin of a pig, could fail to perceive the emotional difference between the painless insult 'filthy goy', which had no punishment attached to it, and 'kike bitch', one of those terms of abuse which turned into death sentences for millions. Yet we are expected to believe that a death camp survivor herself made such an equation and reacted with *passionate caresses* to being called a 'kike bitch', so soon after her family, friends and neighbours were exterminated for the crime of being 'kikes'.

As I've argued in another context, people who do violence to others almost invariably believe that their victims repay pain with love, and it is the Nazi version of this pathological conceit – the fantasy about the beautiful Jewess who adores the anti-Semite – that is offered to us here. Before the 'kike bitch' there was Stella, the rich, sophisticated Rumanian-Jewish wife of a British diplomat. According to the narrator, Stella loved him so desperately that she risked and lost her life for him.

Like the author, the nameless fictional narrator is born in Rumania, lives in Vienna in the 1930's and spends most of the war years in Nazi Germany; Stella, his mistress from earlier days, is safe in Switzerland for the duration, but misses him so much that in 1942 she slips across the border to see him in Berlin and disappears into a death camp.

Stella's husband, Sir John, whom the narrator admires beyond measure ('he is a fine nobleman . . . his breeding is better than anyone else's . . . he has the best manners a person could possibly have') is very civilized about the whole affair. He offers these words of comfort to the narrator for the loss of the young woman they both loved, the woman murdered in an extermination camp: 'An excellent poke, indeed, a most exquisite fuck – didn't you think so? Poor girl, what a shame she had to die so soon – although she, too, would be fairly close to her forties today. And you know, they don't age so well, those Bedouin Jewesses; they become skinny and grow moustaches – oh, come on, you wouldn't roll her as eagerly now as you did back then, would you?' This vicious drivel is described as 'an impressive object lesson in elegant unabashment'.

If it turned out that the narrator was actually an erstwhile Gestapo informer, some of the text might make sense. But the swine is presented to us as a genius, as the new Proust who is finally completing his *Remembrance of Things Past*. He claims the virtue of absolute candour and all-inclusiveness: 'I want to say

[138]

everything in this book: everything I know, presume, believe, recognize and sense: everything I have gone through and lived through; the way I have gone through it and lived through it; and, if possible, why and to what end I went through it and lived through it. . . .' Only he never gets around to saying what he did for a living in Germany during the war.

What he does say is that there is 'no more guilt'. The enormity of the Nazis' crimes, he tells us, means that 'the causality of guilt and atonement, crime and punishment is cancelled . . .' He speaks of 'the anonymity and ubiquity of evil', as if murderers had no names. Millions died because of 'the continuous existence of murderousness in the human condition', as if a condition and not people had killed them. The crimes of the Nazi regime did not call for judgment: on the contrary, they put 'an end to any further attempts at distinguishing good and evil . . . There were no murderers any more and no victims.'

These are the concluding assertions of the book, which ends with an attack on the Nuremberg war crimes tribunal for its 'meaningless' arraignment of the surviving Nazi leaders – seedy, pathetic individuals who (like the whole Nazi regime) were nothing but an expression of the murderousness in the human condition. Having declared that it is impossible to distinguish between good and evil – that is, between helping one's fellow men and slaughtering them – the narrator finds it easy to deride the Nuremberg tribunal as 'put on too hastily, with too much governessy indignation and idealism and on a very flimsy legal basis', and with nothing to put forward but 'moralistic reflections on history'. It was 'built upon claptrap', and not least because of the war crimes committed by the victors. There is much to be said on the subject but the main point is this: what gave the victors the legal and moral right to judge at Nuremberg was not their own innocence but the crimes of the accused.

One of the many admiring reviewers of this book recommended it as a legitimate expression of Germany's desire to make the past easier to live with. This strikes me as a slander on most Germans today. How many people would want to feel comfortable about the systematic extermination of millions?

Neo-Nazis around the world produce pamphlets claiming that there were no death camps. The photographs, newsreels, films, eyewitness reports, confessions, testimonies of survivors, the Nazis' own records, they say, were all faked by the Jewish media. In their simplicity they can conceive of only one defence for genocide: it didn't happen.

On a more sophisticated level, historian David Irving allows that the Holocaust did happen, but insists that Hitler knew nothing about it.

Gregor von Rezzori enters a 'no contest' plea to all the charges, writes contemptuously of Hitler and the rest as deluded drug-addicted incompetent vain fools – *losers* – yet he manages to arrive at the same conclusion as the slimy little pamphlets which deny the existence of the gas chambers: no one could be fairly blamed or punished.

*

Since all literature is invention, many readers, and critics too, fail to appreciate that there is such a thing as lying in fiction. Swift's philosophizing horses, Mark Twain's angels, Kleist's ghosts embody profound truths about human nature and society (it's in this sense that all the Grimm tales are true), but by the same token an apparently naturalistic novel in which nothing physically impossible occurs, and which at times is presented as reportage of historical events, can be nothing but a tissue of lies. Though this may appear a contradiction, Rezzori's novel is both mindless and devious – as indeed it has to be in order to persuade his readers that there is no way to tell the difference between good and evil. This is the ultimate defence of all evil acts, but the truth is that we not only can tell the difference, we do so *instinctively*. All normal people are sickened by brutality, they recoil from the infliction of pain on others. Rezzori seems to be aware of this, and he consistently tries to make his readers mistrust their visceral responses. His death camp survivor who reacts with passionate caresses to being called a 'kike bitch' is an impossibility in a way that Kafka's human cockroach is not; she is a lie aimed at deadening the reader's moral sense. Why should you be repelled by racial abuse if even a Jewess from the Holocaust finds it a sexual turn-on?

In Rezzori's book revulsion and moral outrage are *bad manners*, proof of *lack of culture*. This lie is the very essence of the culture of oppression; neither fascism nor an apologia for fascism could succeed without it, and Rezzori does not hesitate to fake the evidence to make it more credible.

The reader is led to believe that the victims themselves – or rather, the more sophisticated and cultured victims – disapproved of excessive emotional reaction to Nazi atrocities. In November 1938, on the day after the *Kristallnacht*, the narrator and Stella go to Salzburg to visit her cousin, who is married to an Austrian official. Entering the cousin's elegant parlour, they are unpleasantly surprised to find it occupied by a group of Berliners ('to judge by their names, noses and accents they are all undeniably Jewish') loudly complaining about the persecution of the Jews in Germany. These 'Berlin Jews, rich ones' (refugees, in fact, though the narrator calls them 'émigrés') can't even speak German properly, and the 'obnoxious' Hungarian among them 'yiddles' when he talks. But they have the impertinence to go on railing against Hitler as if he were 'the arch-villain and enemy of mankind'! Stella 'has skillful objections and intelligent arguments ready' against their crude outbursts, and 'whenever she can, she mellows the fervour which lets justified indignation *degenerate into tongue-lashing*'. Still, she cannot make much headway against 'the passionately concentrated Berlin snottiness' of her fellow-Jews.

Moreover, they are complaining about 'hair-raising cruelties' *which they haven't even witnessed, much less experienced*. 'The host (quite reserved anyhow) occasionally ventures to ask, "Did this happen to you personally?" or "Did you witness it?"'

The Berlin Jews not only overreact to Hitler but are vulgar, pushy and ill-mannered (they come uninvited and stay to supper!). By contrast, the host, who finally becomes exasperated beyond endurance and announces that he worships Hitler as a saint, is a model of good manners: he 'is incapable of rudeness under any circumstances'. He, too, is adored by his Jewish wife; they are a couple of 'extraordinary musicality and literary culture'.

Rezzori sustains this picture of reserved, well-bred, civilised fascism by not allowing his reader to witness any of the horrors visited upon the victims. Although Stella is supposed to be the narrator's great love, and he is supposed to be ready to testify about her fate before the war crimes tribunal at Nuremberg, there is no indication that he knows anything about it or is even interested in finding out how she died and where. We never learn exactly what happened to her, what she went through or what she felt. Her disappearance 'into one of the death camps' is a one-line news item.

Jews suffer off the page in this book. There is only one glimpse of the Holocaust, and then it is the victims who are seen as revolting. A group of prisoners are let out of some derailed cattle cars and crouch beside the tracks to relieve themselves; when one of them tries to escape ('hops away from his pile . . . glancing around with bulging eyes') a shot rings out and 'the shitting frog simply keels over on his nose'. On the other hand there are whole chapters, rich in descriptive details, about the 'ineffable, inconceivable horror' of the Allied bombings, the devastation of Nuremberg and Hamburg and the hunger and poverty of the German people at the end of the war. There are good novels which focus on their wartime sufferings, but there is something deeply wrong with a novel that uses this suffering to bolster the assertion that no one was guilty of genocide.

There is simply no room to list all the devices the author uses to soften up the reader for his conclusion that the Nazis cannot be held responsible for their crimes against humanity. Among other things, he is a master of misdirection. The narrator's disclaimers of Nazi guilt are interspersed with lengthy ruminations about his own guilt, his responsibility for various deaths which he was clearly not responsible for at all. 'I KNOW THAT I AM A MURDERER' he tells us in block capitals, blaming himself for the death of his cousin Wolfgang, who shoots off his thumb, is bitten by a rat and dies of blood poisoning. He also blames himself for the death of one of his postwar mistresses who dies of cancer. And above all he blames himself for the death of his editor, Schwab. I bet you thought the title *The Death of My Brother Abel* was a reference to somebody who was actually murdered. Not a bit of it! 'Abel' is Schwab, an alcoholic who is constantly gobbling pills of various kinds and who dies of a combination of drink and drugs; the narrator feels he 'murdered' Schwab because he didn't finish this novel for him, because he survived him, because he didn't love him enough, etc. etc. He shows himself a fellow just too scrupulous for this world, a man whose tender conscience gives him no peace. Would he tell you that there were no murderers in the Third Reich if it wasn't so?

All the same, I would still like to know what he did for a living in Germany during the war.

*

One reviewer praised *The Death of My Brother Abel* on the grounds that it 'illuminates anti-Semitism from the inside'. If that's what is needed, *Mein Kampf* does the job even better, especially in retrospect, because we know who Hitler was, we know what he did. But we don't really know who this narrator is. Only his missing actions could have put his thoughts and feelings into perspective.

By their deeds shall ye know them is the basic law of fiction; there cannot be a good novel which is not founded on it. Actions alone reveal moral choices, action alone defines a character – and of course nowhere so clearly and dramatically as on a life-and-death terrain such as existed in Hitler's terror state.

To cover the gaping hole in the narrator's past, there is a lot about the theory of the modern novel. The modern novel that is without significant action or plot, and therefore without perspective on the inner world of its characters, is eminently suitable for expounding the kind of moral insanity represented by fascism, which is based on a similar disdain for what people *do*, since they are not accountable for it. Indeed, it doesn't even matter what a writer writes. 'Damn it, it's not so important *what* a man writes. People want to know *how* he brought it about.' Accordingly we are given the narrator's discussions with his ailing editor, Schwab; we are told about the hotel he writes in, how much paper he uses, what he stores it in, etc. etc. This still leaves hundreds of pages for biblical-historical-literary-philosophical-scientific-topographical name-dropping.

Take Stella's accomplishments, for example. 'Stella, who, in Berlin – the legendary Berlin of the late twenties! – had been friends with Paul Flechtheim, Gottfried Benn, Max Reinhardt, George Grosz; who had studied sociology in Heidelberg, psychology at the Sorbonne, art history in Florence and Freiburg, and was as well known in Prague as in Madrid. Stella, who had her winter chalet at Saint Moritz, her summer villas in Saint-Jean-Cap-Ferrat and Biarritz, and regularly won the prize for being the most elegant "Lady in Her Car" at the autumn races in Baden-Baden as well as first prize in the golf tournament. Stella, the indefatigable denizen of nightclubs, the chain smoker whose collection of lovers was as important as her collection of Futurists. Stella, who had read her Marx as passionately as *The Divine Comedy*, who knew her Einstein as thoroughly as the writings of Lilly Braun. . . .'

How could such nonsense be so widely published and praised? I think the answer lies in the power of pretentiousness. There are millions of people who think that having heard about something is the same as knowing it, and their notion of culture is a mixture of elegant lifestyle and big names. The very mention of Marx, *The Divine Comedy*, Einstein and Saint Moritz makes them feel cultured – and they will overlook a lot in a book that gives them such a wonderful feeling.

USA Today, September 20, 1985

The Letters of Thomas Mann

translated by Richard and Clara Winston (Secker and Warburg, 2 volumes)

In a letter to Feuchtwanger, Thomas Mann speaks of 'the brightness of an individual's destiny (which) wins out against the gloom of circumstances'. I can't think of a better way of summing up Thomas Mann's own life.

By 1929, when he received the Nobel Prize at the age of 54, Tomas Mann had written *Buddenbrooks*, *The Magic Mountain*, *Death in Venice*, *Tonio Kröger*, *Tristan* and many other novellas and short stories – an impressive enough achievement for a lifetime. Yet he grew better as he grew older, and he wrote his two best books, *Doctor Faustus* and *Confessions of Felix Krull*, in his seventies. This alone is an indication of the fantastic creative energy which possessed him. Moreover, he was appreciated: no writer of this century since the death of Tolstoy has been such a world figure – and none took so much pleasure in the laurels the world had to bestow. In his eightieth year he writes of his great delight in receiving from Queen Juliana 'a magnificent thing, Commander Cross of Orange-Nassau, the prettiest plaything for big children'.

The smouldering resentment against his reputation (according to *The New Yorker*, as he himself writes, 'he might be a major author, but "*not that major*"') has made him less talked about since his death in 1955, which is a pity, for he is not a bit less timely or pertinent than he used to be. To mention only *Doctor Faustus*, it is still the most illuminating book on the political and intellectual fanaticism of our age, a tragedy which stems 'from cleverness . . . a pact with the devil springing from a craving for an inspired breakthrough'. Another of his letters analyses his own work in a way that indicates his continuing relevance. His favourite device is

> a parody, not cynical but affectionate, of tradition. Such may well be the attitude of a writer who in an age of endings and transitions finds himself at once playing the part of a straggler, consummating and completing the past, and the part of an innovator undermining and dissolving it. It is the role and situation of the ironic conservative . . . The fact is that I consider myself primarily a humorist. . . . Humour, I am inclined to think, is an expression of amiability and comradeship toward those with whom we share this planet – in short, of fellow feeling, of an intention to do good to men, to teach them an appreciation of charm and to spread liberating merriment among them.

This collection of his letters (excellently selected, translated and annotated by Richard and Clara Winston) would be good news in any case, but it is in fact the fullest self-portrait that we have of Thomas Mann, far surpassing in scope his own brief and premature autobiography or his account of writing *Doctor Faustus*, and gives us invaluable insights into his work.

Still, it would be a mistake to seek too direct a connection between the artist and his art: in between there is the magic of genius, which often takes little heed of the author's mind or body. 'Obstinately and inexorably nemesis takes its course, following the vilest laws,' he writes from his California home in 1951, 'and sometimes I catch myself thinking: just as well; let it come the way they insist on having it. Human wickedness deserves a visitation such as the earth has not yet seen – and this civilization of grabbers, fools and gangsters deserves to perish.' In this very same letter he reports, 'with my energies plainly dwindling and a sense of depression growing, I have taken up the ancient *Felix Krull* again'. *Felix Krull* turned out to be one of the sunniest masterpieces of world literature.

[146]

Mann's attitude towards suicide is perhaps most revealing of the qualities which made him a great novelist. Both his sisters killed themselves, and so did his eldest son Klaus. Thomas Mann's response is always primarily a concern for the survivors, rather than pity for those who took their lives. On the occasion of Stefan Zweig's suicide he writes to Zweig's first wife: 'Was he conscious of no obligation towards the hundreds of thousands . . . upon whom his abdication was bound to have a profoundly depressing effect?' If the harshness repels, it should be remembered that much of modern literature has contributed to the moral insanity of our times by viewing actions only in subjective terms. Mann measured what people did in terms of the effect they had on others. This epic view of life is also the only moral one. (It failed him in the Schönberg affair, which is a novel in itself.)

The letters afford glimpses of Mann's extraordinary family, particularly his wife Katia and their brilliant daughter Erika, who risked her life going back into Germany to retrieve the manuscript of *Joseph and His Brothers* from their house in Munich and forfeited a career of her own to labour as her father's researcher, editor and best critic.

There are also letters to his brother Heinrich, about whom he had this to say to an Italian critic:

> . . . it was an indescribable shock to me, and seemed like a dream, when shortly before his death Heinrich dedicated one of his books to me with the words: 'To my big brother, who wrote *Doctor Faustus*'. What . . . ? How . . . ? He had always been the big brother. And I puffed out my chest and thought of Goethe's remark about the Germans' silly bickering over which was greater, he or Schiller: 'They ought to be glad that they have two such boys.'

These letters are fascinating on many levels, and not least as the record of a famous public figure whose life encompassed several historical periods and whose changing political attitudes epitomize the sad history of this century. As a patriotic German, Thomas Mann (in bitter opposition to Heinrich) welcomed the First World War: 'this great, fundamentally decent and in fact stirring people's war' – only to become a tireless anti-Nazi and fervent admirer of America as defender of Western civilization. 'I do not think,' he wrote to Beneš upon giving up his Czech passport in 1944 to become an American citizen, 'that I shall turn my back upon this country whose libertarian traditions and humanely beneficent atmosphere I sincerely appreciate.' But in 1952 he returned to Europe and settled in Switzerland, having come to see America as 'supporting the old, worn-out, rotten and corrupt forces throughout the world', as a power which 'in a time of inexorable change plays the policeman of the status quo'.

This last quotation is from one of his many letters to Agnes E. Meyer, wife of the publisher of the *Washington Post*. Thomas Mann's correspondence with this formidable lady testifies to the paradoxical quality of fame: she admired and helped him a great deal but continually castigated him and even his children for failing to live up to her idea of perfection. In this she was not alone: as Mann's achievement and reputation grew, so did the attacks upon him from all sides for his failure to take the 'proper stand' on a great many issues.

He was too famous to be left alone. His irate reply to Mrs Meyer is an exception rather than the rule, reflecting his exasperation with forever having to explain and justify himself. As these letters clearly show, fame is a lot of work and trouble, and it had a wearing and at times intimidating effect on him. He was more than a great writer, he was a symbol, an idol. And worshippers make their idol their alter ego: they come to believe he is exactly like themselves, and when he shows himself to be different, they turn on him with the rage of people who feel betrayed.

There was a shadow over the brightness of Thomas Mann's destiny: he could never think in solitude, without at least a subliminal awareness of the effect of his words on the hordes of touchy admirers – critics, editors, columnists, professors – who kept up his reputation yet were ready to pounce on him if he failed to live up to their literary, political or moral expectations.

Mann showed a great deal more integrity than Goethe as the favourite of the powerful and the influential, yet he was understandably not eager to offend his supporters. One begins to see the reason for the wooden passages in some of his novels, the occasional ponderousness, the balanced view instead of the daring leap that is called for, when one reads his careful letters to authorities of state, press and academia. How much easier it was for unrecognized geniuses like Stendhal or Kleist or Italo Svevo to say exactly what they thought and felt! Because *it did not matter*: no one gave a damn *what* they wrote, except a few close friends. Failure is a kind of luck, as long as it doesn't kill you.

The Times, December 14, 1970

The Genius Whose Time Has Come

Heinrich von Kleist
(18 October 1777–21 November 1811)

As far as I can tell, the first printed reference in English to Heinrich von Kleist appeared on 28 December 1811 in *The Times*, which published a disapproving obituary.

> The attention of the people of Berlin has lately been very much occupied by the tragical adventure of M. Kleist, the celebrated Prussian poet, and Madame Vogel. The reports which were at first circulated with regard to the cause of this unfortunate affair, have been strongly contradicted by the family of the lady; and it has been particularly denied that love was in any respect the cause of it. Madame Vogel, it is said, had suffered long under an incurable disorder; her physicians had declared her death inevitable; she herself formed a resolution to put a period to her existence. M. Kleist, the poet, and a friend of her family, had also long determined to kill himself. These two unhappy beings having confidentially communicated to each other their horrible resolution, resolved to carry it into effect at the same time. They repaired to the Inn at Wilhelmstadt, between Berlin and Potsdam, on the border of the *Sacred Lake*. For one night and one day they were preparing themselves for death, by putting up prayers, singing, drinking a number of bottles of wine and rum, and last of all by taking about sixteen cups of coffee . . . This done, they repaired to the banks of the *Sacred Lake*, where they sat down opposite each other. M. Kleist took a loaded pistol, and shot Madame Vogel through the

heart, who fell back dead; he then reloaded the pistol and shot himself through the head . . . The public are far from admiring, or even of approving, this act of insanity. . . .

The article, translated from *Le Moniteur*, contains some errors of fact. Kleist and Frau Vogel may or may not have been lovers, but they were positively not drinking heavily or singing in the last hours before their death; in fact, what is most striking about their behaviour is their propriety, well documented in the statements given to the police by the innkeeper and his wife and servants. The two guests spent most of the night writing letters in their adjoining rooms, and in the morning dressed with care and went for a walk; in the afternoon they asked to have coffee served to them by the lake, and the workman who carried the table and two chairs down to the lakeshore later testified that when the gentleman asked him to fetch another tot of rum (he had already bought a small flask at the inn), Frau Vogel objected.

The lady remarked: 'Do you really want to drink any more rum today, dear child, don't you think you've had enough?' And the gentleman answered: 'All right, dear child, if you don't want me to, then I won't. So don't bother, good fellow, don't bring anything.'

Possibly Frau Vogel, who had been told that she had cancer of the womb, was afraid that if Kleist got tipsy he would fail to kill her promptly and painlessly. There were two pistols, which she carried in a basket over her arm, covered with a white cloth, and Kleist charged both with just enough gunpowder to kill but not disfigure.

In his stories there are several characters who commit suicide (like the hero of *The Engagement in Santo Domingo*, who 'stuck the pistol right into his mouth' and whose 'skull was completely shattered, with fragments of it clinging to the walls') and Kleist's death has often been referred to as a case of life imitating art. But while, among weightier, despairing considerations, Kleist may have been curious to undergo the experi-

[151]

ence of suicide for the sake of checking on the validity of his earlier descriptions of it, he was determined not to leave a mess like his characters. Though he shot Frau Vogel at close range and stuck the other pistol right into his mouth, the only marks on their bodies were a small round bloodstain under her left breast, and a few flecks of blood around his lips.

This end leaves us with the same dominant impression as Kleist's whole oeuvre: desperate, violent acts executed with the utmost precision, with uncanny finesse. 'In art everything depends on form, and everything that has to do with form is my business,' he wrote once. His mastery of form, like all great skills, involved an irrepressible love of play. He was last seen from a distance, only minutes before the shots were heard, skipping stones on the water.

For those who condemned his 'act of insanity' there is a reply in *Penthesilea*: writers can argue back from beyond the grave.

> Yet man rebels, shaking his shoulders free
> Of all that weighs him down beyond endurance;
> There must be a limit to pain or he won't bear it.

During his short and terrible life this genius was a poor and unsuccessful writer. He became a 'celebrated poet' only after his death; it was the scandal of the double suicide by the Wannsee which began the slow process of rescuing from obscurity his eight plays and eight stories, his essays, anecdotes, epigrams, poems and translations. He may even have foreseen this; the notion of violent death begetting posthumous fame is very Kleistian. '*Immortality, now you are truly mine!*' exclaims the hero of his last play, *The Prince of Homburg*, awaiting execution.

*

Kleist was not, as suicides are often thought to be, a weak character – only one overly familiar with death. His father, a major in the Prussian army, died when the boy was ten, his mother when he was fifteen; on his eighteenth birthday the cousin who had been his closest companion killed himself. Besides, he lived in an age when children weren't protected by law from growing up. He entered the army at fourteen, was a fighting soldier at fifteen. It was the sort of adolescence that produced Napoleon and San Martín: for those who have the inborn gifts, early encounters with death and the practice of doing one's duty under fire seem to be conducive to the sudden growth of extraordinary will-power, courage and intelligence, qualities which are observable in every great man, be he a commander of armies or of words.

In many ways Kleist is akin to his near-contemporary Stendhal, who was also an adolescent soldier. Though Kleist fought the French and Stendhal was bored by the Germans, and though their preoccupations were different, their sensibilities were similar – both were profoundly responsive to music, painting and mathematics – and their shared formative experiences of parental death and war must have helped to give their style its rare decisiveness and briskness. Neither of them wasted time on nonsensical problems, and they both wrote with the objectivity of intelligent officers who knew that misleading information could be deadly and there was no point in telling anything but the truth.

Such conduct in literature is usually punished by critical abuse and public indifference. 'Just to describe the plot is to banish oneself from polite society,' wrote the first reviewer of *The Marquise of O*. The trouble with the truth about anything is that it tends to be offensive, either because it's bad news or because it's confusingly different from received notions (and people get very offended and spiteful when they don't understand something) or because it punctures a successful pretence. And somehow sex is usually involved.

In his very first play, *The Schroffenstein Family* (1802), his version of Romeo and Juliet, Kleist brings sexual longing on to the stage in one of the most potent love scenes ever conceived – so potent that I doubt it could have been freely performed before the 1960s. Kleist's Romeo undresses his Juliet and exchanges clothes with her while describing how he will undress her on their wedding night. At the age of twenty-five Kleist is already master of simple actions which express great passions. In an earlier love scene the girl, still suspecting the lovely boy of being her deadly enemy, drinks the water he brings to her although she is sure it is poisoned. If he wants to kill her, then she wants to die. The clothes-changing scene at the end is charged not only with sexual longing but also self-sacrifice (each emotion strengthening the impact of the other): the boy, knowing that his father is coming to kill the girl, talks her into exchanging clothes with him to save her life. Kleist's young lovers do not kill themselves; they are murdered by their fathers – each killing his own child, thinking it's the other. It's hatred that destroys, not love. This masterpiece is in some ways superior to Shakespeare's (certainly in its concept), yet apart from a couple of untypically favourable reviews and one single performance in Graz it went unnoticed in Kleist's lifetime and has inspired belittling comments for nearly two centuries. I can see no other reason for this than the 'vulgar', 'tasteless', 'clumsy' undressing scene in which an adolescent is curious about and thrilled by the body of the girl he loves. I'm convinced, however, that this very same scene will help to pack the theatres in the third century of Kleist's immortal life.

But then it is possible to understand the classics. We can have a clear perspective on characters if our ego is not involved in their beliefs and actions, in their habits and way of life – in other words, if they are far removed from us in time and place. There may be great contemporary writers, but there can be very few great contemporary readers; we are too involved in present conflicts, too mesmerised by the dominant falsehoods of the day, too accustomed to what happens to be 'right' or 'wrong' at the moment, to be able to match the clear-sighted impartiality of great literature. This is as true of us as it was of the prim Germans of the 19th century. What could they possibly have made of the hero and heroine of *The Earthquake in Chile*? They are a couple of exceptionally nice and decent youngsters – there is absolutely nothing wrong with them – yet they make love! They make love even though they are not married. Worse, the girl is a novice nun and they commit their mortal sin in the garden of the convent. It is obvious that readers who viewed their conduct as sacrilegious and depraved could not fully grasp Kleist's portrayal of the insolence and brutality of those who set up to be their judges. The girl is condemned to death and her lover thrown into prison; just as she is being led to the scaffold and he is about to hang himself in his cell, they are liberated by the earthquake – only to be killed by an enraged mob for *causing* the earthquake with their sin.

Even among liberal-minded readers for whom sex held no terrors, there were few who could see the point of the story. The lynching is such a shocking evocation of righteous stupidity and sanctimonious cruelty that it could hardly be appreciated by those who believe that human beings are basically good. To mention but one telling detail, when friends try to protect the lovers by pretending that they are not the couple the mob are looking for, 'the instigator of all these horrors' kills by mistake a lady of spotless reputation.

> 'Monster!' a stranger cried out. 'That was Donna Costanze Xares!'
> 'Then why did they lie to us!' the shoemaker retorted. 'Find the right one and kill her!'

If Stendhal tells us how people become lovers, Kleist tells us how people become murderers. It is hardly ever for a good reason.

Having killed his son, believing him to be his enemy's daughter, the father in *The Schroffenstein Family* asks his vassal why he did it. He cannot remember. 'Why, of course, it's Agnes,' says the vassal.

RUPERT   Agnes, yes, that's right,
> She did me harm, she did me great harm,
> O, yes, I know that well . . . What was it, now?

[155]

```
SANTING                         I don't know
            What you mean. The girl herself
            Has done you no harm.
RUPERT                          No harm? Santing!
            Why did I kill her, then? Tell
            Me quickly how she injured me, I beg you.
            Put it as spitefully as you like. – Basilisk,
            Don't look at me, speak, Devil, speak,
            And if you do not know, lie!
SANTING                         Have you gone mad?
            The girl was Sylvester's daughter.
```

*

When Rupert learns that in fact he has killed his own son,
that's another moment.

The play, published anonymously in a faulty edition, earned
Kleist nothing; he hoped to do better. 'I swear to you,' he wrote
to his sister Ulrike, 'that I could do better than that idiot
Kotzebue,' (referring to a very famous and successful playwright of the period). 'Only I must have time. *Time* is what I
need. If you would only let me work beside you in peace for a
couple of months, without driving me mad with anxiety about
what will become of me . . .'

But whatever he wrote, it did him no good. There is in every
culture a deep divide between what is alive and what is
praiseworthy, and the first decade of the 19th century was
already cursed by the army of literary experts who would
discard the living and praise the rest. If Kleist had been the
vulgar author the critics claimed him to be, he could have
succeeded, but in order to attract the attention of intelligent
readers, he would have needed the recommendation of the
official guardians of literature who thought he was vulgar. As
he wrote once:

The pimping, the tale-bearing of reviewers – and especially
the fact that this has become a necessity for the public –
shows me how iniquitous and impure literature and taste

[156]

must be in Germany. I have yet to meet a reader who was properly ashamed of having bought some lovely child of literature second-hand. As if they were bound by tradition to leave the first bloom of love to the reviewers, just as noblemen in certain countries had a similar right over the brides of their serfs. Yes, truly! – there are such enervated readers in Germany, who no longer think of direct intercourse with the works of the mind and are content year in year out with the literary journals and their role as spectators.

It was in such a predicament, familiar to every struggling writer, that Kleist sought the blessing of the man who counted most, addressing him with obligatory deference as 'Hochwohlgeborner Herr, Hochzuverehrender Herr Geheimrat, Ew. Excellenz' and saying, in all sincerity, that he approached him 'on the knees of my heart'. Unavoidably, however, his realism – in particular his portrayal of destructive passions – earned him the disapproval of Goethe, the demigod of German culture, whose own aesthetic standards could be judged from his boast that 'the heroines I have drawn all turned out very well, for *they are all better than women in real life*'. (Italics mine throughout.) Goethe's expressions of 'horror and disgust' did more than anything else to deprive Kleist of a living, and they still carry enough weight to deprive him of his rightful place in German literature. True, Goethe produced *The Broken Jug* at Weimar, turning this broad comedy (a play very much like Brueghel's *Village Wedding*) into the most resounding flop of the decade, which he later referred to as 'helping' Kleist and 'making him known'. But of course this arbiter of literary worth, this complacent, timid and hypocritical lawyer, the author of that much admired poem describing how he spent a night at an inn in bed with a beautiful, willing chambermaid, doing nothing but thinking of his true love – the author of a Faust who sells his soul to the devil and then goes to heaven – couldn't help being offended by Kleist, a writer more like Marlowe, whose Faust is torn limb from limb by devils at the end. Kleist's works are shocking warnings that we cannot escape the consequences of our actions, while Goethe's offer the deadly lie that nothing is decisive or final on this earth. Goethe thought Kleist's works were 'diseased' because they showed 'the unlovely and frightening in Nature', while I believe it is Goethe's 'beneficent high-mindedness' (as Thomas Mann puts it with due reverence) that is sick as well as outdated, and Kleist is bound to emerge from Goethe's fading shadow as the greatest German writer.

In the meantime, however, we are stuck with Goethe's opinion that it is 'impossible for a *mature understanding* to enter into the violence of Kleist's themes *with any pleasure*', and even a recent English reference book on German literature condemns Kleist for finding life 'a labyrinth to which reason, faith and feeling were uncertain guides'. There could be no more accurate description of life than that, but it can still be dismissed as the product of a diseased imagination, proof positive that Kleist was 'born without a sense of direction or balance'.

To listen to this sort of inane criticism, which condemned him to economic death, yet continue to portray life according to his derided vision (until the age of 34 – and even then commit suicide rather than turn into a hack) required the rarest kind of toughness and tenacity, which are manifest in his soldierly style.

Indeed, among all the giants of world literature, it is this Prussian officer who writes most like a general. Cities burn, people are killed in a sub-clause, and he's already off on another track.

. . . While his men were plundering the suburbs, Kohlhaas stuck a notice up on the door post of the church saying that he, Kohlhaas, had set the city afire, and, if the Junker were not surrendered to him, he would raze the place so thoroughly that, as he put it, he would not have to hunt behind any walls to find him.

The terror of the Wittenbergians at this unheard-of outrage was indescribable; and no sooner had the fire, which luckily on that rather still summer night burned down no more than nineteen buildings (among them, however, one church) been partly extinguished towards morning, than the elderly Sheriff, Otto von Gorgas, dispatched a company of fifty men to capture the savage fellow.

(Michael Kohlhaas)

But nothing could illustrate Kleist's tough-minded objectivity more strikingly than *The Engagement in Santo Domingo*, a love story from the bloody days of the race war in Haiti at the beginning of the nineteenth century, when it was still a French colony. The story begins with a list of a plantation owner's good deeds toward his most trusted slave, who is freed, made overseer of the estate, given a house and a pension and even provided for in the master's will, and who 'in the general frenzy of revenge . . . was one of the first to reach for a rifle and, *remembering the tyranny that had torn him from his native land*, blow his master's brains out'.

The short-lived engagement between a Swiss officer and a mulatto girl who have been fighting on opposite sides is recounted by Kleist in such a manner that no reader black or white could find it uninformed, incomplete, sentimental, patronizing or unfair. I don't know of any other literary work reflecting the race conflict of which this could be said, and even if Kleist hadn't written anything else, *The Engagement in Santo Domingo* alone would make him one of the most relevant writers of our age. We can learn more from this story than from all the well-meaning novels by our own contemporaries about our racial predicament.

One of the reasons for Kleist's unique achievement is of course that he does not *aim* at promoting better understanding between the races; such aims are corrupting, because they lead to tampering with the evidence. Whatever the implications, we get them by the way, as it were – by way of the lovers' fatal encounter. In great literature as in life, everything is by the way of something else; nothing stands in isolation.

*

Kleist chose his life as much as his death. As a scion of a Prussian military family, counting among his ancestors sixteen generals and two field marshals, he could have had a secure career as an officer of Friedrich Wilhelm III, but in 1799, at the age of twenty-one, he quit the army, signalling his departure with his first literary work, *An Essay on Finding the Certain Way to Happiness and Enjoying It Undisturbed – Even Among the Greatest Afflictions of Life!*

At first he thought that happiness was to be found in Knowledge and a Good Wife: he became engaged to a general's daughter, Wilhelmine von Zenge, nearly killed himself with study at the university in his native city of Frankfurt an der Oder, and then continued his studies while holding a post as a trainee civil servant in Berlin. But as his sister Ulrike recalled, 'one day when his chief gave him a boring book in many volumes with the order to read it through and make a report on it, Heinrich made up his mind: he would go away'. There is a clue here to the development of a genius; Kleist may have ended up killing himself but while he lived he knew how to guard his spirit and his intelligence; he had a keen sense of how boring books corrupt the brain. There is nothing to be got out of books that bore us; they affect the mind as rape affects women's bodies; what should be great joy is nausea. I often think if students weren't compelled to finish books which don't speak to them, literary education wouldn't leave them so unfeeling about literature.

In any case, at about the time Kleist quit his job he was reading Kant, who inspired him to the discovery which was to be one of the chief motifs of his life's work – the ultimate incomprehensibility of things, or rather, the deficiency of human understanding. He wrote to Wilhelmine about it, hoping 'it will not shock you as deeply and painfully as it shocked me'. (It is one of the characteristics of a genius that he can be deeply and painfully shocked by an idea.)

If everybody had green glasses instead of eyes, then they would necessarily form the opinion that the objects which they see through them *are* green – and they would never be able to decide whether their eye shows them things as they are, or whether it doesn't add something to them which belongs not to them but to the eye. So it is with the mind. We cannot decide whether what we call truth is really truth, or whether it only seems so to us . . . O, Wilhelmine, if the sharp point of this idea does not strike into your heart, do not smile at someone who feels wounded by it . . .

This was a tremendous insight – tremendous because he felt it so tremendously that he saw its bearing on all aspects of life and could create from it a whole series of powerful characters who are driven to extremes by their own misjudgments or deceptive appearances. With all the fury of a woman scorned *Penthesilea* sets her dogs on Achilles, whom she loves; she drives an arrow through his throat, tears his armour from his body and sinks her teeth into his flesh – only poor Achilles wasn't scorning her. The hero of *The Engagement in Santo Domingo* kills his lover for betraying him – but far from betraying him, she has just saved his life.

There is very little pleasure in this and a great deal of horror, but Kleist horrifies us for a purpose. We cannot understand anything profoundly unless it moves or shocks us so deeply that it touches our subconscious; great writers are not those who tell us we shouldn't play with fire, but those who make our fingers burn.

Kleist does not smooth over anything, either to excuse his characters or to tidy up his story. Nor does he confuse depth with mystification, as many modern authors do; there is never any doubt in a Kleist work who does what to whom and why. But what he leaves alone, or rather, spotlights like no other writer, are life's unresolved contradictions. Goethe, like Hollywood producers in the old days, believed in processing reality with *Ausgleichung*, *Aussöhnung* and *Abrundung* (balancing, reconciling and rounding-off) in the interests of reassurance and uplift; Kleist rendered life as he found it – unsettled, unsettling and inexplicably absurd.

[161]

The Marquise of O is pregnant, she doesn't know how or by whom; at the end we have the answer, but in the meantime Kleist gives us the most haunting evocation of bewilderment, of that maddening feeling of *how can that be!* which intelligent people are condemned to suffer every day. In *St. Cecilia, or the Power of Music* a Catholic nunnery is saved by an authentic miracle, only to be secularised, as we learn from a sub-clause, 'at the end of the Thirty Years' War, by the terms of the Peace of Westphalia'.

One way of describing Kleist's masterpieces might be to quote from his *Amphitryon*:

> This is a fiendish business, a goblin's tale,
> Yet it's as true as sunlight.

*

No writer can create a single character or a single scene beyond his emotional range. Kleist, whose works are charged with suddenly swelling passions, had an abnormal capacity for extreme emotions – for extreme joy as well as extreme despair, extreme love as well as extreme hate. He lived, in the words of an army friend, 'exposed to the storms of his inner self'.

After losing his faith in knowledge and the curative power of explanations at the age of 23, he sought relief in travel. 'I do not deserve to be unhappy, and will not always remain so,' he wrote to Wilhelmine from Paris. Happiness, he now saw, was to 'till a field, to plant a tree, to father a child'. He soon renounced these simple ambitions, but he felt them so deeply that they survive everywhere in his work, and all the 'fiendish business' of his stories and plays is set against the soundest longings of the heart for love, a home and family. From Paris he went to Switzerland, planning to buy a plot of land and become a farmer, but then spent all his capital, a small inheritance from his parents, on writing his first two plays. This marked the beginning of his labours 'to pluck the garland of immortality' and the beginning of his lifelong insolvency. 'I must now set myself to writing whether I like it or not,' he wrote to Wilhelmine, breaking off their engagement. 'In all probability I'll be penniless within a year . . . Dear girl, do not write to me any more. My only wish is to die.'

The first play was *The Schroffenstein Family*; the other was the first draft of *Robert Guiskard*, about which Wieland wrote that 'if the spirits of Aeschylus, Sophocles and Shakespeare united to produce a tragedy, it would be like Kleist's *Death of Guiskard the Norman*, so far as the whole accords with what he allowed me to hear . . .' Kleist, dissatisfied, burned it. After burning it he walked from Paris to Normandy, planning to join the invasion of England which Napoleon was organizing in the fall of 1803. He hated Napoleon, the conqueror of Germany, but was sure the invasion would fail, and thought he might as well take the opportunity 'to die the glorious death of battles'.

According to Thomas Mann, Kleist's 'ambition and wish to die are difficult to reconcile', but it seems to me that he no more wanted to die than the moth wants to get burned: he wanted to be near the flame. Graham Greene records in his auto-biography *A Sort of Life* that when he was a student he played Russian roulette, not just once but a number of times, all on his own; he must have seen deep into himself in those dark flashes when he pulled the trigger. Kleist, I believe, got addicted to the thrill of bullets that just missed him when he was an adolescent soldier; this thrill, repeatedly sought in his best creative periods, unlocked his subconscious and gave his work the intensity of last moments lived at the peak of health and unclouded perception. The excitement and inspiration which he derived from the thought of death, talking of suicide, planning various ways of suicide, eventually cost him his life when poverty and humiliation and the eagerness of a woman to join him pushed him into the act, but while he lived he created a body of work which positively glows with the heightened sense of self-awareness most men feel in the presence of death.

Life is worthwhile only when we don't value it . . . we can use it to great purpose only if we're ready to throw it away lightly and joyfully. Anyone who clings to life is already morally dead; the willingness to sacrifice life is the essence of vitality, and it rots away when one is taking care of oneself.

(letter to Wilhelmine)

There is a joy of freedom, dignity and even power for those who are not afraid of death. Michael Kohlhaas, the horse dealer, who raised a rebellion when the Elector of Saxony denied him justice in the matter of a pair of stolen horses, is caught and condemned to death, but when the Elector's emissary comes to offer him his life and liberty in exchange for a piece of paper on which a fortune teller has written the future of the Elector and his house, Kohlhaas answers:

'Noble sir, if your sovereign should come to me and say, "I'll destroy myself and the whole pack of those who help me wield the sceptre" – destroy himself, mind you, which is the dearest wish of my soul – I would still refuse him the paper, which is worth more to him than his life, and say, "You can send me to the scaffold, but I can make you suffer, and I mean to."'

At the place of execution:

Kohlhaas, striding up in front of the man with a suddenness that took his guard by surprise, drew out the capsule, removed the paper, unsealed it and read it through; and looking steadily at the man with the blue and white plumes, in whose breast fond hopes were already beginning to spring, he stuck the paper in his mouth and swallowed it. At this sight the man with the blue and white plumes was seized by a fit and fell unconscious to the ground. While his dismayed companions bent over him and raised him, Kohlhaas turned around to the scaffold, where his head fell under the executioner's axe.

These are the chief Kleistian motifs, in his life as in his work: bewilderment, elation in the presence of death, and the sense of annihilating surprise.

It's strange how . . . whenever I decide to take a firm step the ground vanishes from under my feet.

(letter to Marie von Kleist)

*

Today the fact-bound view of life which leaves out most of it is no longer as fashionable as it used to be a couple of decades ago, and I believe the supernatural elements in Kleist, far from proving a barrier, will increase his popularity in the coming years. At any rate, I don't think many people would argue today, as Martin Greenberg did in his 1960 introduction to the stories, that the end of *Michael Kohlhaas* is 'with its fairytale supernaturalism, a good deal less forceful and serious' than the rest.

Mr Greenberg is referring to the fairytale-like intervention of the old gypsy woman, evidently a reincarnation of Kohlhaas's wife, who gives him the paper foretelling the future of the Elector's house. The Elector's desperate desire to obtain the paper gives Kohlhaas the power to choose between life and revenge on 'the man with the blue and white plumes'. I can't see anything wrong with that. Literal-minded people who think the ghost in *Hamlet* is a mistake will not follow, but ideally a literary incident is like a law of physics, identifying not a single occurrence but a universal process in a definitive way that holds good for all times and places. It is real or not depending on whether what it signifies is true or not. Thus the devils at the end of Marlowe's *Dr. Faustus* are real and right – as is the magic paper in *Michael Kohlhaas*, which, by granting him choices, renders visible what is otherwise invisible but nonetheless real: the inner freedom of the character. Man is spiritually free even at the moment his head is chopped off. What could be more forceful or serious?

Mesmerized by the glitter of wealth and power and by the horror of misery and helplessness, most of us tend to assume that there is a stage on the social scale below which a man must suffer all indignities, and a stage above which a man can be vile to his fellow men and get away with it. True enough, Stalin died in power and in bed and Dr Mengele lives a contented old age in South America, and we are all acquainted with lesser known evil men who should have gone up in flames and didn't, but *Michael Kohlhaas* reminds us that they are exceptions to the rule. The Elector's agony over his inability to prise out the secret of his future from the man he has ruined embodies the law of interdependence; it asserts in the most amazing and thrilling way that there are no heights from which it is possible to strike at those below with impunity. As Kohlhaas exults over the power the magic paper gives him 'to wound his enemy mortally in the heel at the very moment it was treading him in the dust' we recognize the true fact – without which the soul shrivels – that we are not fully defined by our social situation, that the prince is never fully a prince and the pauper is never fully a pauper – indeed, that the condemned man is not only a condemned man.

People find it comforting to think that they are trapped, they must go along, they are victims of circumstances and 'have no choice', but such falsehoods are tranquillizers that deaden the spirit. This is proved by the depressing books which are based on the notion of victimised humanity, even if they are written by such gifted writers as Kafka. Kafka's K. has no choice but to submit to his executioners and hand them back the knife to kill him with; his spirit has been destroyed by the system. But such images are the daydreams of would-be Hitlers and the night-mares of the weak, and have very little to do with real life. In real life there is no power which could inescapably prevail over our vitality and love. Even on the way to the gas chambers mothers laughed, sang and played with their children to dis-tract them until the last possible moment from the horror of the end. Kleist is one of the most eloquent writers on tragic fatality and on man's inhumanity to man, showing human beings at the mercy of chance and evil powers and passions, yet he is never depressing or demoralising, for his works are lit up by choices. We are not masters of our fate, but we are free to choose what meaning we give to our life and our death.

*

It is unfortunate that the rediscovery of Kleist occurred at a time when 'modern' was the greatest praise and he could be recommended most effectively, if misleadingly, by comparing him to fashionable modern authors. Martin Greenberg, in his introduction to the stories, compares Kleist not only to Büchner and Stendhal, which would be fine, but also to Nietzsche, Freud, Lawrence and Kafka, as 'a hero of the modern spirit'. Whatever one thinks of these last-named heroes of the modern spirit, it seems beyond dispute that they were obsessed with exclusive concerns. Freud, for instance, throws a great deal of light on the subconscious and sex, but at the expense of the importance of everything else. Kleist is different in kind; his genius is a scale which measures everything at its true weight.

Only the desire to read 'modernism' into Kleist could have prompted Mr Greenberg to claim that *The Beggarwoman of Locarno* carries 'the implied statement that the moral order is not rational and just, but cruel, impatient and insensate'. That would be a very modern implication indeed (as well as false) but it has nothing to do with Kleist. He does not rail against the moral order; he defines it. A Marquis of Locarno, having other things on his mind, inadvertently causes the death of an old beggarwoman through unthinking callousness, and thereafter is haunted by her spirit until he goes mad and burns down his castle with himself in it. This ghost story carries the implied statement that indifference to others is self-destructive, which may be very harsh but appears to me quite logical; as ye sow, so shall ye reap. This is an older and truer notion than the complaints of the moderns. The modern idea is that the world is so full of cruelty that a little more or less won't make any difference; Kleist shows that it's enough to be a little mean to bring upon oneself the most terrible retribution.

As I write Professor Ilse Graham is saying on the BBC that Kleist offers us 'Kafkaesque images of man's imprisonment in his shell'. Man's imprisonment in his shell is a neurotic condition that has been elevated into a world view by some of the moderns, or rather their critics; Kleist was in no way guilty of that. He is very unmodern and profound in defining people in their relationship to others. It was Stendhal who said that 'a man can acquire everything in solitude except character', but Kleist might have said it too. His portrayal of his characters' inner world shows the depth of their involvement with others: if the moderns present subjective fantasies which are allowed to run their course unopposed by reality, the subjectivity of Kleist's characters is constantly thwarted and reshaped by other people and events. Kleist is not about solo runs but interplay. The 'modern' hero may be seen as a loner; Kleist's characters live in society.

Kleist is a classic writer in the Greek sense. The best guide to him is Aristotle, who said that of all the elements of tragedy 'the most important is the plot, the ordering of the incidents, for tragedy is a representation not of men but of action and of life, of happiness and unhappiness – and happiness and unhappiness are bound up with action'. One need only add that men too are best represented through action, particularly as Aristotle himself says that 'character is that which reveals personal choice . . . preferences and aversions'. And of course we have no idea of the strength of any preference or aversion until a person acts upon it. It is only when we know what a person does that we can know what he really wants, how he really feels: action alone verifies the character.

I stress this because it's still fashionable to assume that plot is a sort of inferior element of the literary art, instead of the most important and most difficult one, as Aristotle insists. Kleist practises almost exclusively what is most difficult: he writes almost nothing but plot, noting only those actions which reveal his characters' deepest aversions and preferences and relating only those events which have a decisive bearing on their life or death. He is the supreme author of fate, discarding all details which are not fateful. If the weather is mentioned in a Kleist story it is mentioned because it matters: Kohlhaas is about to set a convent on fire when he is brought to his senses by a thunderbolt.

The fateful and the characteristic are forged together in the same dramatic moment; Kleist's characters are tested to the limit, through the most extreme reversals of fortune. In his mediaeval story *The Duel* a lecherous count, accused of murdering his brother, claims that he spent the night of the murder in the arms of a young widow. Cast out by her family, the widow appeals to her friend Sir Frederick for help to defend her honour. Sir Frederick, who is in love with her, challenges the count to holy combat, claiming the widow is innocent; the count accepts the challenge, still insisting that he has slept with her. By law and tradition the trial by combat will reveal which of them speaks the truth: God will grant victory to the righteous and defeat and the stake await the perjurer. Sir Frederick is defeated and is condemned to death along with the sinful woman for trying to prove a lie by invoking God's judgment. By the lights of the age and by his own lights, he has every reason to conclude that the widow lied to him and thus sent him to his death. What man, however much in love, would not turn on the woman who so fatally betrayed him? But Sir Frederick's love makes him doubt not the lady but God's judgment, and his first concern is to comfort her.

Creating characters whose passions triumph over their despair at the very moment of their unexpected and terrible defeat, Kleist evokes the traumatic moments of the reader's own life and helps him to live with them.

*

Kleist is a supreme dramatist but more flawlessly so in his stories than his plays. The exposition in *Penthesilea*, for instance, takes up the whole first half of the play. No such structural criticism could be made of any of his stories. Just the same, there is no question that he is Germany's greatest playwright. Even Thomas Mann, who bowed towards the beneficently high-minded Goethe, asserted that in the whole history of the German theatre 'it is Kleist's works alone . . . from which emanate the force, the primitive dramatic shock, the shudder of myth, the holy dread of ancient tragedy'.

His most successful play during his lifetime was *Das Käthchen von Heilbronn*, which had a few performances in Vienna and then a few more in Graz and Bamberg that he didn't even know about.

Käthchen is usually derided as a wildly romantic drama of chivalry in which an armourer's daughter is so smitten by a knight who drops in at her father's workshop that she jumps out of a window to follow him, breaking both her legs. This would indeed be an absurdly romantic, not to say ludicrous, business – but it's not what Kleist puts on the stage. He presents a mediaeval court scene in which the knight is on trial for his life, accused by the armourer of practising black magic on the girl, and her jumping from the window is cited as proof.

True enough, Käthchen is madly in love, but her madness is presented through the father's equally mad jealous rage and the formal proceedings of the court. Unlike the Romantics, who could not match their strong feelings with strong-minded judgment, Kleist puts passions on trial, placing them within a critical context, giving the exact measure of their distance from ordinary behaviour.

Goethe, who was given a copy of *Das Käthchen von Heilbronn* by his secretary Riemer, threw it into the blazing stove with the words:

'A great mixture of sense and nonsense! The cursed unnatural! I'll not produce that even if half Weimar demands it.' Riemer was horrified, because he had borrowed the copy.

Once again, much of the power of this play comes from Kleist's free use of supernatural elements, which are often the most moving or shocking way to express a truth about fate, a secret of the soul. Though far apart and unknown to each other the knight and the armourer's daughter meet in a dream in which it is revealed to them that they are destined for each other. When they do meet in the waking world Käthchen falls in love at first sight and goes through fire and water for him because she recognizes him as her intended; the knight rejects her at first because he does not remember.

Mann's favourite Kleist play was 'the one colossal act of *Robert Guiskard*, which is simply too good to be surpassed or allow the play to continue'. Guiskard, the Norman Duke of Sicily, has led his army to the gates of Constantinople; the city is about to fall, they are on the brink of victory, but so is pestilence: the Normans are dying, and Guiskard spends the entire act in an attempt to maintain his authority and the morale of his troops, sending one emissary after another to meet their deputation and finally appearing himself to try to dispel the just fear that he too is infected by the plague.

The depth of this dramatic conception may be measured by comparison with Camus's *The Plague*, in which a community struck by pestilence struggles with the problems of dying or surviving. Camus's characters are vividly drawn, yet there is something both all too obvious and slightly false about people trying to make the best of a bad situation. It is as if human beings were endowed with the kind of judicious intelligence that would make them address themselves to their real and urgent problems instead of busying themselves with trifles – as if we were the sort of creatures who, threatened with nuclear war, the blighting of our environment, terrorism and anarchy, would spend our lives trying to overcome these dangers, instead of rushing about in cars and watching television. In *Robert Guiskard* the plague, though spelling the death of everyone on stage, is just a distraction for characters preoccupied with such eerily inappropriate matters as the conquest of Constantinople and rival claims to the Sicilian dukedom. People are fighting over all the things they will never live to keep.

There is here, as always in Kleist, 'a confusion of effects', which Goethe thought was his weakness as a writer. The truth is of course that when we react with a single feeling to what we see or read, it is a sign that we are confronted with something contrived and simplified. If we were invited to see only the irony of the Normans trying to seize what is about to fall from their dead hands, there would be no 'confusion of effects' or truth in the presentation. By showing us also the grandeur of Guiskard's fighting in the shadow of death, as if he had a future, Kleist moves us both to pity and awe.

*

Kleist never saw any of his plays performed. He wrote, he hoped, he failed. Once, despairing of his vocation as a writer, he decided to apprentice himself to a carpenter in Koblenz; then he wound up as a civil servant in Königsberg – a job in which he held out for twenty months. Twice he attempted to secure himself a 'position in life' as an editor: in 1808 in Dresden, with Adam Müller, he founded the arts magazine *Phöbus*, which gained a few admirers (among them the Brothers Grimm and Goethe's secretary) and a great many detractors and lasted for a year; then in 1810 he founded and brilliantly edited the first German daily, the *Berliner Abendblätter*. Since then both journals have become classics because of Kleist's contributions and are read in book form; the *Berliner Abendblätter* was even a popular success at the time, until it ran afoul of the censors chiefly on account of Kleist's opposition to the peace with Napoleon; thereafter half the articles were banned and the police were ordered to stop supplying the paper's most popular item, the police news. The *Berliner Abendblätter*, Kleist's last source of livelihood, folded in March 1811; eight months later he was dead.

His suicide, like the death of his tragic heroes, had a ghastly inevitability yet could have been so easily avoided.

After the newspaper folded he set himself to finishing what was to be his last play, *The Prince of Homburg*. It is an often-revived classic, the *Hamlet* of the German stage; but while *Hamlet* is about to kill or not to kill, *The Prince of Homburg* is about to be or not to be.

The prince, full of ardour, dreaming of glory, risks his life leading a victorious cavalry charge against the invading enemy – and against his orders. He is condemned to death, and the brave soldier is unmanned by the prospect of the firing squad; he begs ignominiously for mercy, he offers to give up his fiancee in exchange for his life; but in the end his pride gets the better of him and he would rather face execution than buy his life with a lie. The mechanics of the plot have a lot to do with the rights and wrongs of military discipline, and there is a happy ending which aborts the catharsis; this is Kleist's only work which is marred by the drawbacks of his Junker background and his pressing need to flatter the rulers of Prussia. (He hoped the play would get him a yearly pension of a hundred thaler.) Yet this unsatisfactory framework contains some of the most moving, most dramatic scenes ever written about a man wavering between fame and death, shame and death, between love and life, pride and fear – about a prince who is discovering the terms on which he is willing to live or die.

PRINCE: O, Mother, you would not talk like that
If death had chilled you as it chills me!
You seem endowed with heavenly powers
Of salvation – you, your ladies and the
   Princess.
I could hang on the neck of the basest fellow,
The camp follower who tends your horse,
And beg him and everyone around to save me.
On God's wide earth I'm the only one who is
Helpless and forsaken, and there's nothing I
   can do.

ELECTOR'S WIFE: You're beside yourself!
What has happened to you?

PRINCE: Alas! On my way over here I saw
By the light of the torches the open grave
Which tomorrow will have my corpse.
See, Aunt, these eyes that look at you,
They will shade over with the dark of night,
Murderous bullets will pierce this breast.
In the marketplace the windows are sold
Which overlook the dreary show,
And he who still today surveys the future
Like a fairy kingdom from the heights of life
Tomorrow lies stinking between two narrow
   boards,
And a stone tells you of him that – he was!

[173]

ELECTOR'S WIFE:	My son! If it be heaven's will
	You will arm yourself with courage and
	composure.

PRINCE:	O, Mother, God's world is so fair!
	I beg you, do not send me down to those dark shades
	Before the hour strikes! If I did wrong
	Then let him punish me some other way,
	Why must it be the bullet, why?
	Let him dismiss me from my command,
	Cashier me, if the law so wills,
	Discharge me from the army: God in heaven!
	Since I saw my grave, I only want to live,
	And ask no longer whether it's with honour!

Then how calmly Kleist himself would take his life at the age of 34! He finished the play in the late summer of 1811 and dedicated and presented it to the King's sister-in-law, a princess of Hesse-Homburg, in the hope that a play about her ancestor would move her to grant him a pension. The Princess was greatly offended by it and far from helping Kleist in any way made sure that the play would not be published or performed in her lifetime. The second volume of Kleist's incomparable stories was published at the beginning of August and caused so little stir that not even his devoted sister Ulrike, without whose help he would have starved many times, felt justified in lending him any more money, just to let him go on writing.

In his last frantic efforts to secure himself a living Kleist also applied to the King for a pension or a post in the Civil Service or reinstatement in the Army, and received a half-promise that he would be appointed an adjutant to the King if the peace with Napoleon broke down. On 19 September he wrote to Chancellor Hardenberg (with whom he had been involved in a bitter correspondence over his claim to compensation for the suppression of the *Abendblätter*) asking for an advance of 20 louis d'or on his hoped-for appointment as adjutant to the King. It seems to me that if he had only received those 20 gold sovereigns, they could have made all the difference.

... I am taking the liberty, trusting in Your Excellency's often-tested patriotism, of applying to you, my Lord, for an advance of 20 louis d'or for which I will be personally responsible to Your Excellency. The granting of this request will give me the reassurance, which would be most soothing to my spirits, that Your Excellency's heart is no longer filled with animosity towards me; and meanwhile I beg Your Excellency to accept my assurance that immediately after the end of the war I will arrange for this debt of honour to be discharged, but for my everlasting debt of eternal gratitude, and so I remain unto death,

Your Excellency's most humble and obedient servant,
H. v. Kleist

His Excellency, however, did not respond. How Kleist must have waited for the post, dying a little each day as nothing came.

At the end of September he went to Frankfurt an der Oder to see his sisters Ulrike and Minette and ask them for his share of what their parents had left them. They were horrified by his audacity; he had spent his share years ago, writing *The Schroffenstein Family* and *Robert Guiskard* in Switzerland, and they had been helping him ever since. They had a meal of recriminations: why hadn't he stayed in the Army, why hadn't he kept his job with the *technische Deputation*? He would have had a secure position in life, and if he wanted to write, he could have written in his spare time.

Afterwards he wrote about the meeting to Marie von Kleist, a more distant relative:

I assure you, I would rather endure death ten times over than experience once more what I felt in Frankfurt at the dinner table, between my two sisters . . . I've always loved my sisters very much, partly on account of their well-formed, excel-

[175]

lently constituted personalities, partly because of the friendship they had for me . . . and one of my most heartfelt and earnest wishes was to bring them honour and joy one day with my works. Now it is indeed true that it has been dangerous of late to have dealings with me, from several points of view, and I blame them all the less for having withdrawn from me, the more I bear in mind the poverty of the whole family, which rested in part on their shoulders. Yet the thought of seeing whatever merit I have finally earned, be it great or small, not acknowledged in any way and to see myself regarded by them as a completely useless member of the human community, not worth taking any further interest in, is extremely painful for me. It robs me not only of the joys I hoped for from the future, it also poisons the past.

Yet the man who was so alone in the world had a horror of dying without company. Whenever he thought of suicide he thought of doing it with a friend (he proposed it to several of his friends, men and women, at various times), and he would have had to go on living if he hadn't met Frau Vogel, who was eager to exchange a lingering death from cancer for a sudden and romantic end. 'My soul has become fully ripened for death through contact with hers,' he wrote to Marie von Kleist.

The dispassionate objectivity of a true writer didn't desert him even in his last day of despair. In a parting letter to Adam Müller's wife he wished her well, reminding her that 'it is indeed quite possible to be very happy on this earth'.

On 22 November 1811 Chancellor Hardenberg made a note on Kleist's unanswered letter of 19 September: 'H v Kleist requesting a private loan of 20 Friedrichsdor. To be filed, since the aforesaid v Kleist is no longer alive as of 21.11.11. Hardenberg.'

It is impossible to write about Kleist without paying tribute to Helmut Sembdner, the editor of the complete works in German and various volumes of biographical documents. There were several dedicated Kleist scholars before him, but Sembdner has done for Kleist what Martineau did for Stendhal; works and life left in disarray are rescued, ordered and clarified once and for all. Ever since Sembdner did his work Kleist's reputation has been steadily growing.

As for Kleist in English, I used my own translations when quoting from his plays, letters, etc., but I couldn't possibly improve on Martin Greenberg's rendering of the stories published in New York by Ungar. Greenberg's translation of *The Marquise of O and Other Stories* is an immortal work: it makes Kleist a native author in the English language.

The Times, November 26, 1977

POSTSCRIPT: Is it possible to overpraise a great writer? When this article appeared in *The Times* Professor Uriel Dann of Oxford wrote to the paper saying that

> Mr. Vizinczey's eulogy of Kleist cannot pass without a modification.
>
> Kleist's genius and power are beyond dispute. But surely, Mr. Vizinczey, by his own standards, glosses over those traits of Kleist which are obnoxious to the collective mind of the West in 1977: His insane hatred of the French ('Schlagt sie tot! Das Weltgericht/ Fragt euch nach den Gründen nicht!'); his penchant for cruelty and bloodshed; his social prejudice – natural to his background, but a strain on dramatic truth and, of course, ridiculous from our viewpoint (Käthchen becomes acceptable as her knight's bride when she is revealed as an imperial by-blow). And, on a different plane, Kleist's mannerisms of style with its interminably meandering sentences. Mr. Vizinczey knows all this. He would carry more conviction if he had taken honest issue with these points.

I do gloss over Kleist's 'insane hatred of the French', as I don't think it was all that insane or all that important. Kleist learned French, he made translations from the French, he was deeply attached to French writers (Froissart, Molière, La Fontaine, Montesquieu, Rousseau), it was to Paris that he went to seek happiness and enlightenment before turning into a writer, but he loved his country and during the years of Napoleon's victories he called for death to the invaders of his nation. To my mind this was just as pardonable, indeed admirable, as French patriots' hatred of the Germans during the Occupation.

True, when Kleist hated he hated like no ordinary man, but as far as we are concerned we can only be grateful for it, because it was this capacity for extreme emotions which created the intensity of his works, and it spoiled possibly only some of his patriotic poems and his play about the Germans driving out the Romans. (Even in regard to *The Battle of Arminius*, Professor Heibling has convincing arguments to the contrary.) But even if Kleist had written innumerable diatribes against the French and even if he had eaten two of Napoleon's corporals every day for breakfast, this wouldn't detract from the importance of his masterpieces. There is a kind of academic philistinism which equates literary greatness with good behaviour and thereby produces a pathetic crop of university graduates who are intimately familiar with the real or imaginary faults of great men without having the slightest idea why these men were great or why they matter to us. Reliance on this sort of irrelevant criticism robs England of Kleist's 'genius and power' which Professor Dann acknowledges: with the solitary exception of *The Broken Jug*, published by Manchester University Press, none of Kleist's works is in print in English in this country.

Professor Dann's most representative objection is to Kleist's 'penchant for cruelty and bloodshed'. It is one of those notions which go back to the great charlatan of Weimar and it has been echoed even by Thomas Mann, who did so much to inspire the recent revival of Kleist's works without feeling able to challenge directly conservative academic opinion or the almighty Goethe. On the face of it, there appears to be something to the charge: most of Kleist's works are indeed concerned with violence and hate. Yet to say that he had 'a penchant for cruelty and bloodshed' seems to me as absurd as to say that Balzac had a penchant for swindling or that Dostoevsky had a penchant for drunkenness and wifebeating.

As for Kleist's style, as can be seen from what I have quoted, his sentences run on but they cover a lot of ground – indeed, one would be hard put to find a single redundant word. Once Kleist praised a friend for *saying even what he does not say*, which is perhaps the best description of his own dense, suggestive style. His stories are the swiftest prose ever written. No other writer has quite his pace. This of course limits his appeal; most readers like plenty of time to get involved, to picture a scene, to share a character's feelings; hence the popularity of fat books and music like Ravel's 'Bolero' in which a few notes are repeated a hundred times over until they penetrate the thickest skull. Kleist makes a point, paints a scene for only so long as it takes the most quick-witted and imaginative readers to grasp it. But to them he gives the thrill of letting their brains race at a genius's speed of thought.

The Times, November 26, 1977

Extracts from Kleist

Feelings in front of Caspar David Friedrich's Seascape

It is splendid to stand on the seashore, in an endless solitude, under a gloomy sky, and gaze out over a boundless wilderness of water. To feel this splendour, however, you must have gone there, you must be compelled to go away again, you must want to cross over to the other side and be unable to do so, you must miss everything in life and yet hear the sound of life in the rush of the tide, the sighing of the air, the drifting of the clouds, the lonely cry of the birds. To be so perceptive, your heart must seek compensation from Nature for some injury.

All this, however, is not possible in front of the painting, and what I ought to find in the painting itself, I find between myself and the painting: namely, my heart makes demands on the painting, and the painting does an injury to me. Thus I myself become the figure of the Capuchin monk, the picture becomes the dune, but the sea I am supposed to gaze at with longing is entirely absent. Nothing could be sadder or more unpleasant than this position in the world: the single spark of life in the vast realm of death, the solitary centre in the solitary circle. The picture with its two or three mysterious objects lies there like an Apocalypse, as if it were having Young's Night Thoughts, and since in its uniformity and boundlessness it has nothing in the foreground but the frame, when you contemplate it you feel as though your eyelids have been cut off.

All the same, the painter has doubtless broken new ground

in the field of his art; and I am persuaded that through his genius a square mile of sand from the Brandenburg Marshes could be presented, along with a barberry bush and a solitary crow ruffling its feathers, and that this picture would make a truly Ossian effect. Yes, if you could paint this landscape with its own chalk and its own water, I believe you could make the foxes and wolves howl with it: which is the most that one can manage to say in praise of this kind of landscape painting.

But my own feelings about this amazing painting are too confused; therefore, before I dare to express them fully, I have decided to be advised by the comments of those who pass by it in pairs from morning till night.

Extracts from *Letter from One Writer to Another*

My dear friend!

Lately when I found you reading my poems, you expatiated with extraordinary eloquence about the Form . . . Permit me to say that your mind is dwelling here on merits that would have proved themselves more valuable if you had not noticed them at all. If when I write I could reach into my breast, grasp my thoughts with both hands and lay them in yours without further ado, then I confess the dearest wish of my heart would be fulfilled . . . I strive to the best of my ability to give clarity to the expression, meaning to the metrical structure, charm and life to the sounds of the words, but not for their own sake at all, rather simply and solely in order that the thought they enclose should become apparent. It is the characteristic of all authentic form that the spirit comes through it immediately and directly, while defective form holds the spirit bound like a bad mirror and reminds us of nothing but itself . . .

What do I care about the wit of the puns that are exchanged on the Field of Agincourt? And when Ophelia says of Hamlet, 'What a noble mind is here o'erthrown!' – or

Macduff says of Malcolm, 'He has no children!' – what do iambics signify, or rhymes or assonances or suchlike devices for which you are always pricking up your ears, as if they were all that mattered.

Letter from a Painter to His Son

My dear Son,
   You write me that you are painting a Madonna and that your feeling for the finishing of the work seems to you so fleshly and unclean that you would like to take the holy sacrament every time before picking up your brush. Listen to your old father, that is a false exaltation which sticks to you from that school you spring from. According to the training given us by our worthy old master, the thing is completely settled by a vulgar but honest pleasure in the sport of bringing your fancies on to the canvas. The world is a wonderful arrangement, and the most godlike effects, my dear son, result from the most lowly and insignificant causes. The human being, to give you an obvious example, is a sublime creation, but it isn't helpful to think of this with holy awe at the moment when a child is made. Indeed, anyone who took the sacrament at such a time and went to work with the sole purpose of constructing his notion of perfection in the material world would inevitably produce a pitiful and sickly creature; whereas a man who kisses a girl on a cheerful summer night, without further thought, will undoubtedly bring into the world a lad who afterwards scrambles around between earth and heaven in vigorous fashion and makes plenty of work for the philosophers. And so God be with you.

On Reflection: A Paradox

People praise reflection to high heaven, especially cold-blooded protracted reflection before action. If I were a

Spaniard, an Italian or a Frenchman, then I might agree. Since however I am a German, I intend to make the following speech to my son, especially if he should decide to become a soldier.

'Reflection, you know, finds its point of time far more appropriately *after* than *before* the act. If it enters into play before or at the decisive moment, then it seems to confuse, inhibit and repress the strength needed for action – strength which springs from unhindered feeling. It is afterwards, when the action has been performed, that you should feel the need to reflect, to become conscious of what was faulty and weak in your conduct and to regulate the feeling for other cases in the future. Life itself is a fight with fate, and it is with action as with wrestling: in the moment when he has a grip on his opponent, the athlete simply cannot act according to any other consideration but the inspirations of the moment; and any fighter who calculated which muscles he ought to strain and which limbs he ought to set in motion in order to win would unfailingly get the worst of it and be overthrown. But afterwards, when he has won or is lying on the ground, it may be useful and appropriate to reflect about which thrust it was that threw down his opponent, or which leg he should have tripped him up with in order to hold himself upright. Anyone who doesn't hug life like a wrestler and sense and feel it according to all the twists of the fight, all the delaying actions, thrusts, feints and reactions, will never get his way in a conversation, much less in a battle.'

Excerpts from *On the Gradual Formation of Thoughts Through Speech*

. . . The French say *appetite grows with eating* and this empirical principle remains true even when we paraphrase it and say *ideas come with speaking* . . . It is strangely inspiring to speak to someone directly facing us; a glance which proclaims that our half-expressed thought has already been grasped often gives us the expression for the whole other half. I believe that many a great speaker did not yet know at the moment that he opened his mouth what he was going to say. But the conviction that the profusion of ideas that he needed could be drawn from the situation and from the resulting stimulation of his mind made him bold enough to begin, trusting to good luck. I'm reminded of Mirabeau's 'thunder-bolt', which sent packing the master of ceremonies who came back to the assembly hall after the last session of the Estates-General was dissolved by the King. The master of ceremonies returned to the council chamber where the deputies still lingered and asked them whether they had heard the King's order to disperse. 'Yes,' answered Mirabeau, 'we heard the King's order.' (I am certain that at this civil beginning he had not yet thought of bayonets.) 'Yes, Monsieur,' he repeated, 'we heard it.' (You can see that he still had no idea exactly what he wanted.) 'But what entitles you,' he continued – and now suddenly a whole torrent of tremendous ideas welled up in him – 'to give orders to us here? We are the representatives of the nation,' (that was what he needed) 'the nation gives orders and receives none,' (to vault at one leap to the pinnacle of audacity) 'and to explain myself quite clearly to you' (only now for the first time does he find words to express the defiance for which his soul stands prepared) 'go and tell your King that we will never quit our places unless at the point of bayonets.' Whereupon, content with himself, he sat down on a chair. . . .

La Fontaine, too, gives a noteworthy example of the gradual formation of an idea from a beginning dictated by necessity. In his fable, *Plague Among the Animals*, the fox is compelled to pacify the lion, without knowing how he is going to do it. You know the fable. Plague reigns in the animal kingdom, and the lion assembles all the beasts and informs them that a sacrifice must be offered up to heaven, if heaven is to be placated. There are many sinners in the nation and the death of the greatest sinner among them must save the rest from destruction. They must therefore frankly confess their transgressions to him. He for his part acknowledges that under the stress of hunger he has put an end to many a sheep; also to the sheepdog, if it came too near him; yes, in his lickerish moments, it had even befallen him to eat the shepherd. If no one has been guilty of greater frailties than these, then he is ready to die. 'Sire,' says the fox, who wishes to deflect the storm away from himself, 'you are too magnanimous. Your noble zeal leads you too far. What is it, to strangle a sheep? Or a dog, that useless beast? And as for the shepherd,' he continues, for this is the main point, 'you might say' (though he still doesn't know what) 'he deserves the worst' (by good luck – and then he gets involved) 'being' (a bad phrase, but it's what occurs to him at the moment) 'one of those humans' (and now for the first time he finds the thought that snatches him out of danger) 'who imagine that they can rule over the animals.' And then he demonstrates that the donkey, that bloodthirsty creature who devours all the cabbages, is the most fitting sacrifice, whereupon they all fall on the donkey and tear him to pieces.

A speech such as this is really thinking out loud. The train of thoughts and the words for them move along side by side, and the mental acts for one and the other coincide. Speech is thus not a dragging weight on the wheel of intelligence, but rather a kind of second wheel on the same axle which runs along parallel with it. . . .

Who Killed Kleist?

Kleist: A Biography, by Joachim Maass, translated by Ralph Manheim (Secker)

The translator of this biography and the blurb-writer both crib from my essay on Kleist; in the one instance where there are quotation marks around my text, I am identified as 'a recent article in *The Times* of London'. This sort of thing is common practice: just because people use your work and ideas, it doesn't mean that they are going to acknowledge your existence.

For that matter, the author of the book is scarcely acknowledged: there isn't a word about him. And why would a London publisher describe a London paper as *of London*? Evidently when the printing was ordered from the States, no one bothered to check whether the American text would be appropriate here in Britain.

All this is a fitting reminder, when the subject is Kleist, that the literary world is as rife with meanness and incompetence as any other business. Heinrich von Kleist (1777–1811) couldn't make a living in it simply by writing masterpieces, and committed suicide at the age of 34.

What I am actually quoted as saying is that 'Kleist is bound to emerge from Goethe's fading shadow as the greatest German writer'. The two certainly typify two distinctly different kinds of literature. Goethe elevated complacency and wishful thinking to sublime heights; Kleist rendered the world as he found it.

Goethe wrote a Faust who sells his soul to the Devil, enjoys all the benefits of the deal, then gets to heaven on the strength of a good girl's love: Kleist, by contrast, communicates the terrible irrevocability of our actions. His *Beggarwoman of Locarno* will shock you into recognising that you can destroy yourself with a thoughtless word or gesture, never mind a pact with the Devil.

In his *Kleist* the late Joachim Maass complains that the outcome of this story is 'unduly harsh, compatible neither with Kleist's nor with anyone else's principles'. But Kleist did not invent stories to illustrate principles (what a notion of literature!): he wrote to demonstrate the conditions we live under, which more often than not are unduly harsh indeed.

Maass is also bothered by Kleist's 'immoderate feelings', unable to perceive that it is the extraordinary force of his emotions that gives him the power to move us. Critical studies and biographies process genius through mediocre minds, and this one is no exception.

Maass often sounds like Kleist's contemporaries, though he quotes them with disapproval. 'I do not like a writer to base his work on the real world,' one of them complained, 'for it is precisely to escape depressing realities that we take flight into the realm of fantasy.' The first reviewer of *The Marquise of O* wrote that 'merely to describe the plot is to banish oneself from polite society'.

Then of course there was Goethe, who produced Kleist's *The Broken Jug* so disastrously at Weimar that Kleist could never live it down. This joint theatrical fiasco turned Goethe's jealousy of the younger writer into undying hatred, which was tantamount in today's terms to the enmity of the entire literary establishment of London and New York.

Thomas Mann called *Michael Kohlhaas* the most powerful story in the German language, but this was too late for Kleist; it was Goethe's opinion of it that counted: 'It is nicely told (and cleverly constructed . . .), but on the other hand it takes a great spirit of contradiction to generalise from a single instance with such unvarying and deep-rooted pessimism: there are unlovely and frightening things in Nature with which literature should not concern itself.' It was 'impossible for a mature understanding to enter into the violence of Kleist's themes with any pleasure'.

But literature *is* single instances embodying general laws! And Kleist is so far from being a pessimist that all his defeated characters have the opportunity for spiritual triumph. Kohlhaas had the power to 'wound his enemy mortally in the heel at the very moment it was treading him in the dust'! What could be more exhilarating? We may not choose our destinies, but we can always choose the meaning we give to our life or death. We are not fully defined by our social situations.

But Goethe said Kleist gave no pleasure, and, with all the mindless hacks and prigs echoing Goethe, Kleist's magazine *Phöbus* went under and saddled him with debts he could never repay. The popular paper he started so brilliantly, the *Berliner Abendblätter*, folded in six months under official displeasure. His stories were published but earned him neither money nor reputation.

He never saw any of his plays performed. *The Prince of Homburg* could not be staged because the condemned prince goes to pieces at the sight of his grave. Imagine a play in which General Montgomery is on his knees pleading for his life, and you may have some idea of the exasperation Kleist inspired by portraying *everybody* in an unguarded moment. Every time he wrote something great he was worse off than before.

Yet this was the Golden Age of the incomparable Goethe (whom Maass calls 'the wisest of men') and it goes against the grain to admit that Kleist could have been driven to suicide by poverty, neglect and humiliation in this best of all literary worlds.

So a great deal is made of Kleist's fascination with death, his habit of proposing joint suicide to his friends. Even Thomas Mann, who did so much to popularise Kleist, but who had no idea what it was like to be without money, harped on Kleist's 'desire for annihilation', asserting that 'Kleist died because he was weary of his incompleteness and eager to return his botched self to the universal flux'.

Such notions, even when supported by despairing passages from Kleist's letters, are given the lie by his actions, which are the last word on every emotion. Kleist, the descendant of 16 generals and two field-marshals, spent his last months begging for money or a job: from his publishers, from Chancellor Hardenberg, from the King's brother Prince Wilhelm, from the King himself; and only when he was rebuffed by everybody, including his sister Ulrike, who was sick of him wasting his life and disgracing his family by writing immortal works instead of earning a living, did he decide to shoot himself with a woman who had cancer (or thought she had) and wanted to die with him.

Maass is not alone in portraying Kleist as a born suicide, but what is unforgivable is the way he tries to reconcile us to the destruction of a young genius, turning a tragic loss into a matter of little consequence. He belittles Kleist's last stories in order to make the point, totally without foundation, that Kleist's creative powers were declining.

During his last night, not wishing to leave his works to a world which didn't give a damn, Kleist burned everything he could lay his hands on, including the only copy of his two-volume novel. Maass puts 'novel' in quotation marks, as if it were something less than a Kleist novel that was lost to us. He claims that Kleist had 'ceased to love his art, and they were vegetating in a kind of ruined marriage'. In other words, the great writer was burnt out, so it didn't make all that much difference that he died at the age of 34. This is the reasoning of a small soul in flight from a sense of loss; it is an expression of the ignoble desire to feel good at all costs, which (typically) involves the denial of something we really could feel cheerful about – i.e. Kleist's genius. When you close your eyes to tragedy, you close your eyes to greatness.

Kleist's creative faculties were at full strength when he put a gun in his mouth and pulled the trigger. He did it without damaging his teeth, his tongue or his brain. According to the autopsy report, 'the brain was unusually firm'.

The Sunday Telegraph, January 5, 1984

[189]

Sex, Society, Politics

The Lessons of Robert Kennedy

The Heir Apparent, by William V. Shannon (Collier-
   Macmillan)
Robert Kennedy, by Margaret Laing (Macdonald)

Both these books benefit from having been written while Robert
Kennedy was alive. The dead hero appears all the more
dramatic for being viewed as a living person with an open
future, and the authors' objectivity is a relief after the obituaries. As for the defect of this objectivity (the determination
to stick to facts and avoid concern with their meaning), this is
highlighted but also partly counteracted by the reader's hind-
sight. Knowing something the authors didn't know brings its
own reward of fascination: the reader can add his own perspective to the printed record. The very title of Shannon's book, *The
Heir Apparent*, illustrates what I mean.

   William V. Shannon, a member of the editorial board of *The
New York Times*, knows much more about the New York political
scene than about Robert Kennedy, and his book, which is
concerned with Kennedy primarily as a New York Senator and
contains whole chapters about his rivalry with Senator Keat-
ing, Governor Rockefeller and Mayor Lindsay, is not for those
who want a portrait of the man and a comprehensive review of
his career.

   From Shannon's account the former rackets-investigator
and Attorney-General emerges as a politician whose greatest
emotional commitment is his hatred of gangsters. About this he
would never compromise, and he fights a long, arduous and
successful campaign in Manhattan to prevent the election of a

Surrogate Judge who once supported a lawyer stooge of the gangster Frank Costello. Considering the role of organized crime in American society in general and the corruption of the New York courts in particular (of which Mr Shannon paints a frightening picture), Robert Kennedy's passionate hatred of executive criminals was a virtue that could not be valued highly enough, and it seems certain that if he had become President he would have fought the Mafia with more zeal than his predecessors.

Otherwise, however, he appears as a rather vacillating and temporizing Senator: his heart is in the right place, he would rather side with the reformers than with the old establishment, but his actions and alliances are finally formed according to the dictates of power politics. In sometimes fascinating detail, Mr Shannon's book shows more of the Kennedy we all knew, opposing-supporting-opposing President Johnson and the war in Vietnam.

The clue to the enigma of the good crusader and the politician with his eye on the main chance is in Margaret Laing's *Robert Kennedy* and specifically in her brief but telling picture of his childhood. Joseph and Rose Kennedy raised their children in the kind of puritanical Catholicism peculiar to Ireland and North America and in a personal code which was opposed to emotionalism, snobbish but just, and from Miss Laing's account it becomes obvious how both John and Robert Kennedy came to react passionately against misery, oppression and corruption while at the same time remaining strangely insensitive to the rights and feelings of individuals.

Indeed, how could Rose's children learn anything much about personal liberty under the rule of Joseph Kennedy? The pious mogul of Hollywood and Wall Street emerges from this book as a loving bully who exploited traditional religious and family loyalties to cement his authority and used his power to drill into his children his own faith in competition, with tragic success. Like so many largely self-made American millionaires of his generation, he was a King *Fix-It* who had made it and thought he had the answers to all the problems of life; so he made sure that his success formulas were passed on to his children, and that they would not be distracted by anything else. As Miss Laing writes, 'the philosophy he taught them was as effective as it was simple – Win, win, win . . . don't come in second or third – that doesn't count . . .'

The Kennedys of both sexes were sent into all kinds of athletic competitions from the age of six and they had to come first in every field or they were no good. That kind of training may help children to learn how to make a fortune or rise to the top in politics, but it is a poor guide to living, because it tells them nothing about life beyond success. What was being ignored was precisely the curse of the Kennedy family: they were given no perspective of death, the only perspective that can measure the true value of any action, any principle or any way of life. Certainly JFK, who did not want to run for political office at all, and RFK, who seems to have been happiest as counsel to the Senate committee investigating organized crime, are archetypal heroes of the American tragedy. The religion of success didn't seem to work for anybody.

The theme that recurs most poignantly in Miss Laing's book is Robert Kennedy's defiance of physical danger, his reckless risk-taking in the full expectation of an early death – and the complete absence of this awareness of mortality from his political-moral decisions. Miss Laing quotes Ethel Kennedy's description of her husband taking the family by plane to Hyannisport in a storm which kept every other plane on the ground, though making the same trip by car would have made only twenty minutes difference. Yet the same man, haunted though he was by the violent deaths of two brothers and a sister, would ally himself with people he despised, abandon just causes and reluctantly support bad ones, for the sake of getting ahead – ahead to what?

This mixture of physical courage and moral cowardice looks less paradoxical to anyone who reads Miss Laing's description of the pace of Kennedy's life, 'heightened by the knowledge that a second spent idly is a second lost forever'. He had television in his bathroom and Shakespeare recordings in the shower, was briefed by his aides while he dressed, ate while he travelled, relaxed by racing his children up and down the pool, improving his position by improving his strength; and every regular working day, when not campaigning across the continent or travelling around the world, he flew from New York to Washington and back, made several speeches, appeared at several meetings, attended several parties, often late into the night. 'Every time I come across him he's tired,' one of his critics told Miss Laing. 'I go to a lot of parties where he is, but he doesn't stay long – he's too busy.'

In such an efficient, well-organized life there can be no time for reflection. If Robert Kennedy had had time to sit down and think, all by himself, he might have considered the threats to his life in relation to the problem of how he should spend it, he might have decided that the 1972 election was less important than what he could do in 1967. In the light of tragically early death is it not obvious, for instance, that it would have been personally more satisfying for him as well as more helpful to the causes he always wished to fight for, if he had begun his campaign at least a few months earlier than he did, even though he saw no chance of success?

These two books reveal a man of terrific vitality and will-power, who did a little good but intended to do much more, and whose tragic misconceptions about life and courage can teach us a great deal. Robert Kennedy remains a salutary hero.

The Times Saturday Review, July 13, 1968

Condemned World, Literary Kingdom

The Armies of the Night, by Norman Mailer
(Weidenfeld and Nicolson)

Who but an American writer (if not a Chinese or a Russian) would today describe his country as 'the land where a new kind of man was born'? The war against Vietnam is only the ghastliest manifestation of what I'd call imperial provincialism, which afflicts America's whole culture – aware only of its own history, insensible to everything which isn't part of the local atmosphere.

The fairest examples of the parochialism of American literature are perhaps the later novels of Norman Mailer, for Mailer is sometimes, as he claims, 'the best writer in America' and a frequently lucid critic of his country's megalomania. Yet as a young novelist, with all the great writers of the world to choose from, he was trying to catch up with Hemingway; and as he has continued to measure himself against the mores of New York, his novels increasingly conform to the local standards of narcissist hysteria. There is a whiff of it even in *The Armies of the Night*, where Mailer sees his homeland of new men as 'once a beauty of magnificence unparalleled, now a beauty with a leprous skin'.

Still, great talent will out, and when Mailer gets down to the novelist's job of portraying reality, in his technically non-fiction works (*Advertisements for Myself*, *The Presidential Papers* and now *The Armies of the Night*), when he is too concerned with life to bother about the hometown notions of art, he is very, very good.

The central character in this oeuvre is Norman Mailer – a figure much too real on the printed page, too rich in brilliantly illuminated passions, vices, and whims to be confused with the mere person of the novelist. Some critics have used the considerable failings of this hero to dismiss the books, but this kind of reasoning would rob *Richard III* of its merits. The only virtue a character needs to possess between hardcovers, even if he bears a real person's name, is vitality: if he comes to life in our imagination he passes the test. Mailer has in fact built his fictional alter ego into one of the most authentic literary figures of our age.

In *The Armies of the Night* he turns up as a middle-aged revolutionary who made it in the bad world he rejects, a celebrity whose follies are written up in *Time* magazine, a man so comfortably insulated from annoying intrusions that he has others standing by to pick up his phone for him. He is saddled with the worst vice of middle age, the feeling that he has fought enough good fights to be allowed now to worry only about his own problems. May the Lord spare us from such meanness: he 'hated to put in time with losers . . . they passed their subtle problems on'.

There is a great deal in this character that is un-poor, un-young and un-black, that would vote for the law and order of Mayor Daley, that would not wish to hear another word about South Africa. Just the same, he can be prevailed upon to join the October, 1967, march on the Pentagon to protest against the war in Vietnam, and it is through his adventures that the reader can be present at one of those scenes we caught a glimpse of on television from Paris, Prague and Chicago. What makes this re-enactment of the Battle of the Pentagon so poignant (as indeed Mailer spells out in the book: the reader is shown the conjurer's tricks in entr'actes of light entertainment) is that he has chosen a narrator who is 'a participant but not a vested partisan . . . ambiguous in his own proportions' and who can thus convey 'the precise feel of the ambiguity of the event' – the dumb misery of the paratroopers as well as the stubbornness and shame of the students who sit on the ground nonviolently, waiting their turn, while their girls are beaten up. The 'confrontation' is lifted beyond its actuality to become a moral drama, a purgatory where the participants boil in the stew of their own frustrations, trying to save their souls in a condemned world.

But the book works on too many levels simultaneously to allow one to single out the source of its power and beauty. The social novel and moral drama is also an elegy, a lament for the hero's lost youth. Ultimately he joins the protesters not out of ambiguous conscience but because he wants to prove to himself that he is still 'with it'. He isn't – the world has changed too fast and he can recapture neither the fire nor the innocence to be 20 again. The irony of the aging wild boy in a noble freakout cuts both ways: the conflict between generations is fuelled as much by the self-absorption of the young as by the compromises of their elders.

The America that emerges from *The Armies of the Night* doesn't signify only a geographical location; it is a literary kingdom whose inhabitants can be thrillingly familiar to any reader. I read the book twice with excitement, surprise and a great deal of envy.

The Times Saturday Review, September 21, 1968

What Generation Gap?

Culture and Commitment: A Study of the Generation Gap,
by Margaret Mead (Bodley Head)

Margaret Mead's field is cultural anthropology, which is the
most absolutely inoffensive discipline for the study of society,
since it excludes politics. She is of course a gifted and good-
hearted cultural anthropologist, and her new book offers solid
observations about changing family patterns and the resulting
cultural differences between the generations, as well as manifestly honourable intentions and sympathy for everybody's
troubles. One is tempted to let it go at that, except that she
accepts and repeats a great deal of insidious and widespread
nonsense.

To begin with, there is the very notion of a generation gap.
Miss Mead claims that it is 'world-wide' and cites as proof the
youth revolts in various countries, which she views as revolts
against the older generation. This notion has been sold to
people both young and old by politicians, the mass media and
the entrepreneurs who are busy milking the young with all sorts
of merchandise which is shoddy but 'revolutionary'. Neither
they nor Margaret Mead are deterred by the fact that not a
single youth revolt, on or off campus, has been directed against
the older generation.

She mentions the Japanese youth revolts – but these were
about the American-Japanese military alliance, the Vietnam
war and similar issues which have to do with politics, not
generations. The American youth revolts which she also mentions started against segregationists in the south and continue
against military, political and educational powers.

But then Miss Mead lines up everybody over 25 on the side of the powerful. Speaking for them, she writes that 'we still hold the seats of power and command the resources and skills . . . the elders in the advanced countries control the resources needed by the young . . .' She appears to be unaware of the fact that the vast majority of elders have as little control over their own affairs, let alone the national resources, as the young have. There is no gap here between young and old – we are all powerless.

Placing everybody over 25 on equal footing with the Rockefellers, Miss Mead also identifies the elders with all the culture of the past, while the young are identified with the culture of post-nuclear technology. The truth is that it is the old pre-nuclear elites which are unleashing upon the rest of mankind, young and old, the horrors of technology for the sake of maintaining and extending their privileges, power and profits. The nuclear push button is a big change, but the real wonder is the people who can destroy us with it sit on the same committees and councils that sent our great-grandfathers to die in cavalry charges.

For Miss Mead civilization and history and the ancient privileges of the few are all the same thing, as she tells us about 'the repudiation of past and present by the dissident youth of every persuasion in every kind of society in the world'. No doubt presidents, commissars and oil sheiks are comforted by the thought that they stand for everything beautiful that pre-dates the Rolling Stones, and such a notion helps them to keep the support of many of those elders whose shaky hands are kept away from the resources.

The word gets around that the young reject *everything* and civilized people are scared into the belief that if the military-industrial complex goes, that will be the end of Euripides. The contrary is the truth. The survival of human culture past and present, as well as mankind's existence, depends precisely on the success of many of the causes which Miss Mead so wrongly identifies only with the young.

The gap is not between the old and young but between a

radically changed society and culture and the unchanged institutions which control them. To twist the arising conflicts into a conflict of generations is intellectually no more sound and politically just as indecent as dividing the poor along religious lines in Ulster or colour lines in Wolverhampton.

Miss Mead pleads for tolerance while insisting that the young cannot possibly understand the old and that 'nowhere in the world are there elders who know what the children know'. But most of the young understand Mr Nixon very well, and so do most people over 25. Never before in history were the rulers so well understood as in the present: practically everybody watches television and nobody likes poisoned fish.

The Times Saturday Review, September 12, 1970

A True Heroine

The Life and Death of Mary Wollstonecraft, by Claire Tomalin (Weidenfeld)

Mary Wollstonecraft (1759–1797) was the author of *A Vindication of the Rights of Woman*, the first book to argue for equal rights and equal opportunities for the sexes, and it seems that there will never be an end to the unwarranted and deeply felt abuse heaped upon this brave lady.

'A hyena in petticoats,' Horace Walpole called her, 'a philosophical serpent.' She was depicted in the Press as a whore, 'breaking down the bars intended to restrain licentiousness', whose life story would be 'read with disgust by every female who has any pretensions to delicacy'.

In the 18th century, as Claire Tomalin reminds us in her admirable biography *The Life and Death of Mary Wollstonecraft*, even her struggle to make a living as a full-time professional writer was considered a grave offence. The novelist Jane West, for instance, maintained that women were created for 'humble resignation and cheerful content and for the purposes of domesticity, marriage and motherhood', and that writing for women was but

> an ornament or an amusement, not a duty or a profession; and when it is pursued with such avidity as to withdraw us from the especial purposes of our creation, it becomes a crime.

Jane West, of course, made only pained references to the first feminist author, and if you think that times have changed since the end of the 18th century, you should listen to the Auntie Toms today.

Men are even more spiteful. Mr Richard Cobb, Professor of Modern History at Oxford, pictures Mary Wollstonecraft as 'a private nuisance' and 'a public nuisance', a pushy woman who even undertook a 13-day voyage from London to Lisbon to inflict her presence on her best friend who was in the last stages of pregnancy and consumption. '*She managed at least to get in at the death,*' writes Professor Cobb.

Such inane jibes are less likely to be inspired by the person than by the cause she stands for, and it seems that the equality of women is still far from conceded even among scholars. Speaking of scholars – according to a recent Government White Paper, out of more than 3,000 professors in Great Britain in 1969, only 46 were women.

I beg the reader to try to conceive, in the light of these figures from the age of Women's Lib, what a girl with intellectual ambitions was up against in 18th-century England, if she set out to do something less craven than exhorting her sex to 'humble resignation and cheerful content'.

Mary Wollstonecraft's own sentences have a different ring:

> I have a heart that scorns disguise, and a countenance which will not dissemble.

Coming from a girl of 14, this strikes me as evidence of a great spirit.

Her mother had only seven children but six survived; she was meek, humble and resigned, and her husband often beat her. So much for woman's traditional role.

The eldest son received a regular education and became a lawyer; Mary was sent to village schools only long enough to learn reading and writing, but 'had enough wit to flourish under this sort of neglect'.

She sought out educated adults, listened to their talk and borrowed their books, getting to know Milton and Rousseau in her early adolescence. Later she was to write some of the best pages of English literary criticism in her analysis of their work, and not only with respect to their portrayal of women.

But beforehand she served her turn at most of the occupations available to a young woman without a dowry: she was a paid companion ('toad-eating', Fanny Burney called it); she nursed her mother through her last illness; she did sewing at home; she ran a small school for a few paying pupils; and she took a job as governess to a noble lord's children in Ireland.

She had too much vitality and intelligence to fit comfortably into any of these restricting roles, and was often a trial to her employers and associates, to her brothers and sisters. All of which is still used against her – as if her achievements as a brilliant intellectual and important public figure could be diminished by the fact that she was a troublesome relative and an unsatisfactory servant.

It was after being fired as a governess that she became a 'public nuisance', which come to think of it is as good a definition as any of a writer. Encouraged by regular payments from the publisher Joseph Johnson and the stimulating company of Dissenting intellectuals, she set herself against 'the heavy wind of authority' and had a go first at the great Edmund Burke and then at the whole idea of male supremacy. The *Vindication* became the bible of domestic slaves and playthings and made her for a time the most famous woman in Europe.

In her late twenties she had fallen in love with Fuseli, who married someone else. After four years of being the other woman she became so desperate that she called on his wife and suggested that she come and live with them. The wife refused. As Mary Wollstonecraft herself wrote in her book:

One reason why men have superior judgment and more fortitude than women, is undoubtedly this, that they give a freer scope to the grand passions, and by more frequently going astray enlarge their minds.

Going to Paris to see the French Revolution for herself, she became acquainted with the Girondins only to see them overthrown and her new friend Mme Roland sent to the guillotine, along with the courtesans and actresses who had thought that they, too, were free to get involved in politics. There was no republic for female liberty, and she fell in love again.

She was happy, she was pregnant, she gave birth to a daughter, the man would not marry her, she came back to London and tried to commit suicide.

I don't quite see how it is possible to portray a writer while treating her writing as a mere background to her character, as Mrs Tomalin attempts to do, but she is often so wise and precise about her subject that she can move the heart by making a point. 'Women intent on suicide,' she writes, commenting on Mary's parting from her daughter, 'have usually convinced themselves they are performing a service for their children and abandon them with almost exalted feelings.'

The suicide failed; there was another affair, another pregnancy. This time it culminated in marriage to her lover, the philosopher William Godwin, but she died giving birth to another daughter, who became Shelley's wife.

It has often been suggested that this fiery feminist would have been far more successful if she hadn't compromised her cause by her scandalous behaviour and had called for revolutionary changes in society and the family without stepping out of line or forgetting her place.

Mrs Tomalin, however, portrays Mary Wollstonecraft's extraordinary vitality, her pride, her inability to abide condescension, her strong but long-suppressed sexual drive, in such a way that the reader is led to realise that her 'waywardness' and 'tiresomeness' were but the private aspects of her public virtue, of the strength which enabled her to see herself and other women as the equals of men.

The Life and Death of Mary Wollstonecraft is an extended paraphrase of Shaw's dictum: the reasonable woman adapts herself to the world, the unreasonable one persists in trying to adapt the world to herself; therefore all progress depends on the unreasonable woman.

However, it is also evident from Mrs Tomalin's book that this progress could only be very limited so long as women lacked the freedom to live an adventurous youth, to enlarge their minds and develop their characters by 'frequently going astray'. Their attempts to get involved, to take risks, were terminated rather promptly by pregnancy, childbirth, death.

Ours is the first time in history that young girls can live young men's lives, and this is bound to bring about the most amazing changes in the world.

The Sunday Telegraph, September 22, 1974

A Tangle of Anarchists

Daughter of a Revolutionary: Natalie Herzen and the Bakunin/Nechayev Circle, edited by Michael Confino (Alcove Press)

This collection of letters, diaries, memoirs, political manifestos and other documents written by Russian *émigrés* mainly in the 1860s and early 1870s is the sort of book that requires the reading of several other books as well. Each, I should add, is absorbing and illuminating.

To begin with there is Alexander Herzen's *My Past and Thoughts*. He is the 'revolutionary' referred to in Michael Confino's title, though of course Herzen was more of a liberal reformer, and, above all, a great writer. He was not only a rich aristocrat like Tolstoy, but also an illegitimate child: this gave him a double vision of Russian society which Tolstoy strove for but never quite managed to attain.

Herzen's memoirs portray the callous and cruel power the *émigrés* fled from as well as the earnest, absurd and hectic life they led in Paris, Geneva, Florence or London. On the latter subject, E. H. Carr's *The Romantic Exiles* is absolutely and delightfully indispensable supplementary reading.

These exiles were the flower children of the 19th century, combining the joys of political radicalism, incessant travel and free sex. They either had money or knew people who would lend it to them out of political sympathy; they could afford to ponder the moral issues of the day and to indulge their passions.

Herzen's first wife loved a German poet and her husband simultaneously, and when her husband put an end to this 'triangle of love and friendship', she withered away and died at the age of 35. Whereupon the widower got into a triangle of his own, with his best friend's wife.

The friend couldn't have been nicer about it and the wife came to stay, visiting upon Herzen untold miseries, countless scenes and *crises de nerfs*, and three children who died young.

Once one has read Herzen and Carr, Professor Confino's selection of letters and documents, *Daughter of a Revolutionary: Natalie Herzen and the Bakunin/Nechayev Circle*, becomes somewhat more intelligible, though he leaves bewildering gaps and is loftily inclined to dismiss the reader's curiosity with such disdainful footnotes as 'See Herzen to Natalie and Malwida, 20 October, 1869, *Sobranie*, vol. XXX/1, pp. 242, 252.' Thanks a lot, Professor, that's all we need to know.

Still, from the various letters between Herzen and his daughter, Natalie (Tata), we catch a glimpse of a fascinating platonic involvement between her and a blind Sicilian nobleman (nothing very ordinary ever happened to these people), and more than a glimpse of Herzen's determination to keep his favourite daughter all to himself.

When he died, he left her an incurable spinster with frequent migraines and a sufficient inheritance to last her through a long, virginal life.

Not a lady who would naturally come to mind as one likely to become a prostitute in order to raise money for the liberation of Russia. Yet this is what Bakunin, the apostle of Russian anarchism, proposed to her, as well as telling her that she should leave herself only 'the "*stricte nécessaire*" to live on and give the rest to the common cause'. He also expected her to accept the nominal editorship of his new paper to be called after her father's famous journal, the *Bell*, but opposed in every way to Herzen's ideas.

She was to give her money, her name and her body: this was the anarchist way to total freedom, which unaccountably failed to appeal to her.

Bakunin and his *protégé*, the nihilist Sergei Nechayev, are the stars of Professor Confino's volume: slightly mad but nonetheless lethal characters, the forerunners of all amoral and sick political activists.

Through their own letters, as well as Tata Herzen's perceptive comments, we can watch them become petty, dotty and even deranged as their moral indignation is transformed into the delusion of divine power, into the fantasy that they can re-create Russia to their liking.

For sheer dottiness, it would be difficult to match Bakunin's intense curiosity about 'the reactionary activities of Marx and company', or his ecstatic praises of Nechayev ('the most valuable man amongst us all . . . the purest . . . the most *saintly* person in the sense of his total dedication to the cause and his utter self-denial . . . a jewel'), written *after* his discovery that Nechayev was a liar, a thief, a blackmailer and a murderer.

In a different mood, Bakunin warns a friend that Nechayev will

> . . . open all your drawers, read all your correspondence, and when he finds an interesting letter, that is, one that is compromising in any respect whatever, for yourself or one of your friends, he will steal it and keep it. . . .

This warning was followed immediately by a request to another friend the same day:

> It would be splendid of you, and you would be doing the sacred common cause an enormous service if you were to succeed in stealing from Nechayev all the papers he stole and all his papers.

As for madness, Professor Confino includes Nechayev's *Catechism of a Revolutionist*, who must have 'no interests of his own, no affairs, no feelings, no attachments', no scruples and must be totally consumed by one passion, 'terrible, total, universal, merciless destruction'. As Camus commented, 'for the first time, revolution is explicitly separated from love and friendship'.

Nechayev argues that in the right cause *everything is permitted*, even 'the murder of one's brothers', and that revolutionists must view people 'as expendable capital'. Such fanaticism finds its justification in the lists of crimes committed by the Enemy and in big words like Freedom and History, but both here and elsewhere they serve only to free man to be as vile as he wishes and proud of it, too.

There is a most moving and shocking letter in the book describing how this great rebel committed his only act of violence, killing a Moscow student who was a member of his tiny organisation, 'The People's Vengeance', and a financial contributor to the Cause, but who wanted to know where his money was going before he gave more. This was a breach of revolutionary discipline which had to be punished by death.

It was this murder and the character of Nechayev that inspired Dostoyevsky's *The Devils*, the most profound novel on the degeneration of people who, moved first by compassion and rage, are led by their conceit to attempt the godlike task of manufacturing historic convulsions, and are bound to end up as pathetic criminals, victimising the weak.

Dostoyevsky's analysis is borne out by revolutionaries to this day. The Symbionese Liberation Army, in its struggle against white oppression, claims so far only the murder of a black school principal.

To borrow a Marxist phrase, there is an historic necessity about this: outsiders have no choice but to work for reform or to resort to private crime; it's only those in power or with access to power, administrative or military, who can harm a sufficient number of people to set off a revolution.

So it is possible to draw, like Dostoyevsky, too much comfort from the impotence of violent radicals. Bakunin and Nechayev, or Lenin and his little band of Bolsheviks, for that matter, could not destroy old Russia, but the Tsar could, and did.

The Sunday Telegraph, May 19, 1974

Demolition Job on Male Myths and Bogus Social Science

Sexual Politics, by Kate Millett (Hart-Davis)

Whatever the 'real' differences between the sexes may be, writes Kate Millett, *we are not likely to know them until the sexes are treated differently, that is, alike.*

It is this pretence of sameness which bedevils all egalitarian movements: the empty pretensions to special virtues assumed by unspeakably vile rulers call forth from the oppressed the anguished cry *we can be just the same!* Thus ascendancies change without moral progress.

Kate Millett could retort that she does not wish women to be like men. Indeed at one point she states that if the world is to survive men must become less aggressive and women less passive (that is, more active, not more aggressive). One would rejoice at this distinction if it were not blunted by the all-purpose argument that all this female passivity and male aggressiveness are just a product of social conditioning.

She is not so much naive as committed – stuck in the reformer's eternal bind: whatever is asserted about 'human nature' and human differences is used by reactionaries to justify the status quo. She makes mincemeat of those wily psychologists who turn even their inklings of male inferiority into a further rationale for male domination, on the basis of the infantile logic that since men are weaker and meaner, they must be allowed the solace of ruling over women. But the simplest way to put an end to such arguments is to say there are no differences – let the male chauvinists make something of *that*!

Thus Millett can claim that women didn't take their share of power in the Bolshevik Party (despite Lenin's emancipationist views and laws for sexual equality) only because they were hampered by unfavourable social conditions and male resistance. She doesn't pause to consider what it took to get ahead in Lenin's and Stalin's crowd. While there have undoubtedly always been a few sick women everywhere who are able to commit atrocities, I do not believe that the majority of Russian women were capable in any circumstances of making their way to power in Soviet politics through treachery, murder and mass-murder – which a great many normal men, full of jokes and good feelings like Khrushchev, found it quite easy to do.

It is in the sexes' different needs in sexual intercourse that one can find the reasons for the real differences – none of which is in men's favour. Millett is surely right in saying that women's sex problems are planted by men: women's sexuality is free of any built-in neurosis, because they are always capable of intercourse, physically able to perform, if not to enjoy, the sex act at any time – thus they can relax, 'let go', when they make love. A man, however, must *stiffen*, he has to get *worked up* – aye, there's the rub! Hence the need for martial music, for marching off into disasters.

Unable to will an erection, he tries to prove the power of his will over everything else: being at the mercy of his body in his deepest longing, man is driven by the desire and need to dominate, to subjugate, to conquer. Often failing to give satisfaction to his partner, and always uncertain of his ability to do so (he is indeed in need of awe), he conceives the 'inferiority' of women and acquires the psychological deformity which makes him long for slaves whose feelings he does not have to consider. Women tend to long for agreement, for affection, for reciprocity, men for control and power. In my view, erection-anxiety is the psychosexual source of man's dominant position in society and his inferiority as a human being, his irrationality, his cruelty; erection-anxiety is the main source of evil in the world.

Miss Millett cannot accept this 'need' for awe and rampage, for she considers it together with the plea that it should be indulged. The latter does not necessarily follow. On the contrary: the recognition of the male's inferior nature may help to mitigate it.

All this, however, relates only to one aspect of *Sexual Politics*. When Millett does not look at sexual differences as mere excuses for the subjugation of women, she is in fact most eloquent on certain characteristics peculiar to the male. Greater love hath no man than the love of his penis, and this delusive pride in his source of anxiety is conclusively identified by Millett as one of the central emotions of our male-dominated civilization. She achieves this through a kind of polemical literary criticism, attacking Miller, Mailer and Lawrence. (This part of the book is most instructive if read together with Mailer's answer, *The Prisoner of Sex*.)

On Miller and the cult of the rampant he-male, Brigid Brophy's essay is still the last word: Kate Millett lacks Brophy's talent for the dead-on phrase which makes an abundance of details superfluous. Indeed, the author of *Sexual Politics* thinks better than she writes, but if the ponderously academic style makes for a slow trip, it takes us not only beyond Miller and company, but also beyond Freud.

Nor is psychoanalysis the only bogus science to bolster the male ego. Millett casts a few penetrating glances at the social sciences which (in regard to sex as to everything else) consist of rationalizations for leaving things as they are. And while I'd insist that we know a great deal more about the real psychological differences between the sexes than Millett cares to dwell upon, there is no question that she is right in arguing that women have no inner need to be oppressed and exploited, and that social scientists who find the virtues of servility the 'natural' characteristics of women do not know what they are talking about.

She describes their enlightening charts which attribute to women the very same qualities that used to be attributed to blacks – and indeed to all oppressed groups throughout history. She also demonstrates brilliantly (in a chapter on Nazi Germany) how the cult of motherhood is tied to the idea of keeping everybody in his/her place, and that the notion that women should stick to child-bearing is an integral part of tyrannical ideologies.

Sexual Politics is too complex to allow the critic to claim (or the reader to assume) that it can be compressed into a review. While I could go on listing both Millett's virtues and flaws, the essential fact about her book is that it is full of relevant arguments about a vital subject and your time would be well spent in reading it.

The Times, March 22, 1971

Fearless Absurdities

Sex in Man and Woman, by Theodor Reik (Vision
  Press)
The Fantasy Factor, by Peter Dally (Weidenfeld)
Love, by Stendhal (Penguin)

It is rare enough to hear a sensible word about sex, let alone
about the difference between the sexes. The latter subject is still
too much of a political issue for detached reflection. Feminists,
fighting for equal rights and opportunities, tend to view 'femi-
nine' and 'masculine' traits as the result of social conditioning,
while most men who stress the differences are really arguing for
male supremacy.

Theodor Reik is a case in point. His avowed aim in *Sex in Man
and Woman* is to explore the 'emotional variations', the 'diver-
gent psychology' of the sexes, but he is soon off to prove that
men are a higher breed.

To begin with it is only unisex that he opposes ('How would
you like an opera in which only female or only male singers were
heard?') but within a few sentences he is claiming that the sexes
not only do not belong on the same stage but actually 'live on
different planets', and 'even the Ten Commandments are not
conceived as equally binding on both of them'.

Dr Reik is a psychoanalyst of the old Viennese school, which
is to say a male chauvinist pig *par excellence*. There is something
distinctly piggish, for example, in the way he tries to buttress
every self-flattering male notion by quoting a woman.

One of his women patients assures him that men look in the
mirror only to shave; another writes him 'very perceptive and
amusing' letters to complain what horrible voices women have

('what a pleasant sound a roomful of men make. . . . Whereas woman, poor penis-less creature, paltry second-best sex that she is, is sentenced to bleat and to harp, screech and whine. . . .'); a 'mature' woman declares, 'We gladly admit that you men are more intelligent.'

'Would it not be appropriate to assume,' Dr Reik himself asks rhetorically, 'that genius is essentially masculine also when it appears among women?'

Boorishness, according to Dr Reik, is the very essence of manhood: only women worry about whether their lovers will like their clothes, their bodies, their smell – men are supposed to be above such petty concerns. A woman who would want her lover to give her time to enjoy their lovemaking is sternly rebuked on the grounds that delay may be *unpleasurable* for the man, and 'human nature is not made to submit to great sacrifices'.

Much is made of Freud's pathetically vainglorious notion of Penis Envy, according to which girls are supposed to become aware of their inferiority at an early age, when they first notice that they're not equipped with the most worthwhile bit of the creation.

Nothing, of course, is said of Erection Anxiety, which seems to me to explain a great deal about the emotional differences between the sexes. Women are always capable of intercourse, but men must get worked up: hence, I believe, their greater predilection for ego-boosting theories, for monuments, marches and battles, for all kinds of violent activity.

Which brings us to Peter Dally's *The Fantasy Factor*, in which the human race is divided into sadists and masochists and a mixture of both.

To fit us all into these categories, Dr Dally stretches the words until they mean everything and nothing. Thus a sadist is either somebody who merely daydreams about playing 'an active aggressive role', or somebody who is frightened and inhibited by his cruel fantasies, or somebody who actually tortures others.

The masochist, too, is a lot of people. Saints and martyrs,

leading actors in horror movies, successful entrepreneurs ('the masochistic businessman of ability feels he must succeed'), heavyweight champions and chessmasters, Hitler and Stalin and Jesus Christ are all described as masochists.

'Play up, play up and play the game!' is a masochistic battlecry.

Gentleness and kindness, on the other hand, 'are the hallmarks of the man with sadistic fantasies'.

Yet what hurts most in these books is not the onslaught of fearless absurdities but the authors' total lack of professionalism. Dr Reik defines a maiden as a female servant, while his patient *lays* relaxed on the couch; the text is adorned with a great many misspelled French quotations and incorrect literary allusions ('Lady Macbeth had no children').

Dr Dally's forte is the judicious qualification which leaves him saying nothing at all. There is no point in saying 'the sadist is *sometimes* a coward'. Who is not a coward sometimes?

Nor can we take heart from the masochist who is 'often recklessly brave as he hurls himself forward, blind to all dangers . . .' If he hurls himself forward *blind to all dangers* [my italics], he can hardly be called brave for it, let alone a masochist, and the extra qualification 'often' is quite unnecessary.

When Dr Dally makes sense, it is with a mind-blowing commonplace:

In peacetime the chances of a soldier or sailor becoming a hero are limited.

Both authors keep interrupting themselves to discourse briefly on anything that comes into their heads. It is evident that, being psychiatrists, they are used to having a captive audience and are utterly unaware of any obligation to be coherent or interesting.

It's no fun to beat a dead horse, but it is surely a matter of public concern that such works get published. They are in fact only samples of the flood of bad books which, unreadable as they are, are released because they have a ready-made appeal for libraries.

The two necessary qualifications are met by both Dr Reik (pupil of Freud, famous New York analyst) and Dr Dally (senior consultant psychiatrist at the Westminster Hospital): they are authorities who can be sold to librarians on the strength of their position in the world and they write on a serious and fascinating subject.

In the past it required greater skill and effort to write a book than to produce an article: today this situation is reversed. No newspaper editor in Britain would think of printing an article so inconsequential, so muddled, so rambling, so boring, so *incompetent*, as the thousands of full-length books that are issued every year at high prices.

Not wishing to leave you with such a depressing thought, I am glad to be able to report that Penguin are bringing out a great book not unconnected with sex: Stendhal's *Love*. This is shapeless and patchy, too, but it is the work of a genius, a source of pleasure and wisdom, and an inspiration to profound reverie.

It was in *Love* that Stendhal developed his famous theory of consciousness, his notion that the way we see is the way we feel, that the evidence of the world crystallises on the thread of feeling.

In the salt mines of Salzburg a bough stripped of its leaves by winter is thrown into the depths of an abandoned shaft; two or three months later it is pulled out again, covered with glittering crystals: the smallest twigs, no bigger than a tomtit's claw, are spangled with a host of dazzling, shimmering diamonds. No one could recognize the original bough.

What I call crystallisation is that mental process which draws from everything that happens new proofs of the perfection of the person who is loved.

Stendhal's *Love* gives the lie to Dr Dally's claim that 'As civilisation progresses, it is man's intellectual capacity that advances. . . .' A capacity cannot *advance* as if it were a troop of masochists, blind to all dangers.

The Sunday Telegraph, August 10, 1975

An Anthropologist Observes the Ik

The Mountain People, by Colin Turnbull (Cape)

There is a mountain tribe in north-eastern Uganda called the Ik, whose children are cast out at the age of three and grow to feed and amuse themselves by

> prying open the mouths of the very old and pulling out the food they had been chewing and had not had time to swallow . . . [or] they would make as if to take the food and then not take it, so the victim swallowed in haste and surprise and choked on it.

An Ik hides with his food. No husband, parent, child, brother likes to give, and they steal from each other whatever they can. To fall sick and weak among the Ik is to die, for there is no helping hand, and the defenceless cannot even keep the morsel already in their mouths. 'A good man' in the Ik language is defined as 'one who has a full stomach'.

It appears that the Ik were once a normal hunting tribe, but their main hunting ground was turned into a game reserve, and now they are forced to farm barren, burnt-out ravines and mountain slopes. Attending only fitfully to this hopeless occupation, and deprived of their traditional way of life and any useful activity, they are crazed with hunger, boredom and loneliness as they compete against each other for roots, termites and hand-outs.

If the subject of a book could make it good, this one would be great. Indeed, fellow-anthropologists, who seem to react to the theme of the book rather than to the actual text, have nothing but praise for *The Mountain People*.

In my minority opinion, however, it is another depressing manifestation of the belief, increasingly common among publishers and reviewers, that writing books is unskilled work, requiring no special talent, training or practice, a sort of spare-time activity, preferably done by some truly serious people who are experts in other fields, like academics.

The academic in this instance is Colin Turnbull, an anthropologist who has already committed to hardcover the notes and tapes of three previous field trips. On his way to a professorship he has journeyed to the mountains of the Ik, and now would tell us all about it, if only he knew how.

He is both confused and confusing. 'The Ik clearly show . . . that man is not the social animal he has always thought himself to be' – but on other pages the Ik 'still insist on living in villages' and 'do undeniably hold together with remarkable tenacity'.

He finds that they lack 'wholehearted, unquestioning identification' with their environment, while also asserting that 'they prefer to die of starvation and thirst rather than move out of their mountain homeland'. He hardly says anything without also saying its exact opposite, and several times over, too.

It follows that he sees his points confirmed in the oddest ways. 'The overall unsociality of the Ik' is revealed to him even in their last breath. 'Then, true Ik, he let go of my hand . . . and he died alone.' What is so 'true Ik' about dying alone? Dying in company, like my late compatriot Attila the Hun, who had his 600 wives killed and buried with him, seems to me more unusual.

Mr Turnbull is ever ready to state his assumptions as facts, and he always assumes the worst. He claims that the Ik mother working in the fields puts her baby down 'almost hoping that some predator will come along and carry it off'. How does he divine such unspoken almost-hopes? He tells us that a mother whose child was actually eaten by a leopard was 'delighted', without letting us know whether he witnessed her joy, only heard about it, or is relying once more on his intuition.

Above all, I think, Mr Turnbull's mental scales are out of order: he gives the wrong weight to things. It is appalling, if true, that a mother should be delighted when her starving baby is eaten by a leopard, but it is not quite as vile as battering one's children to death. The incidents with which Mr Turnbull tries to prove that the Ik are 'as mean as any people can be' leave me with the uneasy suspicion that he has never seen the front page of a newspaper.

Even when he appears to be informed, there is something faulty in his reasoning. Arguing that it is 'rare for man to shed so much of his humanity' as the Ik, he compares them unfavourably with the inmates of the concentration camps in the Second World War; but if he is so keen to establish degrees of human cruelty, why does he not compare them with the humans who ran those camps?

The Ik don't hang anyone on a meat-hook, they don't burn alive or gas anybody – they are in fact non-violent and rarely resort even to a fist-fight – yet Mr Turnbull, hardened by his own exaggerations, is actually 'hopeful that their isolation will remain as complete as in the past, until they die out'.

Worse, the tragedy of the Ik is drowned by the author's self-pity over the difficulties and discomforts he suffered in the course of observing the ways of a starving tribe. He *thanks* the Ik, no less, 'for having treated me as one of themselves, which is about as badly as anyone can be treated'. He couldn't eat in peace, his things were stolen, they told him lies, they did not love him. For my part, I cannot help admiring the Ik's tolerance and restraint, and am at a loss to understand why they didn't eat *him*.

The Sunday Telegraph, October 12, 1973

Russia

Seeing Through Human Muddle

Gogol, by Henri Troyat, translated by Nancy Amphoux (Allen & Unwin)

There is hardly a page of this book on which there isn't something that I find deeply offensive. Henri Troyat's subject is Gogol, but what this biography is really about is that warm, cosy sense of superiority that mediocre people feel when confronted by genius.

For one thing, this 'little Ukrainian schemer', constantly 'ferreting about in search of new ideas', was ridiculously excitable about art. He *attacked* museums, he *fell upon* ruins, and he wrote a much too enthusiastic article about *Boris Godunov*. Gogol was sincere in his admiration for Pushkin, M. Troyat concedes, 'but, *as usual, he went too far*'. (My italics.)

There you have it in half a sentence, the terrible thing about all true artists: they go too far, they go over the brink and walk on air, while the Troyats of this world must needs advance at a measured crawl, and still get stuck in the mud of their incomprehension.

A great writer is like a great scientist: through his work something vital becomes known which wasn't known before. To Newton we owe our knowledge of the law of gravity; to Nikolai Gogol (1809–52) we owe our awareness of the cosmic gaps in human competence. In the whole literature of the world no writer *went so far* as Gogol in exploring the depths of our ineptitude, the muddle of humankind, the pathos of the misdirected effort.

Gogol was the one who spotted that people think not with

their brains, as they ought to, but with other parts of their anatomy. In *Dead Souls* the public prosecutor

> was quite unable to make sense of the affair, in spite of the fact that he stood on the same spot for some time, squinting with his left eye and flicking his beard with his handkerchief to brush off the snuff.

Earlier in *Dead Souls* there is a weighty discussion of how the hero, Chichikov, should handle the serfs he has just bought; there is a clash of liberal and reactionary views, a serious and illuminating argument about the serf question. The only catch is that the serfs who are to be treated gently or harshly are already dead.

In Gogol everything is absurd yet natural, natural yet absurd: it is absurd of Chichikov to travel about Russia buying dead souls, yet it makes perfect sense, for he buys only those who are officially still alive (that is, are still registered on the Government's files), so that he can use his purchase deeds as collateral for a big loan from the State Bank.

By general consensus, *Dead Souls* is the greatest comic novel in literature, though Gogol reported that when he read the beginning to Pushkin, Pushkin exclaimed with tears in his eyes: 'Oh, God, how sad our Russia is!'

But then these big ones never bother to write anything unless they can reach you in half-a-dozen different ways. Remember the amusing correspondence between two lap-dogs in *Diary of a Madman*? It tells you an amazing amount about lap-dogs and about people's thirst for decorations, as well as about the clerk who imagines it all in the process of going mad.

Madgie writes to her friend Fidèle about the excitement in the house when her mistress's father finally received the honour he had been waiting for:

> All that morning people in formal dress were coming to congratulate him. At dinner Papa was gayer than I'd ever seen him before, and after dinner he picked me up and held me level with his chest and asked: Look, Madgie, what's this?

I saw some sort of ribbon; I sniffed at it but it had no smell at all. Finally, I gave it a discreet lick. It was slightly salty.

Apart from the thrill of salty decorations, in Gogol's world success is either a short-lived misunderstanding (an insignificant young clerk is taken for the Government Inspector and for a brief time can live out his dreams of glory) or the mad fancy of a feverish mind. The office slave in the *Diary* has no other way to become somebody except by going mad – and then he is the King of Spain.

But that's not the whole story either, for once he believes that he is the King of Spain, he truly becomes a great man, acquiring the integrity of the saints and martyrs: no matter how much cold water they pour over him, however much they beat him and torture him, he will not abdicate his throne.

To bring off his sudden shifts and changes, Gogol developed an uncanny style which might have remained forever undefined but for Nabokov's brilliant study (*Nikolai Gogol*, happily still in print). Gogol, writes Nabokov, works with 'a jerk and a glide':

Imagine a trap-door that opens under your feet with absurd suddenness, and a lyrical gust that sweeps you up and then lets you fall with a bump into the next trap-hole.

But to get back to our distinguished member of the Académie Française, M. Troyat notes every manifestation of his subject's extraordinary gifts and then proceeds to ridicule, condemn or patronise him for them. He even finds something distasteful in Gogol's dedication to his work, complaining of his 'hairsplitting' revisions to the manuscript of *Dead Souls*, which rendered the work on the proofs 'interminable'.

No sooner did Gogol learn that *Dead Souls* had finally been passed by the censors than he began '*whining*' about the cuts. (Nancy Amphoux is a faithful if occasionally faulty translator, but she tends to soften the crudities of the original text: here she turns '*geindre*' into 'grumbling'.)

Since M. Troyat evidently writes off the top of his head, tossing off mutually exclusive propositions with the greatest ease (on one page we're told that Gogol could never find any material within himself, on another we learn that 'it is his own inner world that emerges in *Dead Souls*' and 'heroes and walk-ons, humans and animals, furniture and landscapes' are all drawn from inside him), it is not surprising that this biographer cannot understand Gogol's passion for perfection, let alone the more complex aspects of creativity.

One of the mainsprings of Gogol's creativity, it seems to me, was his impotence. Only a sexless life could have enabled him to capture, without the softening hues of love and desire, the absurd features of everyone and everything.

M. Troyat accords neither analysis nor respect to this impotence to which we owe so much. Any reflection on this subject would lead us to think of Gogol's sufferings; it would give us an inkling that achievements like Gogol's don't come cheap, that a man has to give for them all he has got, pay for them with every cell in his body, every waking and dreaming moment of his life. And then we might draw the conclusion that great artists are high above ordinary mortals and have *earned* their place there.

But M. Troyat is not interested in describing the ways in which great artists are superior to other people; he concentrates entertainingly on the half-truths which can make genius appear inferior to the ordinary library reader. So all he gives us on Gogol's impotence is the release Gogol sought in gluttony, with constant sarcastic references to his huge meals and his complaints about stomach-aches.

In fact M. Troyat's Gogol hardly performs any act or has any feeling which he doesn't share with the most dimwitted members of the human race. He eats, he gets constipated, he gets seasick, he is in a bad mood, he is fuddled, he fumes, he pinches himself to make certain he is awake: this is given to us as a portrait of the writer who surpassed Molière.

M. Troyat allows that Gogol is a great writer, but is annoyed that Gogol should be conceited enough to think so too, and reproaches him for *posing* as one. An artist may have enough light in him to create works which shine through the centuries, but he shouldn't know it.

'To hear him talk,' M. Troyat writes peevishly about the young Gogol, who was teaching at a girls' school in Petersburg at the time, 'he had invented an entirely new approach to history.' What uninformed reader could gather that this is exactly what Gogol did? He aimed at seeing 'all mankind at a single glance', and conceived history as a series of deadly blunders.

It is this historic view that enabled him to portray what is eternally wrong in social relationships. Like all great writers he was a profound critic of society, exposing not the evils that could be changed (these are ephemeral and not interesting) but the evils which *can't* be changed. That's why he is still our contemporary: he bequeathed to us, as he himself succinctly put it, 'the laughter that goes to the heart of things'.

According to M. Troyat, however, Gogol felt 'that the world owed him everything and he was entitled to *give nothing in return*'. Masterpieces don't count.

This is the age of the Yahoos, and biographies like M. Troyat's *Gogol* affirm its basic tenet that only mindless activities should be rewarded and respected.

The Sunday Telegraph, March 30, 1975

Grand Master of Despair

Dostoevsky by Leonid Grossman, translated by Mary Mackler (Allen Lane)

If we want to know how the world hangs together, we must read Pushkin, Kleist, Stendhal, Balzac, Tolstoy; if we want to know how the world falls apart, we must read Dostoevsky, the grand master of frenzy, of vile and senseless passions.

While Balzac's monsters, for instance, devour their fellow-men for reasons which make very good selfish sense – out of greed, lust, revenge – Dostoevsky's heroes torture or kill out of deep love for their victims, or for the sake of humanity, or simply to humble themselves. Until you read him, you haven't quite realised how monstrously stupid and twisted human beings can be.

To put it still another way, if Stendhal's world is dominated by lovers, Dostoevsky's dominant characters are ravers – bullies, tyrants and terrorists. A most topical author.

As to method and style, if Pushkin and Kleist could put the universe in an envelope, only Tolstoy matched Dostoevsky for practically endless variations on his themes.

It was Dostoevsky's discovery (put most succinctly in his brief masterpiece, *Notes from Underground*) that the most destructive and dangerous of all religions was the new-found faith in the power of reason, science, industry, revolution and the perfectibility of man. Among the great 19th-century novelists, all more or less tainted with false hopes, only Dostoevsky could stand up today and say to us: 'I told you so!'

His work embodies all our reasons for despair, all the

reactionary facts of life. So a Soviet biography of him is bound to be a most peculiar document.

But let us first pay our respects to the late Leonid Grossman. His *Dostoevsky* is not your run-of-the-mill biography written hurriedly by an underpaid hack who couldn't afford the time to think about his subject; it is the fruit of a lifetime of heroic devotion to a writer whom it was dangerous to recommend too warmly in Soviet Russia. To quote only Lunacharsky, the Commissar of Culture, who used to carry a gun:

> To submit to the direct influence of Dostoevsky in anything is out of the question.

Despite the warning, Grossman allowed himself to become spellbound, and he gives a spellbinding account of Dostoevsky's story. Born in Moscow's poorest district, between a foundling home, a lunatic asylum and an outcasts' graveyard, Dostoevsky suffered from poverty, debts, bronchitis, emphysema and epilepsy. His mother died when he was a boy, his father (first a poor doctor, then a poor landlord, and always a cruel drunkard) was murdered by his serfs.

Dostoevsky himself was sentenced to death by a military tribunal for getting mixed up in socialist company. He had to face the firing squad before learning that his sentence was commuted – which is why we now know, from *The Idiot*, what it feels like to be executed. In Siberia, on top of serving four years at hard labour, he married a sick and stupid woman who despised him.

He had many women fall in love with him but curiously enough they all seemed to turn against him. Indeed it was while reading this biography that it struck me that all the Dostoevsky heroines make violent about-turns, manifesting the psychology of women who were keyed up and let down.

Whatever the reason, this makes for fantastically dramatic scenes in both his life and his fiction. And in fact his second marriage (according to Grossman, who had a series of talks with Dostoevsky's widow in the winter of 1916–17) was a happy one, but for the novelist's illnesses and his gambling fever, which made for a lot of borrowing, begging and pawning.

Grossman subscribes to Balzac's dictum that the main events in a writer's life are his books, and he tells the life in order to throw light on the novels, documenting the connections between Dostoevsky's personal miseries and his unequalled insights into the human tragedy.

Considering the results, Dostoevsky himself was quite pleased with his ill-luck, telling a young writer what a good thing it was that he had to spend ten years in Siberia:

> I really learned to know myself there, my friend. I learned to know Christ, learned to know the Russian man. . . . All my very best ideas came to my head then. . . . Oh, if you could only be sent to penal servitude!

What kept rankling were the lousy publishing deals. His regular publisher declined a novel from him in 1874 because he had just bought *Anna Karenina* (my, publishers were spoiled in those days!) – and, as if this rejection wasn't enough, Dostoevsky learned that the rich Count Tolstoy got paid nearly four times as much as he had been getting, though they were equally popular. 'We are not rated very highly, Anna,' he wrote to his wife. 'They don't think much of me because I live by my work.'

All this finds an ideal chronicler in Grossman. Things start to go wrong when he feels obliged to turn his hero into a forward-looking humanitarian, to make him acceptable to the rulers of the Gulag Archipelago, who like reading-matter to show boundless optimism.

Thus even Dostoevsky's religious mysticism is made to seem preferable to his bitter truths. For if he has the courage of his despair in rejecting the possibility of Utopia, he softens the horror of foul passions and deeds by placing the possibility of spiritual redemption within everybody's reach. Accordingly, as one of his detractors said, 'all sorts of abominations can live together with nobility in a man'.

Grossman himself sees nothing wrong with the conception of Dmitry Karamazov as

. . . the typical arrogant army brute, always ready to insult and hurt someone, always ready for an 'orgy and a pogrom.' But beneath this rough exterior there beats a living, sensitive heart . . . an intellectually and morally gifted individual, a profound and compassionate soul . . . in love with life and art.

Many Russians seem to believe in this kind of thing. But the book becomes really perverse when Grossman laments (let us hope not altogether sincerely) that Dostoevsky failed to foresee the glorious future that the Bolsheviks were to visit upon Russia, and castigates him for prophesying massacres and the worst-ever tyranny at the end of the radical road.

Still, we must be grateful for a book which helps to keep in circulation in the Soviet Union this great exponent of the faith that man does not live by bread alone, and which imparts a great deal of useful documentation as well as the excitement of reading Dostoevsky's 'turbulent and crowded scenes that literally shake the foundations of his novels, scenes of assemblages, arguments, brawls, hysterics, face-slappings and seizures'.

For analysis unclouded by ideology we must look to the West: and I for one await what sounds like an excellent study soon to be published by Alex de Jonge, an Oxford don. But whatever the faults of Grossman's biography, like many of Dostoevsky's characters it is redeemed by love.

The Sunday Telegraph, January 12, 1975

The Tolstoy Tree

The Tolstoys: Twenty-Four Generations of Russian History 1353–1983, by Nikolai Tolstoy (Hamish Hamilton)

A great novelist writes about the whole world and writes as if all the people in it were his relations. With Leo Tolstoy this was very nearly the case, and Nikolai Tolstoy's book about his ancestors throws light on quite a few of them.

I was particularly struck by the pen-portrait of Count Dimitri Andreevich Tolstoy, the novelist's cousin and contemporary, who was Minister of Education and later Minister of the Interior. Possibly even more frustrated than the public by the inert bureaucracy he was supposed to run, Count Dmitri had the brilliant idea of creating a new set of officials called 'land commanders' chosen from the local nobility and empowered to make swift decisions about the affairs of their districts, without reference to other authorities.

Good and intelligent men in these new posts greatly improved matters, but as the majority of the new functionaries with a great deal of power turned out to be good but not intelligent, or intelligent but not good, or neither good nor intelligent, they only added to the general misery and chaos, speeding up the disintegration of Russian society.

Cousin Dmitri is quite clearly the original of the deadly yet intimate portrait of Alexey Karenin, as well as his ministerial colleagues: mean, dry and brilliant men who appear as divorced from life as the insane, because in all their well-intentioned plans for Russia they fail to take into account the incapacities and personal ambitions of the subordinates on whom they depend for the execution of their orders, and expect millions of people with independent wills to pay more attention to decrees and regulations than to their own needs.

In Tolstoy's works, men who try to shape society appear as absurd as if they were trying to shape the waves of the sea, but what might have been trite satire emerges as profound if ironic truth – the distilled experiences of generations and generations of Tolstoys who had been involved in the management of Russia's affairs from the 14th century. The chief virtue of Count Tolstoy's book is that it will serve as a reference work on these ancestors, at least on the father's side of the novelist's family.

However, Tolstoy was far more than a writer of the ruling class, although there was a time when he himself didn't think so. Nikolai Tolstoy quotes an early passage from *War and Peace*, cut from the final version, in which the novelist resolves to write only about

> princes, counts, ministers, senators and their children . . . because I myself belong to the highest order of society and like it. . . .
>
> I cannot understand . . . what a shopkeeper thinks and feels as he invites people to buy braces and ties, or what a theological student thinks as he is being taken to be flogged for the hundredth time, etc. I cannot understand this any more than I can understand what a cow thinks when it is being milked or what a horse thinks when it is carrying a barrel.

In the end he wrote superbly even about what cows and horses thought. He had an almost absolute capacity to identify with all kinds of people, and all the more easily because he belonged to all kinds: there were in truth more poor and obscure Tolstoys than rich and powerful ones. Nikolai Tolstoy notes many of them, though not Tolstoy's half-brother whose mother was a peasant girl and who became a postillion and died a pauper.

With relatives in all walks of life, Tolstoy certainly had an unfair advantage over most modern novelists, who know so little of their own scattered families that they are unable to portray the life of a single class, let alone a whole society, and are restricted to writing about a *set* – the jet set, the university set, the media set, etc. The disintegration of large families has impoverished society in countless ways, even in its literature.

The character closest to Tolstoy was closest to him through her absence. His mother, the rich Princess Maria Volkonsky, married to poor Count Nikolai Tolstoy, died when her youngest son Leo was only 23 months old. Out of his longing for her Tolstoy created Princess Maria Bolkonsky of *War and Peace*: bullied by her father and married by poor Count Rostov partly at least for her money, the plain but clever and noble-hearted princess bewitches both her husband and the reader; she is one of the most movingly beautiful characters who ever stepped off the printed page to live in our imagination.

Princess Maria notwithstanding, the one great flaw in Tolstoy's works is the naturally and happily subservient relationship of the women characters to the men. Tolstoy, so profoundly observant of men's pretensions in their callous use of other men, seems to fall prey himself to the self-justifying delusions of a selfish lover.

Sonya Tolstoy confessed to her diary, 'I can never get used to the dirt, the smell.' Through a combination of religious horror of lust and the male's natural impatience and laziness, Tolstoy had become so inconsiderate of his wife's pleasure that he didn't even bother to wash.

Yet *he* was the one who complained that sex was 'disgusting', 'humiliating', 'repulsive'. As Nikolai Tolstoy writes, he was subject to 'exaggerated remorse', experiencing 'post-coital revulsion more than most'. I submit that there is no lover who can be all that repelled, humiliated and remorseful with a happy woman in his arms, and Tolstoy felt wretched because he sensed his wife's disappointment, however much he refused to acknowledge it to himself.

This lie and self-deception left its mark on almost everything Tolstoy wrote about the relationship between men and women and may also have had something to do with his veering towards ideology later in his life, but his portrayal of the world of men is second to none in the history of literature.

A brief review is necessarily unfair to the dozens of fascinating Tolstoys described in this book, but possibly I'm forgiven for concentrating on the one who matters most.

The Sunday Telegraph, September 11, 1983

Where Are Pasternak's Royalties?

Pasternak: A Biography, by Ronald Hingley (Weidenfeld)

Ronald Hingley visited Boris Pasternak in his dacha outside Moscow in 1958 and confessed his unease about addressing a meeting at the university next day in his shaky Russian. 'Never mind that; let them look at a free man,' replied Pasternak.

Pasternak himself preserved his inner freedom against oppression, terror and abuse throughout his life (1890–1960). His parents were Jews from Odessa and belonged to the artistic aristocracy: his mother Rozaliya was a brilliant pianist, his father Leonid was a marvellous and successful painter whose sitters included, among others, Tolstoy, Lenin, Einstein and Rilke.

The couple and their daughters left Russia in 1921 and sought refuge first in Germany and later in England; Pasternak remained at home, but became an internal exile. He wasn't a fighter like Solzhenitsyn: his rebellion consisted in standing aside. Though he wrote a few basely flattering verses, they made him too miserable to allow him to become a Kremlin toady, and he never joined in the group denunciations, in the baying for the blood of the innocents.

An excellent if uneven poet by everybody's account, he managed to survive Stalin to write his only novel, *Dr Zhivago*. Smuggled out of Russia, it swept the Western world and won the Nobel Prize in 1958. Meanwhile it was reviled throughout the length and breadth of the Soviet Empire by people who couldn't possibly have read it.

To tell the truth, I still think that the best novel to come out of the USSR is Bulgakov's *The Master and Margarita*, a comic masterpiece with many romantic and fantastic motifs (the Devil and his minions visit Moscow) which only bring into sharper focus the diabolical reality of Soviet Russia. *Dr Zhivago* is not quite such a skilful or lucid work, but the misery, blood and suffering oozing through its melancholy pages finally get to you and move you to the depth of your soul.

Ronald Hingley writes well about *Dr Zhivago*, his telling of Pasternak's life, if not as lively as in his earlier *Nightingale Fever*, is orderly and succinct, and in general there are many signs to suggest that he is a brilliant man; but he seems to be succumbing to the sloth and conceit of academic life. Much of the book is stupefyingly ponderous and boring.

He quotes Pasternak's remark about the 'contradiction between the brevity of man's life and the immensity of his long-term tasks', but this does not prevent him from offering lengthy descriptions of Pasternak's poems, seasoned with clumsy verse translations. What is the point of anybody reading *résumés* of poems? All this reprocessing serves as a depressing reminder of the appalling way literature is taught. Instead of getting acquainted with great writing, students spend most of their time reading professors' deadly prose about it. It is as if music students hardly ever had the chance actually to hear music and 'studied' it by reading descriptions of symphonies.

But what am I complaining about? Half the books which are being published simply tell you what is written in other books.

The best and most lively book about Pasternak was written by the great love of his life, Olga Ivinskaya. Professor Hingley compliments her with fatuous conceit 'for the modesty with which she speaks of literary matters', while reproving her 'inelegant emotional self-indulgence'; but most things that live are inelegant, and *A Captive of Time* is an absorbing account of Pasternak's precarious existence between his wife and jealous mistress and the ever-watchful GPU.

Olga Ivinskaya spent eight years in forced labour camps (1949–53 and 1960–64) for no other reason than her connection with Pasternak. He, of course, missed her very much during her first imprisonment, did everything he could for her and supported her family and felt guilty that she was suffering on his account, but when she was released after Stalin's death in 1953 he was seized by fear that she must have grown old and ugly, and decided that he owed it to his wife to break off the affair.

Ivinskaya writes that he summoned her daughter Ira to meet him on Chistye Prudy Boulevard in Moscow, and gave her a message:

> She was to tell me, her mother, when I returned from the camp after my four years there, that he still loved me and that all was well, but that a change might now come about in our relationship.

Ira, who was only 15 but a sensible girl, said nothing of this to her mother until many years later, and when Ivinskaya returned from the camps, still beautiful, if thinner, the affair continued as before. With the boundless tolerance of a woman in love, Ivinskaya adds:

> It is a pity that Ira never made a note of the conversation to preserve the full flavour of his words – the mixture of candour, guileless charm and undeniable heartlessness.

Her book is full of striking incidents and images: such as the Nobel Prize-winning author, with his new false teeth made in the West and his jaw reshaped by plastic surgery, standing in front of the mirror and exclaiming, 'What a pity it all came too late, fame and beauty!'

It is heartrending to read of the money problems of Pasternak, his family and his mistress. According to Ivinskaya, they were advised by the head of the Culture Section of the Central Committee to accept royalties from the West 'in a sack' rather than 'create a fuss' by having them go through the State Bank.

This is what they did on several occasions, and two months after Pasternak's death Olga Ivinskaya was imprisoned for 'currency offences'. It seems to me that Feltrinelli, the Milanese millionaire Communist publisher who grabbed the world rights and 50 per cent of all income from the book's earnings outside Italy, could have done a great deal more to ensure that Pasternak and his heirs received at least the other 50 per cent.

I met Giangiacomo Feltrinelli once, when he wanted to buy the Italian rights to *In Praise of Older Women*, and he didn't strike me as a man who believed that writers ought to make money from their works. I don't believe that he could not have sorted out matters with the Soviet State Bank, hungry for capitalist currencies, if he had set his mind to it. Sending suitcases full of roubles into Russia – a clear violation of exchange regulations – was an invitation to have Olga Ivinskaya arrested, which relieved Feltrinelli of the necessity to pay royalties to anybody. When he turned terrorist and blew himself up, I for one shed no tears.

At all events, it is a fact that while *Dr Zhivago* was earning fortunes around the world, Pasternak's widow spent the last six years of her life in the most terrible poverty, begging from everyone she knew, and Olga Ivinskaya, when she returned from the camps, had to go back to earning her living with the hard, ill-paid labour of translation. What *did* happen and what *is* happening to the Pasternak royalties? I am surprised that Professor Hingley doesn't even raise the question. Pasternak was reviled and persecuted in the East, but if he was robbed, he was robbed in the West.

Finally, one cannot talk about Pasternak without mentioning the superb essay *My Meetings with Russian Writers* in Isaiah Berlin's *Personal Impressions*. If you're interested at all in the subject, you can find out almost everything from this portrait of the great Russian poets and their world. Only 54 pages long, it is a little masterpiece, demonstrating Sir Isaiah's own definition of genius: 'The power to do something perfectly simple and visible which ordinary people cannot, and know that they cannot, do.'

The Sunday Telegraph, August 7, 1983

How Brainwashing Succeeds

The First Circle, by Alexander Solzhenitsyn, translated by Michael Guybon (Collins & Harvill)

Alexander Solzhenitsyn's *The First Circle* is one of those books I wish I had never agreed to review. The author is an admirable man, a Russian who endured eight years in concentration camps, recovered from cancer, and still has enough strength left to write books which may, once more, cost him his freedom or even his life. He is also a good writer with at least one book to his credit that everyone who is interested in the best of contemporary literature ought to read: *One Day in the Life of Ivan Denisovich* (now Penguin, 4s). But I plodded through *The First Circle* (too revolutionary to be published in the Soviet Union) with respectful boredom.

The reader should be warned that this is a minority reaction: most critics think the work is a masterpiece, though for reasons which seem more sociological than literary. Indeed, as a sociological survey the novel can hardly be faulted. Within the first circle of Stalin's hell (a concentration camp for scientists and scholars, the Soviet version of the Rand Corporation), Solzhenitsyn paints a panorama of his totalitarian society which leaves few aspects of the Terror unrecorded. To my mind, however, it is this earnest thoroughness that proves the novel's undoing – the longer the ledger of suffering, the weaker its impact.

There is a good novella buried here which underlines what is wrong with the rest of the bulky volume. A young Soviet career diplomat, Innokenty Volodin, makes a telephone call to warn a former family doctor that he is about to be arrested (Stalin is embarking on his last spree of mass-murder, the Doctors' Plot) and although he disguises his voice on the tapped phone, Volodin begins to fear his own arrest for his weak moment of succumbing to a brave impulse. Through his panic he comes to know himself for what he is: a privileged, complacent, opportunistic organization man.

Late one evening, shortly before he is due to leave for his new post at an embassy in the West, his boss at the Ministry calls him back to the office for a last-minute briefing. The new driver who comes to pick him up treats him with all the accustomed reverence due to a state counsellor at the Foreign Office, and respectfully asks for permission to give a lift to a 'mechanic'; only after the second man gets into the car does Volodin realize that he is in the hands of the secret police.

He wonders about the elaborate ploy (why did not they just come straight out and arrest him?) but the joke serves to remind him of the elevated position he is losing, as within a few hours he is reduced to a numbered, bald criminal. Yet his imprisonment is his liberation: he is freed from his fear, he has nothing more to lose.

The police state intrudes on Volodin's story only as far as it is relevant to the change in his character, and so it is moving and shocking. The other 400 or so pages serve only to trivialize the point through repetition. Events are piled upon each other not according to the inner logic of an imaginative re-creation of life, but from a desire to list every sort of crime committed and every type of victim. Which is how brainwashing succeeds: not by making people believe transparent falsehoods but by forcing them to busy their minds with refuting lies and giving them no time to arrive at the truth.

In the end, Solzhenitsyn tells us more about what Stalin's Russia was not than about what it in fact was, because he has set out to expose the system while absolving the Russians who make it work. *The First Circle* is often as painfully naive as the noble pages of our own *Peace News* – too few villains succeed in victimizing all too many good people. Solzhenitsyn curses

Stalinism, but he still harbours the sunny and murderous delusions which are the foundation of communist ideology. He has an old-fashioned, simple-minded view of the human race – a reminder of the suffocating isolation of Soviet literature.

The Times Saturday Review, November 16, 1968

Chronicles of Blood

The Gulag Archipelago, by Alexander Solzhenitsyn, translated by Thomas P. Whitney (Collins/Harvill, Fontana)

'At the Novosibirsk Transit Prison in 1945 they greeted the prisoners with a roll call based on *cases*. "So and so! Article 58/1-a, 25 years." The chief of the convoy guard was curious. "What did you get it for?" "For nothing at all." "You're lying. *The sentence for nothing at all is 10 years*." '

As a matter of fact, the sentence for nothing at all could be as little as five years or as much as death, but the convoy chief evidently wanted to believe that the bosses had some rules.

Alexander Solzhenitsyn himself got eight years (11 with exile) for making derogatory remarks about Stalin in letters to a friend. It was this crime which, luckily for literature, interrupted his career as a Red Army captain back in 1945 and sent him on an odyssey through the prisons and prison camps which were scattered all over the Soviet Union like so many islands of slavery, torture and murder. He has named them for the maps of history *The Gulag Archipelago*.

From what Solzhenitsyn lived through and observed, from transcripts and records, from his own sufferings and the stories of his fellow-prisoners, he has created a richly-woven narrative of historical events and individual destinies – a masterpiece of pain, moral outrage and gallows humour.

There were, he reports, 'not more than 12 million' in the camps at any one time, and 'not more than half of them were politicals'. This fantastic number of inmates was steadily maintained, even though in a busy year such as 1937–38 over 900,000 men and women were executed.

These figures don't take into account the 'wastage': those who starved, froze, suffocated or died of thirst or typhus in overcrowded freight cars and tents on the Arctic tundra. One would have to count separately also those who were tortured to death while being 'persuaded' to confess to non-existent crimes.

As an historical survey, Solzhenitsyn's work (of which we have here only the first two parts, with five more still to come, and which is here translated by an American, Thomas P. Whitney) will supplement but not replace such comprehensive studies as Robert Conquest's *The Great Terror* and Roy Medvedev's *Let History Judge*. One of its chief merits as history is that it lays to rest the still-lingering illusion, shared to some extent even by Mr Medvedev, that the Soviet Union had a glorious beginning under Lenin and that it was only Stalin who drowned in blood mankind's hopes for a just society.

In truth, Lenin was the first leader of this century who set out to build a better world on a solid foundation of corpses. 'Terror,' wrote the great ideologue, 'is a method of persuasion.' As soon as he gained power he proclaimed his aim of 'purging the Russian land of all kinds of harmful insects', including non-Bolshevik revolutionaries and 'workers malingering at their work'.

To carry out the necessary 'extra-judicial reprisals' he founded the Cheka, which was to turn into an ever-growing army of thugs (known successively as GPU, NKVD, NKGB, MGB, KGB, and perennially as 'the Organs' or 'the Bluecaps'), who tortured and killed an ever-increasing number of people.

As for judicial murders, shortly before his death Lenin instructed the author of the Soviet Criminal Code that the articles requiring execution by shooting should be 'as broadly based as possible', and should apply even to 'agitation and propaganda' against paying taxes.

With the manic arrogance of dictators who believe that they can make the world nice and tidy, Lenin no doubt assumed that such laws would teach people that grumbling and malingering were heinous crimes; but what the Leninist laws were teaching was that a man's life was of no special value, and the way to cope with problems was to shoot somebody.

In a largely illiterate country in a chronic state of chaos, where hardly anybody had any idea how to cope with anything, this message had tremendous appeal.

As good Leninists, Stalin and the GPU ran even the railroads on executions. Solzhenitsyn recounts the bad luck of the great engineer Nikolai Karlovich von Meck, who proposed that freight loads should be increased. He was exposed and shot in 1929 for trying to weaken the Republic's rails and roadbeds.

Soon afterwards the new Commissar of Railroads ordered that the freight loads should be increased – and the engineers who worried about the weakening of the rails and roadbeds 'were rightly shot for their lack of faith in the possibilities of socialist transport'.

'If you live in a graveyard, you can't weep for everyone,' says Solzhenitsyn. Still, one must shed a tear for the wife of Captain Sayenko:

'Captain Sayenko (not the Kharkov Chekist carpenter of 1918–19, who was famous for executing prisoners with his pistol, punching holes in bodies with his sabre, breaking shin-bones in two, flattening heads with weights, and branding people with hot irons, but perhaps a relative) was weak enough to marry for love an ex-employee of the Chinese Eastern Railroad named Kokhanskaya. And suddenly he found out . . . that all the Chinese Eastern Railroad people were going to be arrested.

At this time he was head of the Security Operations Department of the Archangel G.P.U. He acted without losing a moment. How? He *arrested his own beloved wife*! And not on the basis of her being one of the Chinese Eastern Railroad people – but on the basis of a case he himself cooked up. Not only did he save himself, but he moved up and became the Chief of the Tomsk Province N.K.V.D.

Yet even cynicism could live with Marxist-Leninist piety, and Solzhenitsyn is brilliant in his portrayal of the righteous spirit of frame-ups and massacres. 'To do evil a human being first of all must believe that what he is doing is good,' he writes.

If I missed anything in *The Gulag Archipelago* it was the comrades' extreme concern about the well-being of people who had lived in past centuries or were living in the West. Their moral sensitivity was constantly exercised by the cruelties of Tsar Nicholas and the Paris police.

Solzhenitsyn describes how Soviet soldiers were condemned as traitors for the crime of having allowed themselves to be taken prisoner instead of fighting to the death, and how they were transported from German concentration camps to Russian concentration camps in sealed cattle cars. But as he is writing primarily for a Soviet audience, he does not think it necessary to mention that at the very same time Stalin and his henchmen and their propaganda machine could not contain their disbelief and agony that the Nazis could treat *human beings* like cattle!

It is, it seems to me, a universal human trait to rest our good conscience on our indignation over other people's wrong-doing. Indeed, the trouble with horror stories from distant parts of the world is that they inspire not so much shocked understanding as conceit and complacency, and there is a certain kind of lazy-minded reader who will derive nothing more from *The Gulag Archipelago* than the conclusion that Communism as a social system provides just too much scope for human stupidity and malevolence.

Yet one of the most appalling episodes in this book is the British Army's betrayal of 90,000 unsuspecting White Cossacks who were waylaid into the hands of the NKGB in May, 1945, in Austria:

The British proposed first that the Cossacks give up their arms on the pretext of replacing them with standardised weapons. Then the officers . . . were summoned to a supposed conference in the city of Judenberg in the British

Occupation zone. But the British had secretly turned the city over to the Soviet armies the night before. Forty busloads of officers drove straight down into the semicircle of Black Marias. . . . The officers didn't even have anything with which to shoot themselves or stab themselves to death, since their weapons had been taken away.

Later the enlisted men were delivered to the NKGB stock-yards in a similarly treacherous fashion. No doubt there was a *good reason* for it. The moral sickness of our century is expediency, and it knows no political boundaries.

The Sunday Telegraph, June 30, 1974

What Matters Most

Leonardo's Regret

Leonardo and the Age of the Eye, by Ritchie Calder
(Heinemann)

One of the pictures in this beautifully illustrated book is
Leonardo's map of northern Italy which he drew about 1503, in
connexion with his plans to build a canal between Florence and
the sea. As Ritchie Calder says, the map looks 'uncannily like
an aerial photograph'. Leonardo could visualize, and correctly,
how the Earth looked from thousands of feet in the air – that is,
from a point of view which didn't yet exist. Literally, he saw
things that no one else could see: to quote Kenneth Clark, his
supernormal eyes could observe details of the movements of birds
in flight which remained otherwise imperceptible until the
invention of slow-motion cinematography.

Leonardo's youthful absorptions included mathematics,
astronomy, physics, geology, botany, mechanics, optics, acous-
tics, physiology and anatomy; and by the time he left Florence
for Milan in his thirtieth year he had made a reputation as the
painter of Ginevra Benci, the *Benois Madonna* and perhaps his
greatest work, the unfinished *Adoration of the Magi*. Yet according to Vasari, this paragon of art and science was recommended
by Lorenzo to the duke of Milan as a musician who sang and
played the lute 'most divinely'. Needless to say, he was tall and
strikingly handsome, an excellent horseman, could break a
sword in two with the strength of his wrist and wore exquisite
clothes.

Back in the fifteenth century, many of his fellow artists pitied
him and his patrons berated him for neglecting his prodigious

artistic talents and wasting his time on scientific investigations and mechanical contrivances. It is this wasteful activity which is the subject of the present book.

Leonardo was running from a brushstroke on *The Last Supper* to invent the tip-up toilet seat, to design a model town or conceive the prototype of the helicopter or the machine gun; the range of his achievements was surpassed only by the number of his abandoned projects. This St Vitus's dance of overcharged creativity, which in itself has its tragic aspects, is extolled by Ritchie Calder as the glory of outward-looking man, such a great improvement over inward-looking types like St Augustine with his 'in the inner man dwells truth'.

The medieval attitude which tried to explain everything in terms of its relevance to God's children and viewed man's abode as the centre of the universe inspires many contemptuous remarks from the author, who has himself been eloquent on other occasions about the monstrous excesses of science in the nuclear age but finds nothing more admirable than Leonardo's scientific objectivity, his passion to discover and invent whatever there was to discover or invent, regardless of whether it was useful, trivial or deadly.

He regrets that most of Leonardo's scientific discoveries were lost or ignored for hundreds of years and his inventions wasted because the means didn't exist to realise them, and had to wait for others to rediscover them. Which is to say that Leonardo's work as a scientist could be and has been duplicated; yet Ritchie Calder can still rejoice over the sad business of a great artist who 'revelled in all kinds of gears', and wonders what 'Leonardo would have done if he had had a hint of electricity or the internal combustion engine'. I have no doubt that man would have already breathed his last in a thick cloud of carbon monoxide and the world would have already ended with a supersonic bang. Lord Ritchie-Calder, of course, is a great believer in Nicholas da Cusa's dictum that ignorance is the cause of error and evil, but the truth is that our race survived ignorance; it is our scientific genius that will do us in.

Nonetheless, he persists in viewing Leonardo's time, when

people began to lose interest in their divinity and started drawing up ledgers of facts, facts, facts, as the dawn of the golden age when at long last 'men saw things and saw their relevance'. But of course the relevance of it all was just what nobody saw until quite recently, when it became apparent that man's ability to tinker with nature is ruining the Earth. It seems to me there is something unduly harsh in Lord Ritchie-Calder's contempt for the age of ignorance and those who wished that Leonardo had given them another great painting to feast their eyes on instead of telling them the length and width of their eyeballs.

Leonardo is close to us, not as an example of the ideal fusion of the Two Cultures, as the author of *Leonardo and the Age of the Eye* would have us believe, but as a tragic figure, the very mirror of our time: man infinite in faculties, carried away by the very magnitude and brilliance of these faculties to betray his most precious gift. In his book *The Early Renaissance* Michael Levey succeeds in describing both the man and his works when he says that Leonardo brings to his (all too few) paintings 'a Medusa touch . . . a disturbing and faintly dissociated air which makes the spectator draw back for a moment . . . nature and the cosmos may prove more hostile than harmonious'.

Lord Ritchie-Calder recalls Vasari's account of Leonardo's last moments with some scepticism, but I see no reason to doubt that the divine Leonardo who knew so much learned to view his activities in perspective. Vasari says that when Leonardo's patron, King Francis I, arrived to witness the passing of the greatest man of the age, Leonardo 'sat up in bed from respect and related the circumstances of his sickness, saying how greatly he had offended God and man in not having worked at his art as he ought'.

The Times, September 21, 1970

The Proudest Genius of this Realm

Jonathan Swift: Major Prophet, by A. L. Rowse
(Thames & Hudson)

'Idiot humans' and 'perfectibility nonsense' are characteristic A. L. Rowse phrases: he is tactless, intemperate, highly subjective and not overly enamoured of the human race. With such commendable but non-academic virtues, the former Fellow of All Souls remains the *enfant terrible* of the academic world even at the age of 72.

He is the odd man out among the professionals of Higher Learning, who, being allowed to devour immense amounts of public money, tend to share a pious regard for the goodness and bounty of their fellow men, embracing the belief, Marxist or simply parasitic, that there is nothing really wrong with people that another grant wouldn't cure.

In this comfortable and complacent world, Dr Rowse is a headstrong loner whose spirited bitterness and intensely partisan approach to his subjects make him an admirable and stimulating figure even when he is wrong – let alone when he is right, which is often.

The only wonder is that he has taken so long to write his biography of that testy genius, Jonathan Swift. 'Swift is not a complete despairer; nor am I,' he writes. 'But we are not subject to illusions.'

This sort of personal comparison is frowned upon by almost all academics (modesty is a mania with mediocre people), but I think that identification with the truly great and their thoughts is a most edifying mental exercise and ought to be encouraged by example.

It is also a sound critical approach to their work. We cannot really understand a writer unless we think of him as a kindred soul, a friend who in some sense is our equal; and though Swift was the proudest genius of this realm and would get cross even with kings and duchesses if they failed to show him proper respect, I would like to see readers follow Dr Rowse's example and treat Swift and his books with familiarity instead of remaining at a respectful distance.

Jonathan Swift: Major Prophet is certainly one of Dr Rowse's best books and a far better introduction to the subject than either of the works he recommends: Middleton Murry's readable but rather soft-centred biography or Irvin Ehrenpreis's exhaustive study, *Swift, the Man, his Works, and the Age*, stuffed to bursting with irrelevant details.

Anyone struggling through Professor Ehrenpreis is likely to think that he has read all he ever wants to read about Swift, or by him – while Dr Rowse's queer, concise and personal account inspires curiosity, sending the reader back to Swift's own works.

Among other things, we owe to Swift (1667–1745) the ending of the War of the Spanish Succession – or at any rate the most effective pamphlet in English history, *The Conduct of the Allies*, which swung public opinion behind the Tories, who wanted to end the war and the career of the Duke of Marlborough.

An Englishman born and educated in Ireland, Swift enjoyed three years as the leading thinker of the Tory party, but received no greater reward for his services than the Deanery of St Patrick's in Dublin, where he spent the rest of his life, turning into an equally effective pamphleteer for Ireland, whose advice, if followed, could have spared us the present violence.

Dr Rowse's particular theme is the contemporary relevance of Swift as a 'major prophet' of the ills that afflict us today – the conceit of scientists and the busy mismanagement of society which Gulliver observed ahead of us in his travels. *Gulliver's Travels* (1726) was an immediate hit with people of all ages and classes who could read – except politicians, who disliked it. They would, Dr Rowse remarks, since the practice of their profession 'depended on political cant and humbug'.

Cant and humbug survive even in the most conscientious critics and political thinkers, and *Jonathan Swift: Major Prophet* is an effective answer to those who have deplored Swift's 'purely destructive' irony and 'expression of negative feelings and attitudes' (F. R. Leavis), and to those who regret, like Orwell, that Swift's hatred of humanity did not allow him to see the true possibilities of social progress or the blessings of science.

Although he has already been chided for it by some prim reviewers, I think it is quite appropriate for Dr Rowse to mention Concorde in this context: that marvel of Laputan technology, which at the cost of hundreds of millions of pounds of taxpayers' money will inflict the terror of sonic boom on defenceless Lilliputians and help to destroy the protective shield of our atmosphere. But then today we would keep even Auschwitz going, because no government would be so callous as to allow the workers who manufacture poison gases to lose their jobs.

But to return to the realm of literature, Dr Rowse is more traditionally right in describing Swift as a prophet in the sense that, among all English writers, he is the one most resembling an Old Testament prophet with his maniacal righteousness. As Hazlitt put it:

> The determination with which Swift persisted in a pre-concerted theory, savoured of the morbid affliction of which he died. There is nothing more likely to drive a man mad, than the being unable to get rid of the idea of the distinction between right and wrong, and an obstinate, constitutional preference of the true to the agreeable.

Thus afflicted, Swift himself often imagined that he hated mankind, but as Bolingbroke wrote to him: 'If you despised the world as much as you pretend, and perhaps believe, you would not be so angry with it.' Though Dr Rowse quotes Bolingbroke with approval, he perhaps pays less than sufficient attention to Swift's intense love for his fellow men, the love that inspired this divine wrath.

It seems to me, at any rate, that despite Swift's own insistence on his loathing for mankind, his considerable capacity for meanness, both in his life and some of his poetry, the lashing-out of a man suffering from a painful disorder of the inner ear that made the world spin, it is not very useful to think of him as anything but an occasional misanthrope.

His disgust with his fellow creatures could hardly be sustained beyond a few lines: and *Gulliver* itself can be taken as evidence of hatred for humanity only if one treats the book as nothing more than the words printed on paper. Surely only a critic not altogether familiar with the art of fiction could imagine that his contrary feelings about a masterpiece have not been predetermined by the author.

A writer's art lies not so much in his understanding of his theme as in his understanding of his readers, for the book is not the dead print but the living world in the reader's head. The reader's feelings are woven into the lines – how else could a novel have its impact?

It isn't just shame that Gulliver's predicament evokes when he is held in the hand of the giant king:

> Then turning to his first minister, who waited behind him with a white staff near as tall as the main-mast of the Royal Sovereign, he observed how contemptible a thing was human grandeur, which could be mimicked by such diminutive insects as I: and yet, said he, I dare engage, these creatures have their titles and distinctions of honour, they contrive little nests and burrows, that they call houses and cities; they make a figure in dress and equipage; they love, they fight, they dispute, they cheat, they betray.
>
> And thus he continued on, while my colour came and went several times with indignation to hear our noble country, the mistress of arts and arms, the scourge of France, the arbitress of Europe, the seat of virtue, piety, honour and truth, the pride and envy of the world, so contemptuously treated.

It is this sort of paradox, the ridiculing of patriotism and its simultaneous evocation, the constant tension between opposites – love and hate, scorn and pity – which make Swift, after Shakespeare, the most universal of English writers.

Certainly I can find nothing in Dickens's which would be so moving, would evoke so much solidarity for our unhappy species, so much feeling for the animal kingdom, as Gulliver's departure from Houyhnhnmland:

> And I often heard the sorrel nag (who always loved me) crying out, *Hnuy illa nyha majah Yahoo*, Take care of thyself, gentle Yahoo.

Dr Rowse's welcome partiality for Swift makes him rather unfair towards the three women in Swift's life: his attitude towards Varina, Vanessa and Stella is at least as peculiar as Swift's own. But neither distortions nor omissions can detract from his achievement, which owes its liveliness and excitement to its partisanship.

Those who read Swift and will read Dr Rowse no doubt have already found their way to Michael Foot's and Nigel Dennis's excellent books on Swift. I find the novelist Dennis the most convincing psychologist and the best on the artfulness of Swift's art:

> The horror of 'A Modest Proposal' is in the modesty with which the proposal is uttered: the tone of it is most beautifully tentative: we are dealing, it appears, with a good man who thinks it would be a good thing to eat babies but will drop the idea immediately if anyone can think of one or two sensible reasons why it should not be done.

Indeed, what could be more beautifully tentative than the proposer's concluding assurance that he has

> no other motive than the public good of my country, by advancing our trade, providing for infants, relieving the poor, and giving some pleasure to the rich. I have no children by which I can propose to get a single penny; the youngest being nine years old, and my wife past child bearing.

The Sunday Telegraph, November 30, 1975

The Greatest of Friends

James Boswell and His World, by David Daiches
(Thames & Hudson)

Johnson called the East-Indians barbarians.

    BOSWELL: 'You will except the Chinese, Sir?'

    JOHNSON: 'No, Sir.'

    BOSWELL: 'Have they not arts?'

    JOHNSON: 'They have pottery.'

    BOSWELL: 'What do you say to the written characters of their language?'

    JOHNSON: 'Sir, they have not an alphabet. They have not been able to form what all other nations have formed.'

    BOSWELL: 'There is more learning in their language than in any other, from the immense number of their characters.'

    JOHNSON: 'It is only more difficult from its rudeness; as there is more labour in hewing down a tree with a stone than with an axe.'

Boswell's *The Life of Samuel Johnson* (1791) is the greatest of all biographies because it is also many other things besides – not least, the classic script for two stand-up comics, written by the straight man.

Boswell's ability to play up to his partner, to let him have the last word on every subject for good effect, to enjoy the other man's wit at his own expense, is such a singular talent that not even Macaulay could fathom it.

Macaulay believed that Boswell was capable of publishing 'everything which another man would have hidden, everything the publication of which would have made another man hang himself', because he had 'a weak and diseased mind' and had no idea when he made himself ridiculous.

According to Macaulay, 'if he had not been a great fool, he would never have been a great writer'. But it is truer to say that because he was a great writer he could portray himself as a great fool. It was by Boswell's own account that Macaulay could characterise him as:

> . . . a bigot and a sot, bloated with family pride and eternally blustering about the dignity of a born gentleman, yet stooping to be a tale-bearer, an eavesdropper, a common butt in the taverns of London. . . .

Most people fear nothing so much as being ridiculous, which is why they don't want to take too close a look at themselves. Fortunately for us, Boswell could bear to be laughed at: his passion for truth and accuracy was always greater than his vanity.

All this is by way of a reminder that the best person to read on Boswell is Boswell. (The next best thing is the splendid biography by the American scholar Frederick A. Pottle, who also edited and annotated the many volumes of Boswell's Journal.)

The reader has no doubt noticed that I have taken my time getting around to *James Boswell and His World*, but this is because my eyes keep glazing over whenever I turn them to the text. There is nothing really wrong with it, except that David Daiches tries to tell us everything and so ends up saying very little.

> He called on, and was called on by, large numbers of distinguished people. For a while he was confined to his room with a venereal infection. All the time he continued his propaganda for Corsica. Johnson returned from Oxford in May. . . .

It seems that Professor Daiches follows Boswell's Journal, summing up dozens of its pages in a few sentences. Thus bad books are made out of good ones. Instead of Boswell's telling details, we get timetables. We are told (wrongly) that Boswell 'was in London from March 19 until May 8, 1772', but at the end of the same paragraph we read that he left London 'on May 12'.

My complaint is not so much that Professor Daiches gives two dates for the same event, but that he clutters up an already lifeless narrative with totally meaningless and irrelevant facts. Not only does Boswell set out for Edinburgh both on the 8th and the 12th, but he does so 'by the west road (Loughborough, Manchester, Shap, Carlisle, Langholme and Hawick)'.

There is also something odd about the author's way of joining things which are contradictory, and contrasting things which are not contradictory, by the misuse of 'and', 'but' or 'yet'. For instance he claims that Boswell

> cherished his wife in spite of her 'being averse to hymeneal rites' *and* searched the Bible for evidence that concubinage was permitted. And *yet* he worked hard, indulged in religious meditations in church, and enjoyed serious and informed intellectual discussion with his friends. [My italics.]

None of these last-mentioned activities appears contrary to searching the Bible for helpful evidence about concubinage.

In any event, the pictures seem to have been selected to greater effect than the words.

The two paintings of Boswell's wife tell a moving tale: in the first, before marriage, she is serene and pretty; in the second, a group portrait with her husband and three of their children, she looks sickly, ugly and morose. Indeed, it is difficult to imagine that any woman could have blossomed at Boswell's side. He was a repressed, guilt-ridden lecher, a wretched male chauvinist who, like many men without female comrades, was doomed to become 'a bigot and a sot'.

In fact, neither Boswell nor Johnson could really relate to women – not with the same deep attention and freedom that they could relate to each other. In this the Scotsman and the Englishman were both profoundly Anglo-Saxon. Deprived as they were of the strength and cheer of a woman who was both lover and equal, their friendship had the poignant fervour of two schoolboys who have no one but each other in the world.

It is perhaps most of all as the story of this friendship that *The Life of Johnson* holds the heart of the reader.

This is how the friends make up after Johnson, in a fretful mood, had abused Boswell in company.

BOSWELL: '. . . Now, to treat me so –.' He insisted that I had interrupted him, which I assured him was not the case; and proceeded: 'But why treat me so before people who neither love you nor me?'

JOHNSON: 'Well, I am sorry for it. I'll make it up to you twenty different ways, as you please.'

BOSWELL: 'I said today to Sir Joshua, when he observed that you *tossed* me sometimes – I don't care how often or how high he tosses me, when only friends are present, for then I fall upon soft ground: but I do not like falling on stones, which is the case when enemies are present – I think this is a pretty good simile, Sir.'

JOHNSON: 'It is one of the happiest thoughts I have heard.'

The Sunday Telegraph, February 8, 1976

Rules of the Game

The Stubborn Structure: Essays on Criticism and Society, by
Northrop Frye (Methuen)

Two of the most important literary critics of our time, I believe,
are Northrop Frye and George Lukács. I voice my opinion as an
example of value-judgment, which usually passes for criticism
and which Frye shows to be a barren practice, for it 'gives us no
knowledge'.

Likes and dislikes, *taste*, as critical criteria are not only
uninformative, they distort the nature and purpose of the art.
'The sense of taste is a contact sense: the major arts are based on
the senses of distance, and it is easy to think of critical taste as a
sublimation, the critic being an astral gourmet and literature
itself being . . . presented for enjoyment and evaluation, like a
wine.' (*The Stubborn Structure*.) The truth of this observation can
be checked out every week on the review pages where the
predominant attitude is condescension and we are given to
understand mainly that the critics (and the philistine community they represent) are superior to whatever they praise or
damn.

Frye is no wine-taster. He sees the critic in the role of the
investigator, not in the robes of the judge; he has a vision of the
arts as the world of the creative imagination which has its own
discoverable processes, for it is both coherent and self-
contained. ('Nature is inside art as its content, not outside as its
model' – *Fables of Identity*.) He believes that criticism ought to be
to literature 'what history is to action and philosophy is to
wisdom', a systematic and organized study with its own con-

ceptual framework (*Anatomy of Criticism*), and he finds that 'what is at present missing from literary criticism is a co-ordinating principle, a central hypothesis which, like the theory of evolution in biology, will see the phenomena it deals with as parts of a whole' (*Fables of Identity*).

The fact that these quotes come from several of his books should suggest that Frye's work is all of a piece and that he is not so much a critic, as the term is generally used, but a philosopher of literature, who has been working (successfully) towards 'a central expanding pattern of systematic comprehension'. Even when he criticizes a single work such as A. L. Rowse's attempt to give a biographical explanation of Shakespeare's sonnets, Frye turns the occasion into a most illuminating analysis of the pernicious habit of mixing up the shapeless stone with the statue, the raw material of life with the content of literary works.

To give some idea of what Frye is about, one might usefully contrast him with Lukács, who is primarily concerned with literature as a reflection of social reality, while Frye's primary concern is with literature as the revelation of man's imaginative power. 'The connexions of literature are with the imagination, hence the ideal in literature is one of intensity and power rather than of precision or accuracy, as in science.'

Frye is annoyed with those who fail to see the social reference of his criticism, but in this volume he lends substance to their complaint with an essay on Dickens, in which he deals with Dickens's servile view of the world simply as a manifestation of one kind of creative imagination. His enthusiasm for the beautiful New Comedy patterns of Dickens's flight from social reality is not what we usually associate with a socially concerned critic. George Lukács, for his part, could praise the appalling novels of Walter Scott, on the grounds that Scott faithfully reflected the pattern of social change from feudalism to capitalism. Nonetheless it is obvious that if neither aesthetic is all-inclusive, between them they cover a lot of ground, if they are diametrically opposite they are also complementary, and they even meet at a metaphysical point.

For there is of course great social significance in viewing literature on its own – indeed, nothing else can be relevant about literature until we understand it in its own terms, in terms of the 'stubborn structure of the language', the shaping forms of the verbal imagination which are autonomous forces and are the final arbiters of the meaning of any creative work.

The arts, in Frye's view, are our most direct guide to the human world, which is far more significant for us than the 'natural world' presented by science. He recalls Blake's attack on Newton ('Blake's main point is that admiring the mechanisms of the sky leads to establishing human life in mechanical patterns too') and one cannot help concluding that Blake, alas, turned out to be correct. Is it possible that I am not alone in believing that in the dispute between Galileo and the Church, the Church was right and the centre of man's universe *is* the earth? At any rate, Frye defines science as the study of the world out *there*, and art as the expression of what is *here*. 'If we remove science from its context and make it not a mental construct but an oracle of reality, the logical conclusion is that man ought to adjust himself to that reality on its own terms . . . what begins as reason ends in the conditioned reflexes of an insect state, where human beings have become cerebral automata. The real world, that is, the human world, has constantly to be created.'

As the real world is what we make of it, and in this sense all human acts are creative, Frye's study of the creative process reaches beyond the confines of the liberal arts.

Methuen, the publishers of *The Stubborn Structure*, commit the impertinence of not even listing Frye's earlier works, so I would like at least to mention and recommend, in addition to those referred to, his books on Blake, Milton, Shakespeare, alongside the present volume which includes essays on the varieties of literary utopias, Yeats's imagery, Victorian educational theories, revolutionary Romanticism, the morality of scholarship, the arts as informing languages for other disciplines, design as a creative principle in the arts.

It may be obvious how such matters are relevant to the study of literature ('the teaching of literature is impossible, that is

[269]

why it is difficult', he writes), but the book's importance for the general reader perhaps ought to be stressed. Many people take the attitude that the analysis of literature is none of their business: all they want to do is enjoy books, they don't want to bother learning 'dull' stuff about literary forms – which is like saying all they want to do is enjoy watching football, they don't want to know about the rules of the game. Those who are willing to concede the absurdity of approaching literature without any idea of the rules of literary activity ought to take to heart Frank Kermode's warning that Frye 'cannot be safely ignored'.

The Times, November 12, 1970

Equivocal Hero

George Lukács, the Man, his Work, and his Ideas, edited by
G. H. R. Parkinson (Weidenfeld and Nicolson)

One of George Lukács's main contributions to the understanding of literature is his extensive analysis of the problem of significance, his argument for the supremacy of literary heroes who are at once uniquely individual and universally relevant, who express their singularity through typical spiritual and social conflicts, thus truthfully reflecting their age. Lukács himself is such a character: at once admirable and contemptible, he is a pathetic hero, all too representative of the equivocal role intellectuals have been playing in the twentieth century.

He is also the most singular person imaginable. A frail, short, almost dwarfish man with a large oval head (an egghead, precisely), he impressed me in my adolescence as a saintly eminence, whose aura of unworldliness and even sanctity was enhanced by his self-effacing kindness and patience. It wasn't a lasting impression. I was 16 when he took me into his Institute of Aesthetic Studies at the University of Budapest, and I felt new worlds opening up to me at his lectures and seminars until I knew enough to notice how he was tilting every literary work toward Marxism-Leninism. This was the 1949–50 academic year, the beginning of the communist terror in Hungary, with mass-arrests, deportations and executions, but Lukács and his assistants (represented here by Dr. Mészáros) managed to ignore all the blood and kept referring to Stalin and Rákosi as great philosophers and critics, while all the time talking about the importance of understanding social reality. I spent a year at the Institute and the main thing I learned was that ideology is where people go to avoid learning from experience. Lukács, this author of a new theory of the complex totality of existence, appeared to spend his whole life inside his head.

Splitting theoretical hairs a great deal of the time (a habit presumably inherited from his Talmudic uncle and ingrained by a surfeit of Teutonic philosophy), he has led a life of cerebration, which explains both his need for a religious faith that answers all questions and also the unlikely contradictions of his career and his life-work.

A rich banker's son, who used to ride on horseback up to the intellectual cafés of Budapest and wrote two brilliant books on aesthetics in his youth, Lukács became a Communist commissar in 1919 and soon, alas, a Moscow ideologue. Like most of his contemporaries, he has revealed an unerring moral sense about crimes committed thousands of miles away, on the other side of the ideological border, and a blissful unawareness of the murders committed in front of his eyes. Like any party hack, he has been for ever ready to eat his own words and to write enthusiastically about the insanities of his leaders: he could even stoop to a rapturous dissertation on the wisdom of Stalin's last and evidently senile contribution to Marxist philosophy – the theory that eventually all languages will evolve into the language of communism (i.e. Russian). Drawing on his immense scholarship, Lukács was just the man to dress up this sort of vicious imperialist fantasy (aimed at the obliteration of the national cultures of Russia's colonies within the USSR) with generous references to Fichte and Hegel.

'Your back is bent from licking boots,' George Faludy wrote of Lukács. When this great Hungarian poet praised *Darkness at Noon* to Lukács, the philosopher's reply was: 'You should be in jail.' Yet, as the editor of the present book reminds us, Lukács cherishes the notion that it is worthwhile to appear in a shady light for the sake of an idea. This isn't an adequate explanation of all the shady things he has been involved in as a bolshevik theoretician, but his time-serving did give him the opportunity to indulge his redeeming obsession with the geniuses of realist literature and, moreover, gave him the *influence* he needed to establish Goethe, Thomas Mann, Stendhal and Balzac as central figures of human civilisation, canonised in the official culture policy of the Communist Party.

If for the past thirty years the German and French classics have been extensively printed and read throughout the Soviet empire, it is largely due to Lukács's efforts; and this accomplishment may yet have significant consequences for the future.

The present symposium edited by G. H. R. Parkinson gives the reader little idea of either Lukács's betrayals or his benign influence. Dr Mészáros contributes a well-thought-out summary of Lukács's dialectic and his concept of totality (though I doubt whether this beautiful logical construct could help anybody to understand anything) but is loyally vague about Lukács's evident insincerities and tries to minimise his rôle in Soviet ideology.

As for Lukács's relevance to Western readers, the book suffers from Professor Parkinson's exaggerated concern with him as 'one of the most important Marxist theoreticians of this century'. Although Professor Parkinson himself summarises Lukács's latest aesthetic theories, too much attention is paid to the limitations and virtues of the Marxist-as-critic and too little to the way we can profit from this extraordinary philosopher of aesthetics, who writes within the framework of a narrow-minded ideology but, even so, often succeeds in making profound and far-ranging observations which (as Dr Craig argues here) can enrich our reading of literature.

The Guardian, January 29, 1970

The Wisest Art

The Realists, by C. P. Snow (Macmillan)

C. P. Snow has the gift of voicing the chief intellectual pre-occupation of a period; he is a trend-setter or, rather, one who gives effective voice to a trend. So it's important news that his latest book deals with the masters of what he calls 'the wisest art', realist fiction. Arguing against modern attempts to turn the novel into 'verbal puzzles', he urges readers to turn to the books in which we can 'discover something about other people and ourselves'. *The Realists* heralds, I trust, a new and wide-spread interest in the classic novelists.

Introducing Stendhal, Balzac, Dickens, Dostoevsky, Tol-stoy, Galdós, Henry James and Proust, the author admits to 'a touch of chauvinism' in his decision to include Dickens, but is admirably cogent about the fatal flaw in his genius: Dickens, he says, 'had little insight about women'. In fact,

> All the Victorian novelists are handicapped by comparison with their European colleagues . . . The English shone in their business deals – but when one thinks of them alongside Balzac, Stendhal, Hugo, Tolstoy, Dostoevsky, they hadn't much knowledge of adult women in their flesh and bone.

Mentioning Hugo blunts the point: there were few English novelists quite so Victorian, quite so corny as Victor Hugo. Still, Lord Snow's main thesis is unarguable, and one of the great virtues of *The Realists* is that it breaks with the literary insularity which confines English readers to English fiction, so much of which is poisoned by an almost unfathomable hypoc-risy about sex. Lord Snow not only praises foreign authors, he has the courage to do so at the expense of English favourites, and this book can be recommended most of all to those readers who are as fond as he is of Jane Austen, George Eliot or Trollope, but who are not yet at home with the French and Russian classics.

Lord Snow gets a fair number of things wrong. It is absurd, for instance, to say that Stendhal's splendid *Life of Rossini* is 'muddled journalism' which wouldn't even be printed today; it continues to be published in every civilised country.

He thinks *The Charterhouse of Parma* shows that Stendhal (*Stendhal*, of all people!) knew very little of politics; he also says that Fabrizio's reluctance to escape from prison, where he is close to the girl he has fallen in love with, though in danger of losing his life, shows that Stendhal lacks 'psychological common sense' and 'has lost contact with any kind of realism'. In other words, he attributes the character's lack of common sense to the author. It is, of course, Stendhal's special greatness to portray with the profoundest realism the irrational behaviour people are driven to by passionate love.

But then, the importance of correct literary opinions is greatly exaggerated; they tend to make readers feel they know so much about a book that they don't need to read it. The only truly correct and full criticism of a work is the work itself.

C. P. Snow the novelist understands this far better than most critics, and he achieves something far more valuable than unassailable literary criticism: he involves his reader in the lives of some of the most amazing people ever born, who also managed to produce some of the most amazing and illuminating novels ever written. He imparts not the illusion of understanding but the thrill of curiosity.

Snow the novelist conjures up images. This on the meeting of Stendhal and Balzac: 'Two men walking amiably down the street, both little, both fat, two of the finest writers on earth.'

He tells stories: he spies on the dreadful Tolstoy marriage, he tells us why Turgenev was always a better-paid writer than Dostoevsky, lets us into the secrets of Galdós's afternoon excursions and Henry James's wound; he gets carried away and makes breathtaking assertions; this on Stendhal: 'You can meet him today at literary parties in New York or London, aggressive, abrasive, amusing, rancorous because the great commercial break hasn't yet come.' Where are those parties? I'd like to gatecrash.

In fact the experience of reading *The Realists* could be compared to a good party where you hear all sorts of gossip, some of it scurrilous, some preposterous, about certain writers, leaving you with an absolute determination to read their books.

Moreover, this Lives of the Novelists is full of biographical comments which provide useful pointers towards the works.

No one ever tried more strenuously to lead a moral life than Tolstoy, and to exhort others to lead the same moral life. No one ever tried less strenuously than Balzac in those directions. All the evidence tells us that everyone who was close to Balzac, including women who were simultaneously his mistresses, felt that he had brought them happiness. To all those close to Tolstoy, his children, most of all his wife, he brought misery.

This is a good way of alerting the reader to Tolstoy's high-minded befogging of the way men ill-use women, as well as to Balzac's talent for making it clear, in however cynical and worldly a manner, who harms whom and how.

The Realists should be on all university courses, ahead of most academic works, which succeed only in boring students away from literature.

The Sunday Telegraph, October 29, 1978

The American Vice President Who Claimed to Be a British Subject

Burr, by Gore Vidal (Heinemann)

'A monstrous claim!' cried Lord Hawkesbury, Secretary of State at the Home Office in 1808, when he heard that Colonel Aaron Burr, who had fought in the American rebellion against the Crown and later served as Vice-President of the breakaway republic, was demanding right of residence in England on the grounds that he was born and still remained a *British subject*.

A wheeling-dealing New York attorney, the first American grandmaster of *chutzpah*, Aaron Burr had no sense of the incongruous.

While in office as Vice-President of the United States, he ran for the governorship of New York, promising to take the State out of the Union. Upon losing the gubernatorial election, he shot his chief political enemy, Alexander Hamilton, in a duel.

Fleeing indictment for murder, he tried to provoke a war between the United States and Spain in order to make himself the king of Mexico. President Jefferson had him prosecuted, but as Burr had been too inept to get very far with his plot, he was acquitted.

It was after his trial for treason that he came to Europe, hoping to persuade the British Prime Minister to help him take Mexico. Urged to leave England, he tried his luck in France with equal lack of success, and eventually ended up back in New York. In his late seventies he married a rich widow, managing to relieve her of a great deal of money before she sued him for divorce.

No doubt this remarkably brazen character could have been the subject of a fascinating novel, but Gore Vidal chose not to write it. His *Burr* is a traditional American entertainment in which villains are glamorised rather than portrayed.

The narrators are Burr's young admirer (who also spies on him and betrays him, but that's just because he needs the money) and Burr himself. We meet him as a lovable old man, whose coughing, wheezing and cheerful liveliness in the shadow of death and betrayal demand instant indulgence, constantly interfering with his reminiscences of his misdeeds.

Before anything nasty can sink in, we are back to his charming old self or an 'I-was-there' account of some famous scene of the American Revolution. The character never quite takes shape, as he is continually dissolving into a living relic of the grandiose past.

Incredibly, for anyone who is familiar with Mr Vidal's other works, *Burr* is a highly chauvinistic exercise for the benefit of American readers. Burr's attempt to disclaim United States citizenship is not the sort of detail that finds its way into the book.

Of course, modern chauvinism is a radical thing: it includes knocking the Establishment. As a new hero takes his place on the pedestal, we learn that Washington and Jefferson were frauds. Young Burr was as good, or almost as good, as Bonaparte, but General Washington knew nothing of the art of warfare.

President Jefferson is condemned as an empire builder for purchasing Louisiana and Florida, but there is nothing to suggest that a Yankee gentleman on the run was doing anything unreasonable in plotting to invade and conquer a foreign country.

Mr Vidal justifies this on the grounds that everybody did it. In a positively Nixonian interview with himself about his novel, he says: 'Every ambitious man of the period saw himself conquering the world, like Bonaparte.' This is not quite true, even of Bonaparte.

But history is neither here nor there; this book really lives in that special way of seeing, feeling and thinking which enables people to injure their fellow men and still hold their heads high. We live in a world full of crime without shame, and books like *Burr* act as guilt-removers.

If poor Napoleon can be mentioned one more time, he called *Manon Lescaut* 'a novel written for lackeys'. Characterising Mr Vidal's work in a similar fashion, one could say that *Burr* is a novel for self-respecting criminals. It offers a whole range of schizoid notions which dominate the public mood and are indispensable to cheating businessmen, hired killers and revolutionary kidnappers alike, if they are to keep up their pride in their work.

For one, *motive is everything*. A man who blows your head off is not really killing anybody: he's providing for his family or striking a blow for freedom. In Mr Vidal's book Burr emerges from the duel not as the spiteful killer of his victorious political adversary, but as a loving father defending his daughter's honour against Hamilton's scurrilous gossip (which Mr Vidal insinuates here and there with all the artfulness of a lawyer planting fake evidence).

As for thievery, when old Burr marries the widow for her money, he does so not only because he needs cash for a land deal in Texas, but because 'he is the most generous of men' and has given away all his earnings to 'veterans of the Revolution, old widows, young protégés'. The reader is actually invited to admire Burr for fleecing the contemptible old hag.

That's another thing: *the victims are always guilty*. The widow is silly and pretentious, she used to be a prostitute, and she may even have killed her late husband; she gets what she deserves. She's repulsive to look at, too:

The small, bloodshot eyes started in the huge sockets; one can imagine her fleshless skull all too easily.

She doesn't need what is taken from her – she's as good as dead.

So who could fail to be on Burr's side? In the end, even the poor old skull has to realise that there is nothing bad about the jovial, witty, worldly and philosophical septuagenarian, just because he intends to strip her of her assets:

> ... the Colonel means to ruin me. ... No, no. It is not wickedness. He is not capable of any meanness. But he is mad with grandeur.

That's what it's all about: grandeur! Nobody is done in out of wickedness these days.

There is another Gore Vidal, of course – the brilliant essayist, the author of *Julian* (an absorbing and often wise novel about the apostate Roman emperor) and *Myra Breckinridge* (a masterpiece). It must be said even of *Burr* that history and human psychology have rarely been obfuscated with so much eloquence and wit.

The Sunday Telegraph, March 24, 1974

Truth and Lies in Literature

But Truth is the silliest thing under the sun. Try to get a living by the Truth – and go to the Soup Societies.

Herman Melville

I read *Billy Budd* some fifteen years ago but the passage of time has not softened its impact: I am still overcome by nausea whenever some admiring reference reminds me of it. Melville's story fleshes out the grossest, meanest lie in all literature, the lie that a man can love his executioner.

Between the preceding paragraph and this one I reread *Billy Budd* to check whether I remembered it correctly. Though short, it is hard to get through because it is written in such clotted, contorted prose – usually a sign that something is deeply wrong. Here is a summary of the plot. In 1797, shortly after the mutinies at Spithead and the Nore, a young seaman named William Budd – a handsome, guileless, cheerful, openhearted boy – is falsely accused of trying to organize a mutiny aboard HMS *Indomitable*, a warship of the British Navy. Summoned to the captain's cabin and confronted by Claggart, the malevolent master-at-arms who is telling these lies about him, Billy cannot utter a word in his own defence: he has a speech impediment which makes him tongue-tied when he is excited. Moved by outraged innocence and his inability to speak, he lashes out in desperation and strikes his false accuser dead. Captain Vere convenes a summary court-martial and Billy Budd is hanged the following morning.

The bare outline of the story shows how little a seaman's life was worth in the 18th century. There was no shortage of men: if more were needed they were pressganged ashore or commandeered, like Billy Budd, from a passing merchant ship. The mutinies of Spithead and the Nore were provoked by the barbarous treatment of British seamen (though Melville is more inclined to put the blame on revolutionary contagion from France – as if kidnapping people, flogging them and feeding them worms were not enough), and conditions were similar on American ships, which were known as floating jails. As late as 1842, on board the US brig-of-war *Somers*, Captain Alexander Slidell Mackenzie hanged three young sailors (one of them the son of John Canfield Spencer, the Secretary of War) without evidence or trial, on mere suspicion of plotting mutiny. The incident is cited by Melville: Captain Vere and Captain Mackenzie both acted to suppress possible mutiny, he says, and they felt the same urgency about it, 'well-warranted or otherwise'. In case some readers might think it makes a difference whether executions are well-warranted or not, Melville quotes an unnamed author to remind them that they know very little about 'the responsibilities of the sleepless man on the bridge'.

From Philip McFarland's *Sea Dangers: The Affair of the Somers* we learn that Captain Mackenzie liked to watch particularly gruesome executions and on this brief cruise administered over *two thousand* lashes to a crew of only two hundred. To defend this pathological sadist from charges of unusual cruelty it was said that, in relation to the punishment records of other ships, the number of floggings on the *Somers* was only slightly higher than average; but to many people then and since this only proved that an unusually cruel system was run by unusually cruel men.

Melville sees Captain Vere as a good man doing his painful duty, hanging a young sailor for involuntary homicide, but it seems to me that a good man would not be so keen to renounce his personal conscience and abdicate individual moral responsibility. At the court-martial he explains to the three officers who will have to pass judgment that they must suppress their natural reluctance to convict an innocent man: they should forget about Nature and think of the buttons on their uniform.

'How can we adjudge to summary and painful death a fellow creature innocent before God, and whom we feel to be so? – Does that state it aright? You sign sad assent. Well, I too feel that, the full force of that. It is Nature. But do these buttons that we wear attest that our allegiance is to Nature? No, to the King . . . In receiving our commissions, we in the most important regards *ceased to be natural free agents* . . . For suppose condemnation to follow these present proceedings. Would it be so much we ourselves that would condemn as it would be *martial law operating through us*? For that law and the rigour of it, we are not responsible.' (italics added throughout)

This is what later became known as the Nuremberg defence, but it was no less shoddy in Melville's time. And in fact it doesn't make sense even in terms of the story. Neither law nor custom required Captain Vere to convene a court-martial.

As to the drumhead court, it struck the surgeon as impolitic, if nothing more. The thing to do, he thought, was to place Billy Budd in confinement and in a way dictated by usage, and postpone further action . . . to such time as they should rejoin the squadron, and then refer it to the admiral . . .

This is also the opinion of the three officers whom the surgeon has to call to the drumhead court. 'They fully shared his own surprise and concern. Like him too they seemed to think that such a matter should be referred to the admiral.'

But the captain insists that the Mutiny Act must be applied, even though he agrees with the officer of marines that 'Budd purposed neither mutiny nor homicide'. He wants a quick hanging, no matter what.

'Can we not convict and yet mitigate the penalty?' asked the junior lieutenant here speaking, and falteringly, for the first.

'Lieutenant . . . consider the consequences of such clemency.'

To the captain, anything less than immediate execution would be clemency. And if he cannot convince his officers to hang Billy for reasons of the law, he will come up with other reasons.

'The people' (meaning the ship's company) '. . . how would they take it? Even could you explain to them – *which our official position forbids* – they, *long molded by arbitrary discipline*, have not that kind of intelligent responsiveness that might qualify them to comprehend and discriminate . . . Your clement sentence they would account pusillanimous. They would think that we flinch, that we are afraid of them . . .'

In other words, there is only one way that he and his officers can communicate with the men under them, by beatings and hangings. He, Captain Vere, has ruled his ship arbitrarily and his men, 'long molded by arbitrary discipline', would not expect him to rule in any other way: they would not understand what was happening – they would *mutiny* – if he suddenly made an intelligent and humane decision based on the facts and circumstances of a case.

Billy Budd, on the other hand, will have no difficulty understanding why he has to be hanged even though he is innocent, and will sympathise with his executioners. So the captain assures the three officers.

'You see then whither, prompted by duty and the law, I steadfastly drive. I feel as you do for this unfortunate boy. But did he know our hearts, I take him to be of that generous nature that he would feel even for us on whom in this military necessity so heavy a compulsion is laid.'

It is difficult to believe that Melville intends us to take the captain's declarations seriously, and indeed when the surgeon first heard about the drumhead court he was filled with 'disquietude and misgiving', wondering whether the captain was not 'suddenly affected in his mind'. But no, it turns out that the captain's utterances are pure wisdom. The officers who venture to disagree with him are 'well-meaning men not intellectually mature', whereas Captain Vere has both the wisdom of books and practical experience.

When speak he did, something both in the substance of what he said and his manner of saying it showed the influence of unshared studies modifying and tempering the practical training of an active career.

The twisted style goes with the twisted thinking. Portraying someone who is savagely cruel in his conduct, Melville perceives him at the same time as a wise, compassionate, decent man. It is this combination which is so false. Captain Vere is the killer with a heart of gold: he *loves* Billy Budd. Duty compels him to hang the poor boy, but the whole business is more painful for him than for Billy. He goes alone to inform Billy of the death sentence and emerges from the prisoner's compartment with his face 'expressive of the agony of the strong'. The senior lieutenant sees it and is startled by it. 'The condemned man suffered less than he who mainly had effected the condemnation.'

If readers will keep a lookout for it, they will find that one of the most frequent lies in literature is the pretence that it hurts more to abuse, torture or kill somebody than it does to *be* abused, tortured or killed. The corollary of this is that the victims have no objection. On the contrary. They understand, they sympathize with their torturers; they respect and even love them.

Melville does not describe the crucial scene in the prisoner's compartment, he only 'conjectures' that the captain, with fearless honesty, would have told Billy everything, not hiding the fact that he was the one who insisted on the death penalty; he explained to Billy all the good reasons why he had to be hanged even though he was innocent, and Billy understood and approved. What is implied in Melville's 'conjectures' is that the likable young sailor *agrees* that his shipmates, who are all fond of him, will mutiny if he isn't immediately strung up. And far from hating Captain Vere for putting him to death without cause, he is honoured that the captain has come to reveal his 'actuating motives' to him. He is proud and even joyful about it, in a way.

> Not without a sort of joy indeed he might have appreciated the brave opinion of him implied in his captain making such a confidant of him.

What a denial of the life instinct! What a betrayal of suffering humanity! What romanticizing of craven submission! Why should we worry about murder if the victims themselves don't make a big thing out of it? Billy Budd's 'cheerful' devotion to the captain does not flag just because the captain decides to blot out his life. In the morning, with the rope around his neck,

> Billy stood facing aft. At the penultimate moment, his words, his only ones, words wholly unobstructed in the utterance, were these – 'God bless Captain Vere!'

And the supposedly mutinous crew assembled to witness the hanging of their young shipmate echo the unbelievable cry. 'God bless Captain Vere!'

It is difficult to lie in clear straightforward prose. Melville's way of relating things which couldn't possibly happen is to both say them and not say them. You can see here the advantage of a tortuous style and poetic images which do not illuminate what is going on but distract your attention from it. Billy Budd is hanged but his body doesn't twist on the rope. The crew shouts its blessing on the homicidal captain, but not really:

> Without volition as it were, as if indeed the ship's populace were *but the vehicles of some vocal current electric*, with one voice from alow and aloft came a resonant sympathetic echo – 'God bless Captain Vere!'

Moments later the crew revoke their blessing – but again, possibly not.

> The silence . . . was gradually disturbed by a sound not easily to be verbally rendered . . . Being inarticulate, *it was dubious in significance* further than it seemed to indicate some capricious

revulsion of thought or feeling such as mobs ashore are liable to, in the present instance *possibly implying* a sullen revocation on the men's part of their involuntary echoing of Billy's benediction.

The captain himself dies with his victim's name on his lips: 'Billy Budd, Billy Budd.' You might think the captain regrets what he has done. But no: 'these were not the accents of remorse'.

Melville at one point compares Captain Vere and Billy Budd to Abraham and Issaac, and it is said that he meant to write a modern version of the biblical tale: so the improbabilities do not matter; the story makes sense symbolically. But if Starry Vere is Abraham and Billy is Isaac, then who is God? Are we to take the rules of the British Navy, and even a captain's possibly faulty interpretation of them, for the Word of God? The very essence of all concepts of God is that God is what is above and beyond worldly power; Melville seems to be suggesting that men of power are to be obeyed as if they were divine. However unjust, irrational or murderous their decisions may be, we should submit to them not only unquestioningly but gladly, renouncing our own reason, conscience and survival instinct. What is false in the first instance becomes even more false if taken symbolically.

Melville might have revised the manuscript of *Billy Budd* if anyone had wanted to publish it, but as it is, the novel appears to be the logical outcome of his lifelong quest for the one big ultimate (that is, non-existent) Truth, at the expense of the numerous smaller but real truths in life. As Alfred Kazin wrote, Melville had 'found a solution to his long search for truth past the chimera of this world. The solution is law, or authority . . . authority must be preserved, though we doom our own children.' Something had happened to the author of *White-Jacket*, which gave such a shocking account of the treatment of American seamen that it is supposed to have led to the abolition of flogging in the US Navy. Prolonged failure, which drove Kleist to suicide, made Melville worship Authority as superior to the best human instincts and feelings. In Melville's last book Authority does not ill-treat its subjects out of indifference, venality, incompetence, callousness, but *for the common good*. However arbitrary and cruel it may seem in its actions, it is always benign at heart.

What disabling misconceptions about human nature and society are inspired by such lies!

*

There are two basic kinds of literature. One helps you to understand, the other helps you to forget; the first helps you to be a free person and a free citizen, the other helps people to manipulate you. One is like astronomy, the other is like astrology.

The trouble with this analogy is that the difference between astronomy and astrology, between science and mumbo-jumbo, is crystal-clear to most people, whereas the difference between true and false literature is not. Flattery, white lies, pretentions, delusions, self-deceptions are constantly taken for great literature, while great literature is more often than not abused, ignored and suppressed.

This has to do with the psychology of reading. Orwell said that most people cannot see artistic merit in novels which contradict their views, and this is the beginning of all aesthetics. I would add that new insights are even more offensive than contrary opinions, if only because they suggest that the reader was mistaken about something. And of course opinions and insights are the least of it. We are so involved with the novelist we're reading that he can offend us in a million and one ways.

Reading is a *creative act*, a continuous exercise of the imagination which gives flesh, feeling, colour, to the dead words on the page; we have to draw on the experience of all our senses to create a world in our mind, and we cannot do this without involving our subconscious and baring our ego. In short, we are extremely vulnerable when we read and are only happy with authors who share our inclinations, concerns, prejudices, illu-

[288]

sions, pretentions, dreams, and who have the same values, the same attitudes to sex, politics, death, etc.

Unhappily for literary astronomers, not many of us have a burning curiosity about the stars as they are, rather than as we would like them to be, with cheering little messages for Monday. Moreover, most readers (including most critics, professors, editors) not only see no merit in books which contradict their views, they can become quite angry and vindictive about it. Mark Twain, the greatest American writer, bowdlerised his language and decided not to publish some of his best work in his lifetime, to spare himself the abuse it would provoke. Both rewards and punishments pressure writers to lie, expecially about sex and politics. It is self-evident, for instance, that the genius of Dickens would not have been quite enough to secure either his immense popularity or his great reputation among his contemporaries, if he had ever uttered a true word about sex and had not pandered to the philistine complacent merchant class of his day. Consider this, among countless examples: without any training whatsoever, Nicholas Nickleby plays leading roles in Shakespeare (there is nothing to it, anybody can do what those charming, feckless, free-and-easy theatre folk do) and then gives up the chance of a brilliant acting career in order to save the virtue of his grown sister. The small value of artistic endeavour and the moronic helplessness of women ran through everything Dickens wrote; and these were no innocent lies, if there are such things, but lies that underpinned the ascendancy of the propertied classes, the political disenfranchisement of women, the domestic tyrannies and domestic crimes of Victorian England.

I first read Dickens as a young playwright in communist Hungary, where we had outright political censorship but at least there was no pretence that literature only had to do with literature. After having three plays banned at various stages of production and writing two others I didn't even bother to submit, I knew from experience that nothing would be accepted which reflected badly on the ruling class of Party functionaries and bureaucrats. They had to be the most selfless characters in every story, motivated by nothing but concern for the common good. Members of the Central Committee could only have faults which did not imply moral deficiency, such as smoking too much; lesser functionaries could have *private* flaws. The local Party secretary might drink in the evening, he might quarrel with his wife, even hit her, once – but any hint that he was turning everybody's life into hell just *doing his job* was vicious imperialist propaganda. Characters who caused real trouble and misery had to be low-level bosses such as a small-town factory manager, or powerless, marginal individuals, like a dispossessed capitalist or a hooligan. The secret police who came for people during the night did not exist in literature, unless they happened on the scene to save a child from drowning or perform some similar act of heroic charity.

At all events, there I was in Budapest, reading *Nicholas Nickleby* while wondering whether the authorities would be content with banning my play or would also arrest me, and it seemed to me, from a literary world presided over by the secret police, that Dickens wasn't very different from a successful Soviet writer, adroitly attributing blame for social evils to the managers of local institutions rather than the rulers of the country. True, no Soviet writer could get away with portraying a member of the Supreme Soviet as a greedy, stingy, lying windbag like Mr Gregsbury MP, but it hardly matters, since Gregsbury, though very funny, is such a crude and obvious caricature that there is no danger of confusing him with the lordly crooks of politics who have impeccable manners and are treated with reverence by what Balzac called 'the ministerial press'. In Dickens' novels as in Soviet literature, the truly high and mighty have only private vices: they are not shown to be evil in the exercise of their political and social functions. Lord Frederick Verisopht, corrupted by bad companions of lesser rank, has designs on Miss Nickleby's virtue – as if the worst sin committed by a British aristocrat in the 19th century was lusting after poor girls' maidenheads, rather than making them work from early morning till late at night for tuppence!

*

Terence Kilmartin's excellent introduction to the recent reissue of Proust's *Contre Sainte-Beuve* (*By Way of Sainte-Beuve*, The Hogarth Press, 1984) sums up the significance of this fragmentary work in relation to *Remembrance of Things Past*, but to my mind it is even more significant as a portrait of the villain in the drama of literary life: the Authoritative Critic who is really a charlatan. Regarded as the champion of literature, he is in fact its deadliest enemy, depriving the best writers of their audience and readers of the best writing, and doing this mainly by virtue of his position, because readers are only too inclined to take his opinion on trust. In every age there are millions of people who are ready to read good books but are busy with their own affairs and therefore turn to the Authoritative Critic in the same way as they go to their doctor when they have the 'flu: they listen to the expert and take whatever he prescribes. They seem to have no idea that medical experts and literary experts have to pass quite different sorts of tests to rise to eminence in their respective professions. Proust spells it all out for you.

To begin with, the Authoritative Critic must be plausible and eloquent. Charles Augustin Sainte-Beuve (1804–1869) was a man of 'immense culture'. He knew the classics ancient and modern and quoted them readily, he knew Latin and Greek, he made striking observations and illuminating comparisons and witty remarks. He was stupid about all the fundamentals of life, and therefore about all the fundamentals of art, but he could be very clever about everything else, and he wrote his famous Monday columns with what Proust calls *un éclat incomparable*. Unfortunately (and it was here that things started to go wrong) his real ambition was to be a great poet: he published three volumes of verse and they all flopped. Proust describes him as a dull, sincere poet and a lively, mendacious critic. 'It is as though he lied so much in prose because it was easy for him to write in prose, so that when he ceased to write in prose and began to write in verse, he stopped lying.' This may be true but I think it was the need to appear calm and impartial while seething with hatred and spite or trembling with the excitement of making and breaking reputations that got his adrenalin flowing and inspired him to eloquence, so that when he turned to writing poems about 'the purity of love, the sadness of late afternoons in great cities, the magic of memory' and similarly harmless subjects, he became colourless and boring. 'When he's not lying,' writes Proust, 'all his advantages desert him . . . all the elegance, the eloquence, the finesse, the biting humour . . . there is nothing left of them, all are gone.'

In March 1830 Sainte-Beuve sent Stendhal a copy of his *Consolations* and received in reply what I'm sure Stendhal thought was a basely flattering letter. 'I believe you are called to greater literary destinies, but I still find a little affectation in your verses. I would like them to be more like La Fontaine's. You talk too much about glory . . . But you will do better than *Consolations*, something stronger and purer.' *The Red and the Black*, Stendhal's first major novel, was published a few months later and ignored by Sainte-Beuve; indeed, Stendhal was never reviewed by Sainte-Beuve in his lifetime — a punishment equivalent to being ignored by all the quality papers and television. Balzac, even less politic, wrote a scathing attack on Sainte-Beuve's *Port-Royal* and was slighted ever after.

The critic as failed artist is a commonplace figure; the interesting question is *why* these envious mediocrities rise to commanding positions in the bureaucracy of culture, to pronounce life-or-death judgments on struggling writers. The answer seems to lie in the establishment's unease about the exuberant self-confidence of talent and the moral authority of artists who presume to judge society by their wits, without having been appointed to a board or commission. This constitutes a challenge to all official wisepersons, so the critic has to be someone who can be trusted not to be carried away by the authority of truth and beauty. Sainte-Beuve knew where authority lay. When Baudelaire was prosecuted for *Les Fleurs du mal* and his supporters asked his friend the great critic to help with his defence, Sainte-Beuve refused to testify or even to have his name used, as it would have shown disrespect to the Emperor Napoleon III. Sainte-Beuve was Baudelaire's *secret* friend.

A secret friend who knew how to be noncommittal even in private. Sainte-Beuve didn't review *Les Fleurs du mal*, one of the greatest collections of poems ever written, but he sent Baudelaire a personal note about it, discoursing on several of the poems and praising two of them. But then he decides one of these should have been written in Latin, or rather in Greek; the other, *Les Tristesses de la lune*, 'is a charming sonnet – it is like something by an English poet, a contemporary of the young Shakespeare'. This sounds like a compliment – Shakespeare is mentioned – but then it's only the young Shakespeare, and not the young Shakespeare either, but one of his contemporaries. It seems to me that an anonymous contemporary of the *mature* Shakespeare would have been just as noncommittal, but Sainte-Beuve wasn't taking any chances.

Here is a passage from Proust's comment on the letter:

I forgot to mention that he remarked earlier on Baudelaire's 'finesse of execution'. And . . . he ends with: 'But again, there is no question . . . of paying compliments; rather, I would like to scold you.' (There is no question of paying compliments to someone who is a friend of yours and who has just sent you *Les Fleurs du mal*, when you have spent your life paying compliments to writers without talent!)

Proust notes that Sainte-Beuve was always lavish with praise for books written by – or written for – people close to the government, but his only real praise for his friend Baudelaire was praise for the person. This, for example, on Baudelaire as candidate for the Académie:

What is certain is that M. Baudelaire is best seen in person: where one expected to see a strange, eccentric man walk in, one found oneself in the presence of a *polite, respectful, exemplary* candidate, a *nice young man who improves on acquaintance, well-spoken and with impeccable manners*.

Proust thinks that when Sainte-Beuve wrote like this he was 'giving way to that kind of verbal hysteria which occasionally made him take an irresistible pleasure in talking like an illiterate tradesman'. It seems to me, though, that the love of good manners, indeed the worship of good manners, is one of the profoundest feelings of liars and hypocrites of all sorts, who are constantly afraid that someone is going to be ill-mannered enough to tell them to their face that they are liars and hypocrites. When Sainte-Beuve finally wrote about Stendhal, ten years after the novelist's death – and then only because he had become too famous to be ignored any longer – he pretended that Stendhal himself didn't think very much of his own work. 'That there should be something like a Stendhal renaissance would have very much surprised him.' (This about *Stendhal*, who was constantly sending messages to his readers in the 20th century!) Sainte-Beuve praises poor old Beyle quite warmly as a travel writer and art historian, but most of all as a congenial and witty companion. 'The fact is, Beyle achieved his greatest triumphs when dining with friends . . .'

My Larousse describes Sainte-Beuve as the founder of modern French literary criticism, and it is certainly true that he perfected the modern technique of mixing useless praise with effective abuse. Learning that Stendhal was a success at dinner parties is unlikely to send you to his novels but it convinces you of the critic's good will. Doesn't Sainte-Beuve go out of his way to praise Stendhal, to record his greatest achievement, his triumphs among friends? He speaks as a friend, he even praises the novels ('there are some very nice things in them'), so you have no reason to doubt him when he tells you that 'all in all' the novels are 'detestable failures'. This kind of criticism goes for making sure that the reader of the review won't read the book, so Sainte-Beuve doesn't hesitate to lie about the plot and libel the characters. Thus Julien Sorel becomes 'an odious little monster' and Mme de Rênal 'a weak woman whom he seduces and does not love'.

As for politics, 'the author's portrayal of the parties of the period *lacks moderation*.' This is a key phrase; it always signals a defender of the status quo in society as well as in the realm of thought. Moderation may be a virtue in action, because the consequences of action are irreversible and can rarely be modified, but when we read, what we require from an author is that he should make his point, sharply and clearly; we can modify it ourselves if need be. But Sainte-Beuve wants moderation in *thinking*: he doesn't want an author to write vigorously about important matters that touch everyone. He wants everything said with so many qualifications that when he closes the book he will find his brain in exactly the same state as when he started reading. He doesn't want his mind tampered with while relaxing with a book, and he wants you to be left similarly undisturbed: at most you may acquire new ideas about unimportant subjects which do not reflect on how things are arranged in the world. In short, he doesn't want you to think at all.

Realistic fiction is liberating because it portrays individuals according to their abilities and treats them with the attention and respect due to their intrinsic worth rather than their social rank. In this sense all true fiction is subversive. In *The Red and the Black*, the highest ranking individual is Julien Sorel: he has greater intelligence, energy, courage, greater capacity for emotion, action, reflection, and in the end greater integrity than the aristocrats placed far above him on the social scale. This is what Sainte-Beuve finds most detestable. He wants riches and rank treated with proper respect in novels, and when Stendhal doesn't oblige he is so affronted that he doesn't even know what he is reading. He imagines that Julien Sorel, 'a scoundrel resembling Robespierre', hates the rich mayor of Verrières '*as his superior*'. In the novel it is actually the other way around: it is M. de Rênal who hates his children's tutor for being younger, handsomer, livelier, more intelligent, more educated, more interesting, better loved, even by the children, than he is himself.

Sainte-Beuve's attempts to belittle Stendhal and Balzac were not literary misjudgments. They were political attacks in the guise of aesthetics, delivered by a porcupine of a man, sluggish and full of quills, whose strongest emotions were respect for status and authority and fear that tutors might be Robespierres. He rose to his commanding position as the Authoritative

Critic precisely because he was this sort of person and could be trusted to defend the pretensions of the privileged against any truthful representation of men and society. Like the philistine bourgeois he represented, he wanted everything left just as it was and had a horror of passion, because passions made people forget their place and drove them to make their own rules instead of obeying the rules that were made for them.

No wonder he couldn't stand Stendhal's passionate characters. He complains that Stendhal spent too much time in Italy and *The Charterhouse of Parma* is *too Italian*. Fabrizio is

> a pure-blooded Italian . . . without shame, without respect for himself or his position . . . Nowhere does he conduct himself like a man, but like an animal at the mercy of his appetites . . . So at the end when he is taken by love for Clélia, he sacrifices everything to it, *even good manners and gratitude to his aunt.*

When Sainte-Beuve writes about Balzac (after his death) he has the same problem. He misses in all of Balzac's work 'the universal charm of purity and wholesomeness, the breath of healthy fresh air that always blows through Scott's pages', and asks himself plaintively, 'Could even the most benevolent criticism . . . have made him accept a few relatively sober ideas, in the light of which the rushing torrent of his talent might have been controlled, contained, or regulated a trifle?' Balzac should always have remembered what Bettina said to Goethe's mother: 'The work of art must express only what elevates the soul, what gives it noble pleasure, and nothing more.'

Sainte-Beuve makes you believe in multiple reincarnation. You see Sainte-Beuves on all the review pages, praising the spurious, the innocuous, the pretentious, and damning everything that is truthful, lively, passionate, unruly – anything that might move you deeply and stir you to think – anything that might change you. Because if you change, who knows, the world might change – and that must not be.

Harper's, March 1986

Christianity, Communism and Poetry

A Revolutionary in Cuernavaca

Divine Disobedience, Profiles in Catholic Radicalism, by Francine du Plessix Gray (Hamish Hamilton)

Divine Disobedience is fascinating to read but difficult to review, for it consists of three brilliant pieces of journalism-as-literature, and the interest and importance of each is different.

The first is about Emmaus House and its founder Father David Kirk and his colleagues, who believe that 'The Holy Spirit works through the people' and 'priests should be the poor's picketers, and that picketing is a form of praying . . . praying, after all, is a form of picketing'. But while they see their East Harlem community house in religious terms, their Bible comes to them via the French Revolution (the house journal is called *The Bread Is Rising*) and they are really the soul brothers of other politically committed social workers (nay, the Black Panthers) rather than of anybody else, religious or atheist.

The book takes off with its second part, which portrays the famous Berrigan brothers and their co-defendants in two trials for the destruction of draft records. The Berrigans themselves come to life as men consumed by moral passion, an addiction to symbolic gestures and a lack of common sense: they are certainly the most confused heroes of the anti-Vietnam War movement, but no less interesting for that. I was more impressed, however, by some of the peripheral characters at the trials. A former Army chaplain in Korea is asked to tell the court who had told him to pour blood on the draft files. 'God told me', he answers. 'And that's peanuts, compared to what He's going to tell me next.'

One of the most striking facts to emerge about five of the Catonville Nine anti-war activists is that they had become radicalized by what they saw of their country's crimes in Latin America. Francine du Plessix Gray conveys their lives of high drama and comedy in a way which reveals not only their own extraordinary characters but also the drastic social changes of recent times. 'We decided', says Thomas Melville, a former Maryknoll missionary, 'that we would join the revolutionary movement in Guatemala . . . myself, Marjorie, my wife, who was a nun at the time . . .'

The Melvilles' changes of vocation, though, were inspired by the Green Berets' execution of Guatemalans. The lives and actions of these men and women are shaped far more by the conditions of American society than by their religion, which is to say that the subtitle 'profiles in Catholic radicalism' is a misnomer. It could more justifiably be applied to the third part of the book, which portrays the truly Catholic figures of Ivan Illich and his patron, the Mexican bishop Mendez Arceo.

In the winter of 1960–61, Ivan Illich walked three thousand miles across Latin America.

When asked what he learned on that walk, he smiles and answers 'I learned the meaning of distance.'

What is faith about? 'Faith is a readiness for the surprise. We must have a sarcastic readiness for all surprises, including the ultimate surprise of death.'

'I am for those who want to deepen life rather than lengthen it.'

'Only God can create values. The United States breeds violence by imposing its values on other nations.'

Ivan Illich was recently asked to define his theological conception of grace. He replied: 'Another form of grace, these days, can be attained through night school.'

This Croatian genius, who was educated in various European universities and intended for the Vatican diplomatic service, but turned into a parish priest in New York and then the Vice-Chancellor of the University of Puerto Rico before establishing his own institute in Mexico, has the kind of style and personality (rendered by Mrs Gray with flawless instinct for the telling detail) which turn men into legends in their own lifetime.

Illich's early career was not very different from that of other radical priests: he ministered to the needs of the poor and attacked and attempted to reform some moribund practices of the Church. Even so, Cardinal Spellman made him the youngest Monsignor in the United States at the age of 29. Through his pastoral experiences with illiterate Puerto Rican youngsters in New York, he became increasingly concerned with the failure of the sacrosanct system of universal compulsory schooling to alleviate either ignorance or poverty. Losing interest in Church reform, he came to view the educational system as the authoritarian and totalitarian Church of our time, and it was in his role as Vice-Chancellor of the University of Puerto Rico that he called for the abolition of the school system as it is known today all over the world.

When the Bishop of Puerto Rico fired him, he looked for a pleasant valley where he could establish his own school and finally found it in Mexico, at Cuernavaca.

The Bishop of the city, Sergio Mendez Arceo, was known for his open-mindedness. One day Monsignor Illich rang the Bishop's doorbell, was ushered into his study, sat down on his couch, and announced: 'I would like to start, under your auspices, a center of de-Yankeefication.'

Thanks to Bishop Arceo, Illich could establish his institute, innocuously called Centro Intercultural de Documentación, which has in fact become the centre for a worldwide educational revolution (Illich sees any other kinds of revolution as short-cuts which cannot really work). CIDOC soon drew the wrath of conservative churchmen and laymen all over Latin America, and he was attacked in the Mexican Opus Dei's paper as 'that strange, devious and slippery personage, crawling with indefinable nationalities, who is called, or claims to be called, Ivan Illich'. A Committee for the Recovery of the Faith in

Cuernavaca was formed in Mexico, which appealed to Pope Paul in public advertisements to purify the Church by purging Illich and his school. Eventually Ivan Illich left the priesthood and withdrew himself and his institute from the Church.

Mrs Gray could not be bettered in her account of the havoc of ecclesiastical struggles and intrigues – which, however, also show (with Cardinal Spellman's unlikely but nonetheless un-equivocal support of Illich and even more so Bishop Arceo's indomitable backing) that at least some princes of the Church are more helpfully receptive to radicals of the new generation than the representatives of secular power.

Bishop Arceo himself emerges from Mrs Gray's book as one of the most formidable men alive: a cheerful and profound man whose bishop's staff is a plain wooden stick, who believes that 'the desire for human power over others is demonic, the clearest manifestation of original sin', and who inspires as much hatred as admiration. Best known in Mexico from vilification by the right wing press and graffiti calling for his death, Bishop Arceo is remembered in Europe for his role at the Second Vatican Council, where he was the first Church father to call for an apology to the Jews. He believes of his own diocese that 'our poverty is our greatest asset'.

Illich and Arceo have turned Cuernavaca into one of the most intellectually exciting and morally inspiring places in the world today, about which we will hear a great deal yet. *Divine Disobedience* flies you there.

The Times, January 28, 1971

POSTSCRIPT: I include this accolade from 1971 as a record of disappointed expectations. At that time Ivan Illich seemed to be setting in motion a radical improvement of the educational system and CIDOC, seen from a distance and through Fran-cine Du Plessix Gray's book, did indeed look like 'an intellec-tually exciting and morally inspiring place', but it soon went into decline after Illich and the Church parted company. The combination of a conservative organization like the Church and an inspired troublemaker like Illich had a kind of paradoxical dynamism which could have produced large results, but on his own Ivan Illich became too odd, too far out to retain social relevance. Inspired and excited by Ms Gray's book and my review of it, our adventurous teenage daughter Mary went to Cuernavaca to study at CIDOC. She reported back that she was glad she had enrolled in the Spanish language school, because the other courses were given by people who *paid* to teach. One of the reasons I had become excited about Illich's criticisms of the certification system of education was that I had met too many PhDs who were so dense that they shouldn't have been allowed to graduate from high school. Still, even a bad diploma is a better qualification for teaching than straight cash. *Have money, will teach* was a grotesque, depressing end to a bright vision of educational reform.

The Bishop of Platitudes

Built as a City: God and the Urban World Today, by David
Sheppard (Hodder)

One is very much tempted to be charitable to a bishop,
especially to David Sheppard, who has shown more than
customary willingness to bear witness to his conviction that all
men are 'members one of another'.

As an England cricketer, back in 1960, he refused to play
against the all-white South African team, and since then he has
repeatedly challenged racism in sport, bearing up gallantly to
abuse. As a minister of religion, he chose to do his pastoral work
in Islington and Canning Town – in depressed inner city areas
and on ghastly new housing estates where people tend to show
very little interest in religion.

Now he is Bishop of Woolwich, and *Built as a City* is inspired
by his continuing concern about the powerlessness of the urban
working class who have no say as to their surroundings, the
nature of their work or the schooling of their children.

He believes that 'the Christian Gospel should both bring
hope to those who are enslaved by urbanisation and challenge
those who, knowingly or unknowingly, contribute to that en-
slavement'. His book is intended to show how the Church could
help the underprivileged to acquire confidence in themselves
and some control over their lives.

He has the best intentions but, alas, only the vaguest
thoughts. Although his main theme is power, he is capable of
writing that 'power has to do with having access to those who
make decisions'. It is impossible to tell whether he has momen-

tarily forgotten that power has to do with *making* decisions, or whether all the power he wishes to obtain for the under-privileged is the opportunity to make submissions and have discussions with their masters.

To tell the truth, the only thing that comes through loud and clear from the Bishop's pleas for more power to the people is his own sympathy with them. He *cares*.

This seems to be the main point also of his reflections on the deadly boredom of most industrial jobs: no sooner does he deplore it than he settles for the easiest solution – a good look at the bright side of things.

It is true that factory workers do not have the joys and dignity of a craftsman, 'yet, there should be more dignity – not less – in recognising yourself to be a member of a great team which is corporately producing a useful product, rather than simply "working for yourself".' If I worked on the assembly line at Dagenham and the Bishop came around to tell me that, I'd defrock him then and there.

The book is full of question-marks. He recognises that 'the shortage and the price of land are the greatest barriers in the way of balanced housing and industrial developments', but only asks: 'Ought all land, or at least all development land, now to come under public ownership?'

He claims that he asks questions in order to allow people to think for themselves and come up with their own answers, but after a while it dawns on the reader that he is rather adroit at asking questions to fit every kind of answer. Somewhere on the road to Woolwich he appears to have acquired a mastery of public relations. He sounds depressingly like a politician who wants everybody's vote.

There is no injustice he doesn't name, no pain he doesn't voice, but he wouldn't like to be pinned down to any solution which might scare some people away.

He conceives even the Lord as a sort of astute public man who is keeping all his options open. ('The Living God will not be tied down to either formula.')

Ultimately, I believe, the trouble is that he sets too much

store by the heart, relies too much on the right attitudes and feelings. Like others who suffered a surfeit of romantic theology, he appears to believe that wisdom is to mean well.

As long as he means well, he feels equipped to discuss any subject. This leads to the sin of mental sloth.

From his main theme of the powerless poor in London today, he wanders off rather aimlessly, now back into the 19th century, now to the present-day Pentecostal Churches in Chile, so that in the end he mentions just about everything under the sun and some things in heaven too.

How barren such random musings are is perhaps best illustrated by his thoughts on education. Concerned about the failure of the present system to give a real chance to the children of manual workers (a 1968 study showed that nearly *one-half* of the lower manual working-class pupils of *high ability* had left school before the age of 16½), he makes one of his few un-equivocal recommendations: that we should abolish the public, grammar and all selective schools, because:

> If there were no choice for parents but comprehensive schools, they would very quickly bring powerful influence to bear to see that the £3,000 million a year spent on the State system was better used.

He must be one of the few people in Britain who are unaware of the fact that we live under the tyranny of various professional groups, and all the 'influence' we could bring to bear on the running of schools, trains or power stations isn't sufficient to move a feather.

I am also surprised that there is anyone outside the executive of the Labour party who hasn't heard that the establishment of all-comprehensive schools in other countries served only to fatten the educational bureaucracy without increasing the opportunities for the under-privileged. Nor does the Bishop seem to have heard of the experiments and theories of Freire and Illich, who have come up with a workable solution, at least for the elementary grades.

Contrary to the Bishop of Woolwich's notion, what disadvantaged children need is not more professional teaching but less; in truth, the only thing they could use from the largesse of the educational establishment is the free milk which was taken away from them.

As for the quotations from the dull and depressing new translation of the Bible, they sent me back to the miraculous King James Version, which I'm sure will have to come back into general use before we hear anything interesting and well said from a churchman.

The Sunday Telegraph, January 20, 1974

The Cardinal's Conscience

Memoirs, by Cardinal Mindszenty (Weidenfeld)

Cardinal Mindszenty is a clear and straightforward chronicler of his tragic life and his *Memoirs*, extracts from which appeared in *The Sunday Telegraph*, are easy to read but difficult to report on, because this is a book from another world.

To begin with, the churches had a more vital role to play in Hungary than in most other Western nations. Since the country was occupied for centuries by some foreign power or other, the churches there were the only genuinely *national* organisations. And as Catholics comprised an overwhelming majority of the population, the Roman Church was the biggest and relatively the most powerful Hungarian institution. The political decrees came from elsewhere, but Hungary lived in her poetry and the sermons of her priests.

To have an inkling of what this meant, imagine Great Britain ruled by the Chinese, with no monarch, parliament, press, political parties or any other associations which were not directly under Chinese control, except the churches. In such a situation even the members of the Humanist Association would find they had a great deal in common with the Archbishop of Canterbury – and vice-versa.

The Church was, moreover, the haven of the poor but talented. In a society dominated by foreigners and rich land-owners, gifted youngsters from the villages and city slums had only one route to the good and civilised life and a more than marginal usefulness to their fellow men: through the priesthood and the religious orders.

As a result, the Hungarian Church has always been a more

distinctly populist organisation than any welfare state bureaucracy. Supported by its own estates rather than by the far more iniquitous system of taxation, the Church provided free schools and hospitals, orphanages and old people's homes; it did the work of psychiatrists, social workers and arts councils; and it was manned for the most part by priests, monks and nuns whose ties and sympathies were with the poorest in the land.

At the same time, since the Church was rich and generous, there were no poor and timid priests in Hungary, constantly talking out of both sides of their mouths to please the squire because the roof needed mending. Freed from material cares, they could become spirited spiritual leaders. This was the secret of all those dashing hussars: they spent their childhoods under the tutelage of dashing monks and nuns.

József Mindszenty grew up in this great Church, and at the end of the war, after emerging from Nazi imprisonment, became the Prince Primate of Hungary, just as the Russian Army of occupation was settling down to stay.

His life and his *Memoirs* reveal him to be a most *unreasonable* person who doesn't have the sense to know when he's beaten: he is the de Gaulle of the Catholic Church.

In fact he is a lonelier and thus more heroic figure. When the leadership of the West fell into the hands of deadly half-wits who decided to draw the defence line of Western civilisation along a row of Buddhist temples in South-East Asia, while abandoning to Russian despotism nations whose whole history and culture were bound up with Graeco-Roman and Judaic-Christian aspirations and values, Cardinal Mindszenty raised the flags of processions and rang the bells of prayer to declare and keep on declaring his country's spiritual independence.

'I stand for God, for the Church and for Hungary,' he affirmed in a pastoral letter reproduced here. 'This responsibility has been imposed upon me by the fate of my nation, which stands alone, an orphan in the world.'

He constantly *provoked* the Russians and their Hungarian collaborators with this kind of talk. They confiscated the Church lands without compensation, they closed the Catholic schools, dissolved the religious orders, expelled and imprisoned thousands of monks and nuns – all amidst a campaign of slander and abuse the like of which had not been seen since the great witch-hunts – and then they reached out the hand of friendship to the Cardinal, wanting nothing but his blessing for everything they had done.

But Mindszenty wouldn't play. As he recounts with a most impressive simplicity, he was arrested, tortured, drugged, put through a three-day show trial and found guilty of espionage, plotting to bring back the Habsburgs and attempting to start World War III. And, of course, the ultimate crime – currency offences.

Even after they had kept him in damp cells for eight years, they were still ready to make friends with him. They were willing to *pardon him* for all the slanders they had heaped upon him and to let him be the puppet head of the Hungarian Church, while Communist officials appointed bishops and priests (known to the irreverent populace as 'peace priests', because they only appeared in public at peace meetings) and ran the Church as a kind of folklore department of the Marxist-Leninist state.

And still Mindszenty would not co-operate. Evidently he was constitutionally incapable of comprehending that the way to get along in this world is to kiss the boot that kicks you and hail the deadliest enemies of everything you believe in and everyone who is dear to you.

No power on earth has ever been altogether happy with Cardinal Mindszenty. Reading his memoirs, one can easily understand why President Nixon, for example, strongly urged him to leave the American Embassy where he had taken asylum after his few days of freedom in the 1956 revolution. Shoddy politicians who fake moral concern only when they can get something out of it are bound to be annoyed by a man who takes the responsibilities of his office seriously.

Pope Paul VI himself, the Harold Wilson of the Catholic Church, came to the conclusion that the clever diplomatic strategy for handling violent bullies was to give in to them and let them have their way, and retired Cardinal Mindszenty from the leadership of the Hungarian Church. I strongly doubt that this decision would be approved by the Hungarian people, if they had a chance to vote on it in a referendum.

But all these comments concern the peripheral virtues of *Memoirs*. The book's true magnitude lies in Cardinal Mindszenty's unconscious revelation of the secret of his strength. No reader who has any kind of inner life at all, regardless of his beliefs, can fail to be profoundly moved by a man who through decades of vilification, torture, solitary confinement and threat of execution, thought continually of those who were truly great in the history of his country and his Church, and measured his own conduct by theirs.

The Sunday Telegraph, March 23, 1975

Double Suicide

Arthur Koestler: The Story of a Friendship, by George Mikes (Deutsch)

'My view of Koestler is on the trivial plane, not on the tragic one – as he might put it. He felt more comfortable on the tragic plane. I am quite happy on the trivial.' So writes George Mikes in the introduction to this account of his friendship with Koestler, referring to Koestler's distinction between the ultimate reality, life and death, and everyday reality, the reality of 'small worries . . . your bank statement and other trivialities'.

If Koestler was a kind of Don Quixote of literature, with his grand visions and his delusions, then Mr Mikes is the Sancho Panza, the commonsense humorist. He observes humanity through his own person, chronicles our times through the humdrum incidents of his own life which nonetheless have a grain of important truth in them; his comic effects are derived from this paradox.

His last book, *How to Be Poor*, funnier and more pertinent than *How to Be an Alien*, extolled the carefree life of 'respectable – indeed desirable – middle-class poverty' and contrasted it with the miseries of the rich, owned by their houses in the country and abroad, unable to go anywhere else on their holidays, while the middle-class poor can roam about where they please in their battered small cars.

And when you are so rich that princesses come to visit you, you are not allowed to relax in your own spacious house. 'A man dreams of going to bed with a princess; instead, he is landed with a princess who does not let him go to bed.' *How to Be Poor* (published by Deutsch at £4.95) is the present to buy before you start your Christmas shopping: it will cure you of anxiety about money for at least a day.

The author of such lighthearted books is virtually a teetotaller, while the sardonic genius of *Dialogue with Death*, who 'found reality always unbearable' (but could also be very funny), was a heavy drinker. For a while Koestler refused to have anything to do with Mikes because Mikes didn't drink enough. They were brought together originally by their passionate love of Hungarian poetry, which is the commonest bond between Hungarians who are otherwise strangers to each other.

They tried to translate Attila Jozsef's poems, and though Auden didn't think much of their efforts, by then they were friends. They had their differences about liquor and the supernatural (Mr Mikes is a confirmed rationalist), but they agreed on food. In *Arthur Koestler* Mr Mikes describes an elaborate Hungarian 'pig-feast' they organised in Norfolk last winter shortly before the Koestlers committed suicide.

As to the charge that Koestler ought not to have allowed his wife to kill herself with him, we learn that in the summer of 1982, when Mr Mikes and his friend Marietta Markus were visiting the Koestlers at Denston, Koestler asked them to witness a codicil to a will in which Cynthia Koestler was the chief beneficiary – so that clearly he meant her to survive him.

Indeed, a suicide note he had written earlier, in June, 1982, ends with an expression of regret for the pain he was causing her: 'It is to her that I owe the relative peace and happiness that I enjoyed in the last period of my life – and never before.'

Koestler's decision to die on March 1 of this year was prompted by his doctor's report that a swelling in his groin indicated metastasis of the cancer (he had both leukemia and Parkinson's disease) and he must go into hospital without delay. Koestler 'was determined to die in his own house', and who could blame him? Mr Mikes is convinced that Cynthia Koestler's decision to kill herself at the age of 55 was inevitable and entirely her own. This is so, though Mikes doesn't say on what grounds he bases his conviction. The sad truth is that by then she too had terminal cancer. The couple wanted to die together.

It seems to me – and it seemed to Koestler himself, judging by his autobiographical writings – that he had a mad streak in him. He believed in omens, at one time he believed in the Communist party (he travelled the length and breadth of Russia in 1932–33 without apparently noticing that millions of people were dying of starvation) and in the end he believed that coincidences were pre-ordained. His irrational longings were fruitful for the novelist, indeed even for the polemicist, and they also contributed to his vital notion of scientific discovery as daydreaming (best put in *The Sleepwalkers*) but, alas, they were also responsible for his obsession with the supernatural.

Iain Hamilton's excellent biography, which paid no attention at all to Koestler's interest in parapsychology and not much to his scientific writings, made Koestler very angry. Loyally defending his friend's reaction, Mr Mikes remarks that if Mr Hamilton was not interested in these aspects of Koestler's work, which took up a great deal of Koestler's life, perhaps he should have chosen another subject for a biography. In my view Mr Hamilton was right to concentrate on what is important about Koestler rather than his popularisations of science or his paranormal aberrations, however much the latter meant to him and however much time he spent on them.

Koestler committed suicide twice. Devoting his last years to painstakingly scientific studies of levitation, precognition and the like, to mumbo-jumbo about the mystical significance of similar birth-dates a century apart, leaving all he possessed to endow a chair in parapsychology at a British university, so that his name will continue to be bandied about in connection with irrational nonsense, he practically made sure no one should suspect this loony Arthur Koestler of having written some of the most lucid and rational books of our time, among them that devastating attack on mysticism, *The Yogi and the Commissar*.

Koestler is one of the few writers who should be constantly talked and written about to make certain that no one who craves the truth can fail to hear about them. *Darkness at Noon*,

Arrival and Departure and *Thieves in the Night* fit his own demanding definition of the novel: they give a portrait of an age yet they have a mythical core. You don't quite understand our world if you haven't read them.

The same can be said of many of his essays (it is astounding to re-read *The Heel of Achilles: Essays 1968–1973* – nothing in them has dated, any one of them could be published in this morning's paper), as well as his first volume of autobiography, *Arrow in the Blue*, his writings on science, his debunking of Communism, determinism, behaviourism. As an essayist he ranks among the best of the century.

The Sunday Telegraph, October 9, 1983

The Way to Disaster

An Opposing Man, by Ernst Fischer (Allen Lane)

Ernst Fischer (1899–1972) called his book *Memory – and Reflections* in German. The English version of the title, *An Opposing Man*, is not only incorrect but grossly misleading, considering that Fischer spent most of his adult life conforming to the party line and opposing, as he puts it, 'the heretic that is himself'.

After an eventful career as a journalist-politician of the Austrian Social Democratic party in the late 1920s and early 1930s, he joined the Communist Party in exile, spent 10 years as a Comintern bureaucrat in Stalin's Moscow, and returned to Vienna in 1945 as one of the leaders of the Austrian CP.

'In the name of a misconceived idea of discipline which amounted to complicity', he remained silent about the 'judicial murder' of communists in Czechoslovakia, and it was only in his sixties that he stopped opposing his heretical sense of freedom and justice and spoke out against Russian colonialism in Eastern Europe. This led to his expulsion from the party and to this fascinating autobiography.

Fischer recounts the fate of his comrades who, fleeing from fascism, were granted political asylum in the Soviet Union, only to be arrested and shot – along with practically all the delegates to the 17th Congress of the CPSU who made the mistake of voting for Kirov rather than Stalin on a secret ballot. (Since Stalin couldn't tell how each one had voted, the simplest thing was to have most of them killed.)

Once it seemed that Fischer himself would become a victim. He describes the mysterious appearance of a letter on his desk in the Comintern, written by his old friend Gustl Deutsch from the NKVD prison, warning him that Deutsch had been unable to hold out and had signed a confession according to which Fischer himself was a Gestapo agent.

Suspecting that only the NKVD could have placed the letter on his desk, he took it straight to Dimitrov, then Head of the Comintern, to protest both his own innocence and that of his unfortunate friend. Dimitrov promised to intervene and Fischer was spared, though his friend was not.

Elsewhere, however, Fischer describes a pamphlet he wrote *at the very same time*, in which he righteously dismissed the 'calumny' of the capitalist press that the show trials were rigged and that Stalin's colleagues who were being executed were not Gestapo agents. He deplores this work in retrospect but excuses it on the grounds that he could not possibly have had any way of suspecting, inside the Comintern in Moscow, that the calumny of the capitalist press happened to be true.

An Opposing Man is introduced by John Berger, who describes the last day of Fischer's life, referring to him as a philosopher. Fischer does have a considerable reputation as a Marxist art critic and commentator, but he reveals himself here as a rather pathetic if gifted party hack who, after decades of brazen lies and betrayals, is trying to rewrite his life in a way that shows even his 'inexcusable' mistakes as the result of some well-meaning ideological misconception.

Whenever it would be time to speak of his fear of torture, or his ambition to be a big shot in the communist movement, he gets distracted by the evils of capitalism.

Yet I would strongly recommend this book to anyone who is interested in politics. Fischer is a good storyteller, he writes well, and it is easy to see when he is telling the truth and when he is lying to himself. The book allows the reader an inside look into the thinking pattern of a troubled true believer desperately holding on to the theories which seemed so dazzling in his youth.

More important still, Fischer gives a vivid and illuminating account of the disintegration of the Austrian Republic before the *Anschluss*. Without doubt, this was the brightest period of his life (he was a young, handsome, well-known radical, a sought-after speaker, on the side of the angels, with nothing yet to feel guilty about), and he writes about the otherwise dark history with the greatest zest and intelligence.

Before reading his account of the self-liquidation of the Left in Austria, I had never fully understood how much Hitler was helped by Marxist ideology. Putting their faith in historical necessity, in the theory of inevitable progress, according to which the worst excesses of capitalism could only bring about the victory of the proletariat, the socialists adopted a policy of noble forbearance while the communists busied themselves abusing the socialists.

Their common faith in the working class as the most advanced people spared them from worrying too much about the impression Hitler might make on the proletariat. It is one of the great unsolved mysteries of wishful thinking, how the most harassed, most deprived, least healthy and least informed members of a community could be seen as the begetters of a just society and superior civilisation.

For their part, conservative politicians still believed that it was possible for the few to live in luxury and peace while the rest went without.

Failing to make the slightest concessions to the socialists, the government spent the last strength of independent Austria in putting down a workers' rebellion. Fischer's account confirms that the surest and quickest way to disaster is for everyone to stand firmly by his particular misconceptions.

These are times for studying the Fall of Rome, but if you don't want to go that far back, you will find the fall of the Austrian Republic equally rich in ominous portents.

The Sunday Telegraph, March 3, 1974

Hungarian Life-lines: The Power of the Poet and the Spirit of a Child in a Classic Tale of Communal Poverty

People of the Puszta, by Gyula Illyés (Chatto & Windus)

Since the poet Gyula Illyés is unknown to English readers, it might be helpful to emphasize that in Hungary circumstances are as favourable for the development of poetry as they are unfavourable from almost every other point of view. Apart from intervals too brief to count, Hungary has been ruled for centuries by people who came to power through perfidy and bloodshed, and more often than not on behalf of a hated foreign power; so official authority is nothing more than police authority and Hungarians look to their poets for leadership. What opera meant to Italians during the Austrian occupation, poetry means to Hungarians to this day. Poetry is their lifeline; it is what they have in place of national self-determination, sovereign parliament, free press, free discussions: all the freedoms hide out in poetry.

At its best Hungarian poetry has the moody ferocity of a locked-up beast – and also a classic clarity and complete lack of self-indulgence, due to the fact that the poets know they are the only ones in the country whom the people believe and want to hear from. Gyula Illyés can write with the awareness that the better part of a nation hangs on his words – in the same way as the British hung on Churchill's words in the hour of peril (a permanent hour in Hungary). If the reader will try to imagine how a genius can respond to that kind of opportunity, he'll have some sense of Illyés's achievement.

In Hungary revolutions have always been spurred on not by songs but by poems. In 1956 we recited Illyés's *One Sentence on Tyranny* to gain courage to risk our lives: his lines have the power to loosen the lid over the subconscious. But perhaps the attitude of the police state toward him tells more about his impact. Despite the prominent part he played in the revolution, he was not harmed even in 1957, the year of revenge, when tens of thousands were killed and practically everybody else who had opened his mouth was put in prison. And now the government even facilitates the translation of his works! Rarely since Fra Filippo Lippi was released from Moorish slavery has there been such an example of the power of art.

People of the Puszta was written in the same decade as *The Road to Wigan Pier* and *Let Us Now Praise Famous Men* and is one of the classic documents on a community of poverty. Its heroes are people who live beyond the end of the world and back in the dark ages: the farm labourers of the large estates on the Hungarian plains, whose masters were authorized by law to beat them and work them 18 hours a day. It was an existence that left them somewhat crazed.

> Up to a certain age parents beat their children, then there is a brief pause. When this is over, the situation is reversed and the children beat their parents.

Their brutalities, their heroic loyalties, the crushing routine and all-revealing incidents that sum up their lives are recounted not only with realism and compassion but also with a brilliant theatrical sense – a vital element in any report from hell. (Illyés is the translator of Jonson and Molière, and no mean playwright himself.)

People of the Puszta is certainly the sunniest of all books on the theme of abject poverty and powerlessness, and one reason for this is the family spirit which unites the agricultural labourers against the outside world. However debased, they are still a community and have its consolations, until progress takes even this away. Far from improving the lot of the dispossessed, industrial development only deepens their misery.

Illyés is not an outside observer. He was born and grew up in the world he describes through the growing consciousness of his own childhood. The horrors come to us through the spirit of a child (and what a child!) who is still full of the new and joyful sensation of being alive. If the book belongs on the shelf with Orwell, it could also be placed beside Nabokov's *Speak, Memory*.

Any work which survives from the thirties has already passed the first hurdle towards immortality. In the original *People of the Puszta* has sold half a million copies among a population of 10 million, and has survived even the change of languages: it is a success, as I hear (and I am not surprised), even in China. I cannot think of a better Hungarian work for Penguin Classics. G. F. Cushing's translation is excellent.

The Times, January 13, 1972

Commentary on a Poem

I knew a man who was hanged. Or rather, I walked beside him for a while on Rákóczi Avenue in Budapest in the spring of 1956. I was among the first to recognize the portly gentleman with the farmer's mustache, strolling in the sunshine, and so I was able to stay quite near him on the sidewalk; those who came by a few minutes later could find room only on the road. Soon there were so many people trying to follow him that they filled the whole avenue. It was a typically Hungarian occasion, the Budapest version of a ticker-tape parade: silent cheers for a man in disgrace.

Only three years had passed since Imre Nagy was appointed premier of Hungary by Stalin's successors in the Kremlin worried about the restlessness in their European colonies in the wake of the East Berlin riots. As the author of Hungary's 1945 land reform and an outspoken opponent of forced collectivization, a veteran Muscovite Communist who nonetheless remained untainted by the blood that flowed during Stalin's reign, Nagy seemed an ideal choice for easing the strains of dictatorship. When he became prime minister, though, he turned out to be more of a liberal than a Communist, more of a Hungarian patriot than a Russian stooge. He invented that policy of reform and resistance later emulated by Alexander Dubček in the 'Prague spring': he introduced democracy into both the one-party system and state-owned industry; he abolished the punishing work norms in the factories, allowed artisans to set up their own workshops and peasants to leave their collectives and take back their lands; he released political prisoners, wound up police tribunals, and did away with most forms of censorship. In short, he went *too far* and in April 1955, was dismissed from the premiership, the party, and even from his post at the university. The papers vilified him daily for his 'anti-party and anti-people policies'. I remember I was surprised that he wasn't in jail.

Imre Nagy was sixty years old at the time. Unemployed and unemployable, he had nothing anyone could envy him for, yet everyone at that sudden gathering on Rákóczi Avenue seemed awe-struck by him. There was no shouting, no unseemly pushing or shoving, no one tried to elbow me aside for a closer look; there remained a magic circle of empty space around him, which no one crossed. People's respect proved to be greater than their curiosity. There were hundreds ahead of us and behind us and most of them could not possibly have seen him, but still they kept walking, evidently content with the knowledge that he was there somewhere at the heart of the crowd.

Hungarians – and this is the first thing to understand about them – love a loser.

*

From a distance, the great puzzle of the Hungarian revolution of 1956 is a small nation's folly in rebelling against the mighty Soviet Union. In fact, this folly was no temporary aberration; it is a national trait. Hungarians have never been sufficiently impressed by imperial power or by the dangers of losing. When it comes to such matters, they think in centuries. As Lajos Kossuth, the leader of the 1848 revolution against the mighty Hapsburg Empire, used to say with a touch of not untypical arrogance, Hungarians have a 'historical personality'. Not only can they look back on a thousand years of recorded history as a nation, but it has been much the same story through the millennium, so that even the dimwitted can remember it; it is a story of losing and enduring.

At the Battle of Mohács in 1526 the Turks wiped out the Hungarian army, and for the next two centuries Hungary was a province of the Ottoman Empire. During this period nearly half of the country's population succumbed to starvation or plague or were carried off to the slave markets of Arabia. But the

[323]

Ottoman Empire is no more, and there is still a Hungary. Like other Magyar children, I acquired such pointers even before going to school. The history of our defeats and survival is a kind of religion with us, as with the Jews; our self-respect depends on it; our heads are full of the calamities that did not destroy us. 'We have already been punished/for our past and future sins,' says the national anthem, expressing that defiant self-pity that keeps Hungarians restless and rebellious no matter how often we are beaten. Our moments of triumph have been too few to give us all the pride we need, but we glory in the fact that we have outlasted the Tatar invasion (1241), the Turkish occupation (1526–1699), the Austrian occupation (1711–1918), and the German occupation (1944–45). Which is why few of us ever imagined that the Russians would be staying for good – the question was only when they would be leaving and how.

Powerful nations tend to believe that victories are forever; Hungarians believe in the decay of power, in being unruly subjects, in making the strong pay for their conquests.

One of the losers whom we learned to admire from earliest childhood – who dominated our imaginations and whose example shaped our characters as much as anything – was Count Miklós Zrinyi, who held out against the Turks in his castle at Szigetvár until finally in 1566 the sultan Suleiman the Magnificent himself decided to mop him up with an army of a hundred thousand strong. Count Zrinyi and his followers withstood this huge army for weeks, and when they had run out of food and ammunition, they dressed up in their parade uniforms, put gold coins in their pockets for the soldiers who would be men enough to kill them, and sprang forth from the ruins on a suicidal cavalry charge. They got quite far into the enemy camp before being cut down, and Suleiman the Magnificent, shocked by the unexpected assault and already suffering from aggravation at being held up for so long in front of an 'anthill', collapsed and died of a heart attack during the commotion around his tent. The resulting struggle for power among the Turkish moguls gave the Hungarians several years' respite.

Moreover, not only did Count Zrinyi manage to be defeated with spectacular success, but his great-grandson wrote a valiant epic poem about it, so that ever since then, the old man has been leading his cavalry charge in the imaginations of every generation of Hungarians, daring them to fight regardless of the odds, demonstrating that even the few can inflict deadly blows on the many. Count Zrinyi was a very powerful figure during the 1956 revolution.

I write this in all seriousness. It is too often assumed, especially by politicians and political commentators, that people act under the spell of the moment, motivated only by recent events and recent pronouncements. It is a received notion, for instance, that Hungarians persisted in their doomed uprising because Radio Free Europe and the Voice of America urged them to fight on, holding out hope of Western intervention. Speaking for myself – and I believe my case was typical – radio broadcasts had very little to do with what I was doing. I was one of several young writers who organized the demolition of the Stalin statue on October 23, 1956, I worked on the first newspaper of the revolution, *Truth*, and after the second Russian invasion of Budapest on November 4, I fought for a week before escaping to the West. During this period I didn't have much time to listen to the radio, but I was thinking a great deal about men like Count Zrinyi, who both spurred me on to rebel and kept me from running away when I got scared. I was more influenced by the acts and words of people who were dead than by anybody alive.

*

I doubt that there was a single person fighting in the revolution who didn't hear Hunyadi's bells ringing in his ears.

János Hunyadi was a fifteenth-century condottiere who started his career as a page and hired out his sword all over Europe until he had made himself the richest baron in Hungary as well as the general of a well-trained, well-paid army which defeated the Turks repeatedly. In 1456 they annihilated the Turkish forces at the southern Hungarian city of Nándorfehér-

[325]

vár (now Belgrade), thereby postponing the Turkish occupation of Hungary by seventy years and saving Austria and Italy
from what had appeared to be certain conquest by the armies of
Islam. To celebrate János Hunyadi's great victory over the
Moslems, Pope Calixtus III ordered the bells to be rung at
noon; and that is why the bells still toll at midday in every
Catholic church in Christendom.

Hunyadi's true victory, of course, wasn't over the Turks but
over time – the way he set the bells ringing and kept us from
despair. Dictatorship is a constant lecture instructing you that
your feelings, your thoughts and desires are of no account, that
you are a nobody and must live as you are told by other people
who desire and think for you. A foreign dictatorship like
Russia's occupation of Hungary teaches you despair twice
over: neither you nor your nation is of any consequence. Now,
imagine people who have to live like nobodies, yet who know
that one of them was so far from being a nobody that his
deeds are honored all over the world every day. Not only did
Hunyadi inspire us to keep up our spirits, but he also showed
us, through our personal experience, the immense scope of
historic actions: win or lose, it was possible to do things that
would keep our descendants from despairing hundreds of
years hence.

The Hunyadis were the creators of the golden age of Hungary, which still glows in our minds. János Hunyadi's son
Mátyás became one of the great Renaissance rulers: Matthias
Corvinus, king of Hungary from 1458 to 1490, patron of the arts
and humanities, protector of the people, the first king to tax the
nobles and better the lot of the peasants, and the hero of
melodious poems and folk songs who made a habit of going
about in peasant's clothes, so that the high and mighty could
never be sure that the poor man they were about to ill-treat was
not the king himself. It was Mátyás's notion that every
Hungarian was something of a king.

The Hungarian who is most often depicted on a throne is
György Dózsa, who was crowned in 1514 on a white-hot iron
throne with a white-hot iron crown – a peasants' king roasted

alive by the aristocrats for raising a revolt in defence of the rights granted to the peasantry by the Hunyadis.

Hungarian history is rich in crimes inspired by greed and love of property; yet when it came to fighting foreign domination, we had heroes who inspired us to risk not only our lives but also our possessions. First among these was Ferenc Rákóczi II, who was born to estates that amounted to something like a fifth of Hungary and in his time was one of the richest aristocrats in Europe. Prince Rákóczi risked everything to lead a protracted war of liberation against Austria (1703–11) and in the end chose to give up all his lands and live in exile rather than submit to the Habsburgs.

'God can dispose of me in any way he pleases,' said Lajos Kossuth in 1848, echoing Rákóczi's sentiments. 'God can make me suffer, he can make me drink hemlock or send me into exile. But there is one thing not even God can do. He cannot make me an Austrian subject.'

As we identified ourselves with our past heroes, so we also identified our oppressors with the oppressors of our ancestors. They were all one and the same lot, foreigners trying to lord it over us. Thus the Habsburgs were hated and resisted not only on their own account, but also on account of the Tatars and the Turks, and the Russians are detested not only on their own account, but also on account of the Tatars, the Turks, the Austrians and the Germans.

*

In 1955, at the end of his first premiership, Imre Nagy did something that was unprecedented among the leaders of the colonial regime: he failed to change with the change of the party line in Moscow. He did not perform the prescribed ritual of self-criticism of his policy of liberalization and did not endorse the new policy of tightening the screws. The press publicized his integrity by railing at him for refusing to renounce his 'anti-people policies'. Which is how we learned that once again there was a Hungarian leader who served notice that the nation had had enough of foreign rule.

Nagy's material interests as well as his spiritual investment in his past beliefs – in the Russian leadership of communism, in communism itself – should have made him conform. He had done so in the past, he had beaten his breast twice before, when party policy required him to speak against nationalism and for collectivization; all he would have needed to do was repeat himself. He could have let Moscow use his popularity to turn the clock back a little and he could have stayed on top; all they wanted from him was *words*. Even so, he preferred to lose a good living and put his life at risk rather than condemn his reforms and the longing for freedom. His publicized silence asserted openly the secret mood of the nation: we were fed up with reverses, with deferred hopes for a freer and better life; his silence expressed what we felt but could not say.

Most Hungarians, though burning with resentment and hate, were nonetheless pretending to love the Russians and playing at being content with whatever was happening; we did as we were told. But Nagy's silence was a challenge to our notion of ourselves as a heroic nation, it was a signal, an evocation of past glory – the glory of Dózsa sitting silent on his white-hot iron throne. Nagy was beaten, but he didn't give in. He set Hungarians thinking in centuries again.

I believe I witnessed the moment when Nagy understood just how much his mute defiance meant to his countrymen's self-respect, and it occurred during that sudden gathering around him on Rákóczi Avenue as he was taking a stroll in the spring sunshine. At first he appeared to be surprised and embarrassed by the crowd. He quickened his steps, then slowed down again, all the while keeping his eyes on the pavement, pretending to assume that we were all solitary passers-by going about our business. Taking part in an unofficial demonstration – let alone inspiring one – is a grave crime against the state in a people's republic. But the quiet reverence finally got to him and he stopped in front of a shopwindow as if to look at the merchandise. The windowpane was filled with people, reflecting us gazing at him. I was only a few feet away from him and could see the old man blush like a young girl. He took off his pince-nez and cleaned it, then put it on his nose again. We were still there on the windowpane. I fancied that he must see himself in our hearts.

In the end he was hanged for the same reason he fell into official disgrace after his first premiership – for his eloquent silence.

*

Imre Nagy is one of those rare figures who make the study and interpretation of complicated events relatively simple: his character and fate explain a moment of history without the aid of voluminous details. During that moment, he was an uncompromised witness who consistently acted against his own interest, leaving the stronger side for the weaker one.

Just as they had the first time, it was again the Russians who approved him as prime minister in Hungary, on the morning of October 24, 1956, the second day of the revolution. He was not the premier of the revolution but the Kremlin's answer to it, confirmed by Mikoyan and Suslov, Khrushchev's personal envoys to Budapest. The rebels were demanding that Nagy should be placed at the head of government, so the Russians hoped that with his appointment and their artillery fire they would quell the uprising. While citizens were fighting Soviet tanks for the streets of Budapest, Nagy tried to calm them with radio broadcasts of his plans for reform. He was by nature a reformist rather than a revolutionary, and he dismissed all demands (such as the demand for the reintroduction of the multi-party system or the even stronger demand for national independence) which went beyond the tenets of liberal communism. He had great respect for Soviet power. He was guarded by Soviet tanks. Whether it was a hangover from his Moscow training or simply tactical consideration, he felt – as his critics did later – the best Hungarians could hope for was a freer and more independent life within the Soviet Empire, and that asking for more would only provoke massive retaliation and the loss of all possible gains.

However, Nagy's pleas for calm reflection and the restoration of order and his announcements of various reforms fell on deaf ears. Too many people had died in the first few days of fighting to allow anyone to be content with concessions that could be withdrawn at any time as long as the Russian troops remained in Hungary. People don't risk their lives for half measures. They cared about only one thing: getting rid of the Russians. The hatred for Russians became more manifest by the hour. And this hatred had to do not only with communism and foreign rule, but also with the Cyrillic alphabet, Slavic folkways, the remnants of Russian Orthodoxy, and the fumes of vodka. If Hungary had been a French colony, no doubt the Hungarians would have hated the French, too; but they would have had a similar culture and more or less similar attitudes to life. But Hungarians share nothing with the Russians; everything about them strikes us as alien and unnerving.

After the first few days neither Imre Nagy nor anyone else could have had any illusions about the possibility of some sort of socialist democracy in Hungary under the Russians – not necessarily because of the Russians, but because of the Hungarians. It was evident that if the Russians were staying, they could stay only with guns at the ready and must suppress the people whose deepest desire was to be rid of them. There could be no love match, only rape.

At one point during the revolution, I was a member of a student group that arrested a street-corner politician for haranguing a crowd with the demand that Soviet troops should withdraw from Hungary flying the white flag of surrender on each tank and truck. We did not want such impossible demands to gain any currency; we would have been only too happy to kneel by the roadside and wave red flags to cheer the Russians, so long as they were going.

Indeed, by the end of October it appeared that the Russians themselves wished to leave the country where they were hated so much. I heard in the corridors of Parliament, while Mikoyan was still in the building, that he had told Nagy that the Soviet leaders could not afford the *time* they were spending trying to sort out Hungary's problems. Mikoyan and Suslov even agreed to Nagy re-establishing the multiparty system. And on October 30 the Soviet government announced their willingness to negotiate withdrawal of all Soviet troops from Hungary.

On the very same day, however, the British and the French issued their ultimatum to Egypt over control of the Suez Canal. Within hours there were reports of fresh Soviet troops invading northeast Hungary. Moscow, in a dramatic reversal, appeared to have decided to crush the revolution.

It was after this, on November 1, while facing a full-scale invasion, the defeat of the Hungarian army, the execution of thousands and the subjugation of all, that Nagy finally agreed to voice the nation's demand for independence and announced Hungary's withdrawal from the Warsaw Pact, asking the UN to guarantee the country's neutrality. It was only in the last days, in effect, that he decided to make his government the government of the revolution, the government for national independence – after it had become obvious that his caution and his determination to preserve Moscow's good will would not avert the total subjugation of the country, and after the British and French invasion of Suez foreclosed even the remotest possibility of Western intervention on Hungary's behalf.

Nagy was universally condemned for this 'folly', even by the most sympathetic commentators in the West, on the grounds that it left the Russians 'no choice' but to retaliate with full force. But the tanks were already rolling to surround Budapest and cut off the western frontiers. Why *not* declare independence? The tanks could not roll any faster because of his declaration. If anything, Nagy may have hoped that his bold move, expressing the desire of all the colonies for independence, might make the Russians pause and consider the possible repercussions in Poland, Czechoslovakia, or even the Ukraine. In any case, there was nothing to be gained by being craven before being hit. The Poles, who had stopped short of revolution and a declaration of independence earlier in 1956, are not, as a reward for their pragmatism, any freer today than the Hungarians.

Whatever the circumstances and considerations of the moment, it seems to me that ultimately Imre Nagy decided to identify himself with his nation's demand for independence because a sense of history is stronger than class or ideology. From the point of view of history even a few days of independence means a great deal: a precedent for the future.

For the present everything was lost.

About 4:00 A.M. on November 4, Soviet army units launched simultaneous attacks against Budapest and other major Hungarian cities. The Hungarian army and the hastily formed civilian National Guard had not the firepower to withstand tank divisions, but the house-to-house battle went on for about ten days. I joined the National Guard and fought with a group of workers whose fortress was a sprawling factory by Szena Square, one of the main entrances to the capital. We couldn't stop the tanks rolling by, but we fought the infantry with our Russian handguns and submachine guns, our provisions being some five-pound tins of cheese, made in the USA – the only evidence of Western support I saw during the revolution, apart from a crate of oranges. I'll never forget one particular tin of cheese. I had just opened it when a new wave of tanks appeared and tried to blast us out of the pile of rubble we were using as a barricade, and I ducked my head down beside the tin. When the tanks moved on and I looked up again, the tin and the cheese were split right down the middle by a big piece of shrapnel. Like most groups, we held out for a week; by then, the country had once more become a colony and we all had to think again what to do.

The new premier appointed by the Russians was János Kádár, a victim of a phony trial in Stalin's time, who had been freed from prison in 1954 by Imre Nagy and who, as a member of Nagy's government, had boasted only a few days earlier of his determination to fight the Russian tanks with his 'bare hands' if they attempted to re-enter Budapest. He was a detested turncoat and greatly needed Nagy to make a similar about-face to justify his own. According to the records of the Yugoslav embassy, where Nagy took asylum with his family and aides after the Russian troops reoccupied the country, Kádár urged Yugoslav diplomats to persuade Nagy to confess his political 'mistakes', assuring them that if Nagy only submitted himself to self-criticism, he could not only safely return home but would be welcomed back into political life.

The offer was all the more tempting for the fact that Tito – who had invited Nagy in the first place to take asylum at his embassy – now began to make speeches in Yugoslavia against Nagy. It seemed that Tito wanted Nagy as his guest only to make political capital out of him in his dealings with the Russians. This wily politician, who has done very well from bending his neutrality now toward the Soviet Union, now toward the United States, played the same on-again-off-again game with the Hungarian leader. Had Nagy sought asylum in the embassy of any genuinely neutral country, he might be still alive. As it was, he soon found himself an unwanted guest among the Yugoslavs and had to take at face value – as Tito pretended to do – Kádár's written assurance to the Yugoslav government that Nagy and his aides would not be arrested or harmed if they left the embassy.

They were arrested within minutes of leaving the building, and Kádár announced on Radio Budapest on November 25 that they had been taken into protective custody because 'the government has good reason to believe that the counter-revolutionary elements hiding in the country might resort to provocation by killing Imre Nagy or one of his collaborators, and then trying to make the public believe that the Hungarian government was responsible for this murder'.

Betrayed several times over and imprisoned, Nagy and his colleagues still had the choice of freedom and the trappings of power in return for denouncing the revolution. Those of his 'collaborators' who saw the light were in fact released and received high government posts. Quislings, however reluctant and belated, were forgiven and welcomed. Stalin was dead, people were no longer required to be true believers, it was enough to be an opportunist. Nagy, General Pál Maléter and several others did not yield. Nevertheless, Kádár continued to refer to 'Comrade Nagy', who had been 'misguided' and 'failed to realize the dangers of fascism', but who would be welcomed back to the fold. The official Soviet lie about the revolution was that it had been fomented by Western imperialists. Had Nagy come forward to belatedly 'realize' this preposterous nonsense, as Kádár did, Hungary could be a more easily and securely managed colony. If Imre Nagy gave in, who was to hold out and for what earthly reason? Imre Nagy could have helped everybody lose heart for at least a generation, and so the Russians understood they could not give up on him easily.

During his two years of detention Nagy was repeatedly offered the opportunity to condemn the revolution and live. Once again all they wanted from him was *words*. Even during the secret trial in 1958, Kádár instructed the judges that those who showed repentance for their counter-revolutionary activities should be spared the death sentence. This message was duly communicated to the accused – as we know from those who took this last chance to give in and are now free. But Imre Nagy, General Maléter, Miklós Gimes, a journalist, and József Szilágyi, Nagy's secretary, would not condemn the people and what they had fought for, even to save their lives. It was this that made them – and Nagy more than the others for his greater political importance – not mere victims, but tragic heroes: they had a choice of destinies. They could beat Nagy, they could threaten him, but they could not make him renounce the freedom of *Magyarország* (*Magyar* – Hungarian, *ország* – country). He would rather be hanged.

*

East and West, we live in a Now civilization; it is assumed that the past is over and done with, and powerful men in particular suffer from the delusion that human beings have no memories. I would go so far as to say that the distinguishing trait of powerful men is the psychotic certainty that people forget acts of infamy as easily as their parents' birthdays. A recent example was President Nixon's brazen assurance: not even the fact that videotapes of his previous statements were replayed on television beside his latest speech could convince him that anyone but a tiny minority of intellectuals would realize he had lied. But infamy is infamy because it affronts our self-respect: it offends our feelings and insults our intelligence – and few of us ever forget an insult.

It is evident that the Soviet leaders hoped the Hungarians would forget the murder of the man who had stood up for them in the most dramatic and spectacular manner in this century. Yet it would not have been possible to double-cross him and murder him more memorably than they did when they offered him safe-conduct to get him out of the Yugoslav embassy, kidnapped him under the pretext that they wanted to protect him, and *then* killed him.

At a time and place unknown, at a secret trial conducted by anonymous judges and prosecutors, Nagy and three of his associates were condemned to death. The world learned of the trial, the verdict, and the executions from one brief announcement on June 17, 1958. No bodies were handed over to relatives; there are no graves.

Is there a nation that could forgive such crimes against its leaders? And, if anything, Hungarians have a keener memory than most nations, on account of their poetry.

Much of Hungarian poetry is historical – and history-making. Both the 1848 and the 1956 revolutions were fought to poems. (In 1848 it was Sándor Petöfi's *Get on your feet, Magyar, it's now or never!* and in 1956 it was Gyula Illyés's *One Sentence on Tyranny*.) In between revolutions it is poetry that keeps people in touch with their past.

Hungarian is an almost uniquely concise language, capable of extraordinary compression. For instance, there are no auxiliary verbs in Hungarian; verbs are conjugated as in Latin, through changes and accretions to the stem; and moreover, object pronouns adhere to the verb instead of following it as separate words. 'I could have fallen in love with you', which takes eight words in English, is two words in Hungarian. There are no prepositions or possessives, either; they are suffixes wedded to the noun itself, altering the sound of the noun and the adjectives connected with it. Thus every word has many different forms, with each inflection, each syllable having its own meaning and resonance, as in music, providing almost infinite possibilities for rhyme and assonance. As in Latin, nouns have five cases, and this apparent difficulty is the greatest possible advantage. In English we know the object of a sentence by the fact that it comes after the verb; in Hungarian the word has its accusative form, and so it may come before or after the verb – at the beginning, the middle, or the end of the sentence. Word order is not a grammatical but a dramatic device, lending emphasis, creating suspense, surprise, a whole extra dimension of meaning.

Poetry is to Hungarians what opera is to Italians, it reaches everybody and is appreciated by everybody. It is their life line; it is what they have instead of national self-determination, free elections, free press, free speech. Because the poets know the whole community listens to them, Hungarian poetry at its best has the elemental force of universality.

The greatest Hungarian poets living today are George Faludy and Gyula Illyés. The very first time I met Faludy he read me his *Ode to Stalin on His Seventieth Birthday* – an occasion that was being celebrated at the time as if it were the second coming of Christ. It said, in part:

> I daydream I'm invisible and run
> – I board a ship, an express train –
> I get you in the dark of your bedroom
> and gnaw through your throat.
>
> Millions are like that. I want nothing
> from life but your death. O you curse of the earth
> who built your Byzantium with dried blood,
> you Constantine the Great.

And this was during the Stalinist terror; in Moscow Khrushchev was still dancing on all fours around Stalin's table to entertain The Father of Progressive Mankind. Faludy had never set eyes on me before: for all he knew, I might have been a

[336]

police spy. But he was so pleased with his poem, he had to pass it on. I still haven't quite recovered from my amazement at hearing Faludy read it; I felt very brave just for listening.

This is a rough prose translation of George Faludy's poem *The Execution of Imre Nagy*.

He made his inventory at dawn,
pacing under the vault of his cell;
everything was in order,
only his pince-nez was missing.
Another minute had passed. His conscience was clear,
and in less than an hour his stubby legs
would catch up with Lajos Kossuth, Rákóczi, Dózsa.

What made him so calm?
Was it apathy, courage, character?
Or did he know that halfway there
he had solved the riddle of the century?
And what made him great and beautiful?
His faith? His intentions? His honesty?
The end? Force of circumstances? I don't know.

Maléter was coughing
in the next cell. Suddenly a cold draught
touched his forehead. Should he ask for
paper and ink? What for?
What for, he thought. Papers drift away
like leaves in a storm,
and among them walks serenely, with measured steps,
a stocky gray-haired man: the deed.

The end. He guessed it would be hard
but by now it made no difference
– the door opened: cursing,
the goons jumped on him with iron bars,
crushed his shoulders
and broke his arms
and then they placed a leather strap
under his chin and tied it around his head

[337]

so that standing under the gallows
he wouldn't be able to say *Magyarország*,
and they kicked him along the corridor
and he stumbled, half-blind
without his pince-nez, then pityingly
he looked around the courtyard
but couldn't make out the hangman's
frightened face, nor Kádár
who stood there cowering, drunk,
flanked by two Russian officers.

Then there was only the lime, butter-soft,
spreading over him like a billowing
toga. Soon it began to sink,
took his shape,
fastened on him and petrified.
It dissolved his skin, his flesh, his face,
but it preserved hair by hair the friendly curl
of his moustache, like the nation.

Since then the days are skinny
hollow-chested seamstresses
and the nights are sweating whores,
though sometimes when I'm half asleep
a gleam of light falls into my eye –
it might be distant lightning
or a playful searchlight
or the lamps from the next street,
but it could be his pince-nez.

George Faludy lives in Toronto now, but his poem is back in
Hungary, spreading by word of mouth, a magic chant that
protects people from brainwashing.

*

Western politicians, guided by commercial considerations and
eager to pacify their sullen electorates with good news from
distant parts of the world, constantly assure us that things are

getting better in the Soviet Union and its satellites. In this world view, the Communist part of the world is tidy and trouble-free, and only in Western countries must we look forward to disorder, ruin, and revolution. No wonder that the author of détente, Henry Kissinger, could argue that the future belongs to the Soviet Union.

The rulers of the Soviet Empire, however, don't feel so confident.

Visitors from Hungary say that all police and army leaves are cancelled and Soviet army units put on the alert for two days every year: on March 15, which marks the outbreak of the 1848 revolution against the Austrians, and on October 23, which marks the outbreak of the 1956 revolution.

In a simpler age, when human beings had a better reputation, I would have said, 'Man's longing for freedom is irrepressible.' In our day this sounds just too noble to be true, but surely we are pragmatic enough to recognize the power of *ego* and *hate*. From the point of view of the present, the relevance of the Hungarian revolution is that there is certain to be another one – and for the same reason why the French and the Americans couldn't win in Vietnam: there is just no way that people are going to be content to be ordered around and have their lives run by foreigners. I wouldn't hazard a guess when the next Hungarian revolution will break out, though I feel reasonably certain that it won't be on March 15 or October 23, when Soviet troops are on the alert, but on one of the other three hundred and sixty-three days of the year.

Horizon, October 1976